Redefining Prosperity

Society today faces a difficult contradiction: we know exactly how the physical limits of our planet are being reached and exactly why we cannot go on as we have before – and yet, collectively, we seem unable to reach crucial decisions for our future in a timely way. This book argues that our definition of prosperity, which we have long assimilated with the idea of material wealth, may be preventing us from imagining a future that meets essential human aspirations without straining our planet to the breaking point. In other words, redefining prosperity is a necessary and urgent task.

This book is the fruit of a long debate among 15 scholars from diverse fields who worked together to bring the depth and nuance of their respective fields to questions that affect us all. The result is a rich, transdisciplinary work that illuminates the philosophical and historical origins of our current definition of prosperity; identifies the complex processes that gave rise to the problems we face today; elucidates the ways in which our contemporary environmental, social, nutritional, economic, political, and cultural crises are interconnected; and explores why a half-century of economic growth has neither increased life satisfaction in the West nor vanquished world poverty. Approaching these broad-ranging questions from the specific standpoints of their disciplines, each of the authors offers thoughts for the future, considering possible escape routes and proposing changes to the way we live, behave, and organise society and public action – changes that actually respond, in an equitable way, to our deepest aspirations.

Ultimately, in laying the groundwork for a public debate on this subject, this book poses a question to its readers: what is your definition of prosperity, and what can be done to promote it?

Isabelle Cassiers is Professor at the Université catholique de Louvain, Belgium, and Research Associate at the Belgian National Fund for Scientific Research.

Routledge Studies in Ecological Economics

1 **Sustainability Networks**
Cognitive tools for expert collaboration in social-ecological systems
Janne Hukkinen

2 **Drivers of Environmental Change in Uplands**
Aletta Bonn, Tim Allot, Klaus Hubaceck and Jon Stewart

3 **Resilience, Reciprocity and Ecological Economics**
Northwest coast sustainability
Ronald L. Trosper

4 **Environment and Employment**
A reconciliation
Philip Lawn

5 **Philosophical Basics of Ecology and Economy**
Malte Faber and Reiner Manstetten

6 **Carbon Responsibility and Embodied Emissions**
Theory and measurement
João F.D. Rodrigues, Alexandra P.S. Marques and Tiago M.D. Domingos

7 **Environmental Social Accounting Matrices**
Theory and applications
Pablo Martínez de Anguita and John E. Wagner

8 **Greening the Economy**
Integrating economics and ecology to make effective change
Bob Williams

9 **Sustainable Development**
Capabilities, needs, and well-being
Edited by Felix Rauschmayer, Ines Omann and Johannes Frühmann

10 **The Planet in 2050**
The Lund discourse of the future
Edited by Jill Jäger and Sarah Cornell

11 **From Bioeconomics to Degrowth**
Georgescu-Roegen's 'new economics' in eight essays
Edited by Mauro Bonaiuti

12 **Socioeconomic and Environmental Impacts on Agriculture in the New Europe**
Post-Communist transition and accession to the European Union
S. Serban Scrieciu

13 **Waste and Recycling**
Theory and empirics
Takayoshi Shinkuma and Shusuke Managi

14 **Global Ecology and Unequal Exchange**
Fetishism in a zero-sum world
Alf Hornborg

15 **The Metabolic Pattern of Societies**
Where economists fall short
Mario Giampietro, Kozo Mayumi and Alevgül H. Sorman

16 **Energy Security for the EU in the 21st Century**
Markets, geopolitics and corridors
Edited by José María Marín-Quemada, Javier García-Verdugo and Gonzalo Escribano

17 **Hybrid Economic-Environmental Accounts**
Edited by Valeria Costantini, Massimiliano Mazzanti and Anna Montini

18 **Ecology and Power**
Struggles over land and material resources in the past, present and future
Edited by Alf Hornborg, Brett Clark and Kenneth Hermele

19 **Economic Theory and Sustainable Development**
What can we preserve for future generations?
Vincent Martinet

20 **Paving the Road to Sustainable Transport**
Governance and innovation in low-carbon vehicles
Edited by Måns Nilsson, Karl Hillman, Annika Rickne and Thomas Magnusson

21 **Creating a Sustainable Economy**
An institutional and evolutionary approach to environmental policy
Edited by Gerardo Marletto

22 **The Economics of Climate Change and the Change of Climate in Economics**
Kevin Maréchal

23 **Environmental Finance and Development**
Sanja Tišma, Ana Maria Boromisa and Ana Pavičić Kaselj

24 **Beyond Reductionism**
A passion for interdisciplinarity
Edited by Katharine Farrell, Tommaso Luzzati and Sybille van den Hove

25 **The Business Case for Sustainable Finance**
Edited by Iveta Cherneva

26 **The Economic Value of Landscapes**
Edited by C. Martijn van der Heide and Wim Heijman

27 **Post-Kyoto Climate Governance**
Confronting the politics of scale, ideology and knowledge
Asim Zia

28 **Climate Economics**
The state of the art
Frank Ackerman and Elizabeth A. Stanton

29 Good Governance, Scale and Power
A case study of North Sea fisheries
Liza Griffin

30 Waste Management in Spatial Environments
Edited by Alessio D'Amato, Massimiliano Mazzanti and Anna Montini

31 The Green Fiscal Mechanism and Reform for Low Carbon Development
East Asia and Europe
Edited by Akihisa Mori, Paul Ekins, Soocheol Lee, Stefan Speck and Kazuhiro Ueta

32 Peak Oil, Climate Change, and the Limits to China's Economic Growth
Manqi Li

33 The Sustainable Economics of Elinor Ostrom
Commons, contestation and craft
Derek Wall

34 Green Industrial Policy in Emerging Countries
Edited by Anna Pegels

35 The Great Transition
Mauro Bonaiuti

36 Redefining Prosperity
Edited by Isabelle Cassiers

Redefining Prosperity

Edited by Isabelle Cassiers

Routledge
Taylor & Francis Group
LONDON AND NEW YORK

First published 2015
by Routledge
2 Park Square, Milton Park, Abingdon, Oxfordshire OX14 4RN

and by Routledge
711 Third Avenue, New York, NY 10017

First issued in paperback 2017

Routledge is an imprint of the Taylor & Francis Group, an informa business

Redefining Prosperity is an update and translation of *Redéfinir la prospérité. Jalons pour un débat public*, La Tour d'Aigues, Editions de l'Aube, 2011.

British Library Cataloguing in Publication Data
A catalogue record for this book is available from the British Library

Library of Congress Cataloging in Publication Data
Redéfinir la prospérité. English
Redefining prosperity / edited by Isabelle Cassiers.
pages cm. – (Routledge studies in ecological economics)
1. Economic development. 2. Wealth. I. Cassiers, Isabelle. II. Title.
HD83.R37913 2014
338.9–dc23 2014006186

ISBN 13: 978-1-138-74402-8 (pbk)
ISBN 13: 978-1-138-02115-0 (hbk)

Typeset in Times New Roman
by Wearset Ltd, Boldon, Tyne and Wear

Contents

Contributors

Isabelle Cassiers, the editor of this book, is a Professor of Economics and Economic History at the Université catholique de Louvain (IRES and CIRTES), and a Research Associate at the Belgian National Fund for Scientific Research (FNRS). She is also Member of the Belgian Royal Academy and the Collège d'études mondiales in Paris. Since 2006 she has coordinated a transdisciplinary research group on *Redefining prosperity*. She is the author of numerous publications in economic history, and on the topic of moving beyond GDP. More on www.icassiers.be.

Christian Arnsperger: Economist. Professor at the Université catholique de Louvain (ETES and CriDIS); Senior Research Fellow with the Belgian National Fund for Scientific Research. His research focuses on economic anthropology and the existential foundations of the economy, the transition to sustainable (post) capitalism, and the socio-economics of monetary reform with an emphasis on sustainable banking and complementary currencies. Among his numerous scientific publications: *Critical Political Economy* (Routledge, 2008), *Full-Spectrum Economics* (Routledge, 2010), and *Money and Sustainability* (Triarchy Press, 2012, joint with B. Lietaer, S. Brunnhuber, and S. Goerner). More on www.uclouvain.be/8588.html.

Philippe Baret: Agricultural engineer, PhD in quantitative genetics. Professor at Université catholique de Louvain (Earth and Life Institute). Leader of a research group in genetics and system analysis. Chair of the contact group GIRAF of the FNRS on agroecology and associate researcher of Etopia. Author of publications on genomics, genetic diversity, agroecology, and innovation. Also see www.philagri.net/.

Tom Bauler is an assistant professor and holds the Chair "Environment & Economy" at Université Libre de Bruxelles. His main research interests are in the area of governance "of and with" indicators; social and environmental innovation, especially at the level of household-consumer practice and the governance "of and with" ecosystem services. He is involved in a series of EU-level research projects and networks. More on http://igeat.ulb.ac.be/fr/equipe/details/person/tom-bauler/.

Robert Boyer is an economist, former director at the French National Centre for Scientific Research (CNRS) and at the École des hautes études en sciences sociales (EHESS-Paris). He is a research associate at the Institut des Amériques. In the 1970s, he co-founded the Regulation school. He is also an Honorary Fellow of the Society for the Advancement of Social Economics. More at http://robertboyer.org/.

Julien Charles is a post-doctoral researcher at the Belgian National Fund for Scientific Research and Université catholique de Louvain (CriDIS). He obtained a PhD in sociology in 2012. His dissertation focuses on self-management, participatory management, citizens' participation, and empowerment, with particular attention to the requirements of those different participatory projects.

Laurent de Briey: Philosopher and economist. Professor in the Department of Political and Social Sciences of the Université de Namur and Associated Member of the Hoover Chair of economic and social ethics (Université catholique de Louvain). Publications include *Le sens du politique* (Mardaga, 2009). More information at http://directory.unamur.be/staff/ldebriey?_LOCALE_=en.

Jean De Munck: Sociologist and philosopher. Professor at the Université catholique de Louvain (CriDIS) and visiting professor at Paris X-Nanterre. Research in sociology of the norm, social theory, and social dialogue. Among his publications: *Renewing Democratic Deliberation in Europe. The Challenge of Social and Civil Dialogue* (ed. with I. Ferreras, C. Didry, and A. Jobert, Peter Lang, 2012). More at www.uclouvain.be/jean.demunck.

Isabelle Ferreras is a sociologist and political scientist. She is Professor of Sociology at the Université catholique de Louvain (CriDIS), and Research Associate at the Belgian National Fund for Scientific Research. She is also a senior research associate of the Labor and Worklife Program at Harvard University. Her research focuses primarily on the capitalism/democracy contradiction and its consequences, with a particular interest in the experience of labour and working people. Her most recent monograph was published in 2012, *Gouverner le capitalisme? Pour le bicamérisme économique* (PUF); she is currently completing a book for Harvard University Press titled *What is Work?* (forthcoming). For more information, see: www.isabelleferreras.net.

Stéphane Leyens is an associate professor in the Department of Sciences, Philosophies and Societies, Université de Namur. He holds a PhD in philosophy and an MSc in biology. His research interests include development ethics, and more specifically meta-ethical issues raised by questions of development and inter-culturality. He recently published *Le médecin qui soignait les postes de radio. Essais sur l'ethnocentrisme critique de Michael Singleton* (Presses Universitaires de Namur, 2013).

Dominique Méda is a graduate of the École Normale Supérieure and the École Nationale d'Administration, an *agrégée* of philosophy, and accredited to direct research in sociology. She is currently Professor of Sociology at the University of Paris-Dauphine and holds the Chair in "Ecological Reconversion, Work, Employment and Social Policy" at the Collège d'études mondiales. Publications include *Le Travail. Une valeur en voie de disparition*, *Qu'est-ce que la richesse*, *Le Temps des femmes. Pour un nouveau partage des rôles*, and, most recently *La Mystique de la croissance. Comment s'en libérer* (Flammarion, 2013) and, with Patricia Vendramin, *Réinventer le travail* (PUF, 2013). She has also contributed to several volumes on social policy.

Thomas Périlleux is Professor of Sociology at the Université catholique de Louvain and a founding member and researcher at the Centre for Interdisciplinary Research *Democracy, Institutions and Subjectivity* (CriDIS), as well as a member-associate at the Centre for Information, Therapeutics and Studies on Stress (CITES, Liège, Belgium). He is a researcher into the clinical sociology of work and of economic sociology. His numerous publications include *Destins politiques de la souffrance. Intervention sociale, justice, travail* (with John Cultiaux, Érès, 2009) and *Les métiers de la relation malmenés. Répliques cliniques* (with Mireille Cifali, L'Harmattan, 2012).

Géraldine Thiry is a post-doctoral research fellow at the Collège d'Etudes Mondiales (Paris) and Lecturer at Université catholique de Louvain (UCL). She was previously (2012–2013) researcher in the FP7 European Project «BRAINPOoL» (BRinging Alternative Indicators Into Policies) at the Université Libre de Bruxelles (ULB). She received her PhD from the Department of Economics at UCL in May 2012. She holds Master's degrees in Economics and in Political Sciences (International Relations) from UCL. Her main areas of research are new indicators beyond GDP, the socio-economics of quantification, critical accounting and ecological economics. More at www.geraldinethiry.be.

Gaëtan Vanloqueren is an agro-economist by training. A Guest Lecturer at ICHEC-Brussels Management School, where he teaches development economics and policy, he is also a former senior adviser to the U.N. Special Rapporteur on the right to food, and Research Associate at the Université catholique de Louvain. Gaëtan is a founding member of the Interdisciplinary Agro-ecology Research Group (GIRAF) of the Belgian National Fund for Scientific Research. His research interests are in the transition towards sustainable and democratic food systems and food policies. His publications are available at http://uclouvain.academia.edu/GaetanVanloqueren/Papers.

Edwin Zaccai is a professor at the Université Libre de Bruxelles, where he is the director of its Centre for Studies on Sustainable Development. He has also been a visiting lecturer at Sciences Po Paris. He publishes on multidisciplinary approaches to sustainable development, with a focus on the socio-political implications of environmental change in societies. His books include *Sustainable consumption, ecology and Fair Trade* (ed., Routledge, 1997); *25 ans de développement durable, et après?* (PUF, 2011). More at: http://homepages.ulb.ac.be/~ezaccai/.

Foreword

Tim Jackson
Author of *Prosperity without Growth*

"Call no one happy, until he is dead" proclaimed the Athenian statesman Solon, some two and a half thousand years ago. It is a curious claim from a modern perspective, where success is synonymous with material affluence. Worth is measured as wealth. Prosperity is cashed out as spending power. How much we have is more important than who we are. And who we are now is infinitely more important than how our lives are seen in retrospect.

The possibility that the story of our lives might be more important than the stuff of our lives is almost inimical to the way we organise society. Modern economics equates happiness with income. More is always better, in the conventional wisdom. This comforting myth sustains the growth-based economy. The more we have in monetary terms, the better off we are deemed to be. This is the basis on which, for over sixty years, politicians across the world have adopted the Gross Domestic Product (GDP) as the single most important indicator of social progress.

Such narrow vision might be forgiven, were it not for the fact that the bigger our economies, the greater their hunger for material resources. And the greater their hunger for material resources, the faster those resources are depleted. The faster resources are depleted, the greater their impact on the ecosystems on which we depend in the long run for survival. Or, to cut a long story short, our idea of social progress is not just unsustainable, it is internally inconsistent. Chasing prosperity through material possessions can only lead us faster towards disaster. The pursuit of happiness can only lead to a profound unhappiness in the long run.

If the vision itself were coherent, if the only route to a greater prosperity really was more material affluence, our prospect for social progress would indeed be bleak. We would find ourselves in a world in which prosperity was only ever available to the few at the expense of the many; only to present generations at the expense of future generations. Short of railing against the malevolence of deity, we would be consigned to an unsavoury power struggle over available resources and an eventual decline into barbarism.

But the vision isn't coherent. Only the briefest reflection reveals that its fundamental premise is false. More isn't always better. When you've had no food for weeks and the harvest has failed again, even a handful of grain represents a massive improvement in the quality of life. When the American-style walk-in fridge-freezer is stuffed with overwhelming choice, more will only make us sick. Obesity, diabetes, and poor cardiac health come not from insufficiency but from over-sufficiency. The diseases of affluence are a symptom of incoherent thinking. Even in something as basic as food, the equation of more with better just doesn't stack up. Beyond this simple example, it is not difficult to show that it isn't so much materiality itself that brings us affluence but the capabilities that we have to flourish as human beings.

The truth is, a genuine prosperity transcends material concerns. It consists as much in our social and psychological well-being as it does in our access to material things. It rests on the love of our families. It is inherent in the respect of our friends. It depends on the resilience of our communities. It resides in our ability to live a life without shame, to participate fully in the life of society. And though the restless marketers of consumerism persuade us endlessly that these vital goals can only be met with their own indispensable products, social psychology itself defies this pathological logic. As Solon slyly suggested, prosperity is as much about our story as it is about our stuff.

The value of the following delightful collection of essays lies in unpacking the deeper nuances of this conundrum. Redefining prosperity demands both accepting the lure of consumerism and also rejecting it. We have both to admit to our own acquisitive motivations and also to delve beneath them, to the living breathing fabric of social desire, to the yearning for meaning that haunts the human condition. Only through such an examination will it be possible to free ourselves from the pathology in which modern society finds itself, and to build – or perhaps rebuild – a more meaningful vision of prosperity.

Preface

Dominique Méda[1]

In 2003, the United Kingdom's Sustainable Development Commission published a report entitled "Redefining Prosperity", based on research highlighting the "dissonance" between economic growth, environmental sustainability, and human well-being. Both the workgroup created by Isabelle Cassiers in 2006 and the present volume have adopted a similar perspective. Previously, Cassiers co-edited a study offering a sustained reflection on "the active social state" and, with Catherine Delain, she published a widely respected article entitled "Growth Can't Buy Happiness" ("*La croissance ne fait pas le bonheur*"), the implications of which she wanted to explore through a collective project. What makes this topic seem so urgent at present? The reason is that it sets out to assess the scale of the transformations that have occurred after several centuries of unprecedented change in our way of inhabiting and utilising our world – a period during which human activity developed in a way that threatened natural equilibriums and promoted forms of behaviour that can no longer extend beyond the places in which they first appeared. Furthermore, the goal is to evaluate the consequences of the unsustainability – in the literal sense of something that cannot continue in its current form – of our model of economic development, our conduct, our way of inhabiting the world, and the relationship that, in the West, exists between nature and culture. These models and behaviours are what we must now try to radically recreate. For ultimately what is at stake is the degradation of the conditions of human life on earth and the need to invent a new relationship to nature, new ways of living, new standards of "comfort", and new forms of "living well". This quest is as old as the search for wisdom itself: recall how Aristotle, in his *Metaphysics*, observed that all men seek happiness and that a government is good if it offers its citizens this opportunity. The goal of "redefining prosperity" is thus not simply to use a familiar word in a radically new way, but also, by introducing a new or forgotten sense, to propose a fresh interpretation of it, one that will allow humanity both to set itself new goals and to find new means for achieving these goals.

Why have we used the term "prosperity"? "Progress" or "wealth" could have served just as easily as the foundational principles of this new interpretation. They, too, could call attention to the reasons it has become necessary to free ourselves from centuries-old interpretations of these concepts and to propose new ones. Indeed, all three terms belong to the same conceptual history: the terms progress, wealth, and prosperity, which can refer either to individuals or groups of varying sizes (for example, a state or society) were, in recent centuries, first seen as the *results* of economic development before being associated with economic development *tout court*. This conception has become so prevalent today that to say that a rich, forward-looking, and prosperous society is primarily one with a high growth rate is now a commonplace. Prosperity has become synonymous with high levels of consumption, the accumulation of material possessions, rising purchasing power, and the intensification of economic exchange. In France, the so-called "Thirty Glorious Years" are considered a particularly "prosperous" era because standards of living and consumption were continuously on the rise. Gross domestic product, in its dual role as an indicator of consumption and production, has become, particularly over the last fifty years, the symbol of prosperity, wealth, progress – in short, of social success.

This is precisely the conception of prosperity – that is, as an abundance of material possessions – with which a recent book by the author of the Sustainable Development Commission's report, based on the work of the "Redefining Prosperity" project, seeks to break. In *Prosperity without Growth*, Tim Jackson, drawing on the work of Amartya Sen, argues that we must renounce two of the most common meanings of "prosperity": prosperity as opulence – i.e. the immediate availability and constant flow of basic products – and prosperity as utility, or the satisfaction that these products provide. The only meanings of the term that we should retain are those of "capabilities for flourishing" and (as Jackson puts) the "bounded capabilities" required for living well within carefully defined constraints (Jackson, 2009). With this reasoning, we leave the realm of means (i.e. growth) to address the question of ends – in other words, prosperity. But once we have entered the realm of ends, it becomes clear that only a new interpretation of the term can legitimate a new development model and perhaps even a new paradigm: if what human beings and society are seeking is prosperity (another word for "living well") and if prosperity consists not simply in an abundance of material goods, but also in the possession, use, and enjoyment of other kinds of goods, activities, and ways of beings, then a discussion concerning the best way to achieve these ends once again becomes possible. In recent years, this has been precisely the goal not only of Jackson's Sustainable Development Commission and Cassiers' workgroup, but also of many other reflection circles, NGOs, academics, and think tanks, including, for example, France's Forum for Alternative Wealth Indicators (Forum pour d'autres indicateurs de richesse), which drew inspiration from a number of studies from the late nineties on the definition of wealth (including Méda, 1999; Viveret, 2003; Gadrey and Jany-Catrice, 2005) that challenged the exclusive reliance on GDP and economic development for assessing a society's performance. If prosperity no longer consists, either for the individual or for society, in the constant need for more, but rather, as Jackson and all of Sen's disciples suggest, in living well, it becomes possible to relinquish the need for ever higher growth rates and to achieve prosperity without growth

It is important to be fully conscious of the scale of the rupture being proposed: it requires us to renounce that the eighteenth century embraced, particularly economics' ascent to the rank of the queen of sciences and abundance as society's primary goal. It was during the eighteenth century – Adam Smith's work, *Inquiry into the Nature and Causes of the Wealth of Nations*, shows this best – that a completely unprecedented configuration was established, in which the wealth of both individuals and society came to play a central role: in the new world described by Smith, individuals who freely sell their labour power devote themselves single-mindedly to the pursuit of abundance, contribute to increasing production, and, through their work, are remunerated in a way that can be precisely calculated (thanks to labour's infinitely divisible properties; see, in particular, Méda, 2010). When this mechanism is extended to society as a whole, it not only brings opulence to "the lowest classes of people", but ensures, moreover, that the social order is civil and, most importantly, stable. This new economic order, based on calculability, predictability, stability, capabilities, and the exchange of goods, kept its distance from an alternative social model, founded on speech, debate, and deliberation. This order would undoubtedly have been much more "democratic", but also far riskier, as it would always have been in danger of drifting off course, leading to disagreement, conflict, and violence. The economic order advocated by Smith, supported by the industrial revolution and the rise of capitalism, proved more stable and ultimately prevailed, but it had the disadvantage of requiring, as a condition of its survival, that production and consumption grow indefinitely. Its key principle was the quest for abundance – which is, of course, never achieved, since human needs, we are told, are infinite – which means that production must always increase. If the abundance of produced and consumed goods and services is central to this social order, then there must always be new needs to satisfy to ensure that new goods and services will be produced and exchanged. Just as the values and ethics of work that Weber believed had helped to create capitalism have vanished even as capitalism itself – which could dispense with its original props – survived, the main reason we still desire growth more than anything else is in order to "sustain" the social bond. The true reason for growth has been forgotten; all that remains is the injunction to grow indefinitely lest our society collapses. To break with the need to always produce and consume more, to renounce what was originally simply a means for achieving an entirely different end means abandoning the eighteenth-century configuration and the need for relentless production and consumption.

Yet on what basis must we abandon this configuration? Jackson offers two main reasons, both of which have long been invoked by people working on these questions. First, it is needed to prevent the destruction of natural resources and the conditions that make the world inhabitable which are the result of two centuries of growth and particularly the past fifty years. The Meadows were already denouncing this problem in 1970s. Second, there is the fact that the abundance of material goods does not necessarily lead – particularly above a certain income bracket – to higher levels of subjectively acknowledged well-being. This issue is, however, a matter of debate. A third point also deserves mention, of which Jackson says little about and which the present volume will address: the meaning of this relentless process for individuals trapped in what Max Weber called the "iron cage", whether in terms of the time devoted to producing goods and services or the quality of work they require – considerations that raise the question of the alternative uses of human time that could be developed. For one forgets that work, which makes the production of goods and services possible, can easily lose its meaning as external pressures increase, especially when human time could be put to other extremely important uses that also generate collective satisfaction and well-being. These include time devoted to public deliberation, caring for others, taking care of oneself, and educating children – in other words, activities involving politics, friendship, love, parenting, and self-development. These activities do not transform the world through production or preparing goods and services to be sold, but rather through a willingness to preserve, heal, listen, and change – but not necessarily in the sense of productive labour or bringing something to the market. They can be grouped together under the terms "culture" or "care" – words that refer to a kind of enrichment or development that is far more respectful of the existing world, and far less aggressive.

Like many other studies from the last quarter of the twentieth century and like many of the authors in the present volume, Jackson proposes that we abandon our desire to always have more – more goods and services, or more of that general equivalency, money, which allows us to acquire the latter; adopt as our goal prosperity defined as "capabilities of flourishing"; and choose relationships over material possessions, allowing us to consume less and to invest in the new technologies and energy sources that we truly need. Such a plea, it must be noted, is obviously addressed to the citizens of developed countries. In so doing, Jackson celebrates, like Jeremy Rifkin in *The End of Work* (1996) along with many other representatives of contemporary thought, a diminished role for consumption in our lives, the cultivation of frugality and sobriety (which he portrays as behaviour that, far from being painful or uncomfortable, can bring us even greater satisfaction), and a shift (or rebalancing) of human concerns from relationships between people and things to relationships between people. To invoke Louis Dumont's important book *From Mandeville to Marx* (1977b), our goal must consist in nothing more and nothing less than a reversal of the key development of the eighteenth century, namely, the replacement of the relationships of dependence between human beings with relationships between human beings and things. This confirms (as if confirmation was needed) that Jackson, along with an entire current of thought that appeared during the final quarter of the twentieth century (and with which I personally identify), is proposing a radical break with the eighteenth-century transition – a break that requires us to minimise the importance of economic growth and consumption, and to abandon the transformation of the world as society's primary goal and developmental principle. This increased interest in human relationships should be accompanied by the transference of our utopian energies from the realm of production and consumption to the realm of relationships.

Louis Dumont called attention to the danger that, in his eyes, such a rupture represented: he believed that sliding back to human-to-human relationships could have dangerous and perhaps event totalitarian consequences if they were not channelled or mediated through relationships to things.

> [T]he facts before us are weighty enough to warrant reflection. They demonstrate that, until the present, the alternative between wealth as an end and compulsory and pathological forms of subordination seem to be our fate. Herein lies, in all likelihood, the drama of totalitarianism. Here, even the generous doctrinaires who claimed to deliver us from "possessive individualism" appear as sorcerers' apprentices.
>
> (Dumont, 1977a: 134, 1977b: 108)[2]

In *Qu'est-ce que la richesse?* (What is wealth?) (Méda, 1999), I tried to explain why Dumont's fear struck me as exaggerated. Yet we should nevertheless recognise this fact: contending that growth, consumption, and incomes (even if Jackson does not dwell on them) should no longer be so important is not an argument that will go over easily. To wean ourselves off the eighteenth-century configuration and to replace the religion of growth with the search for a more stationary condition, we need more than a credible policy of work-sharing. More than anything, we need a radically different form of social organisation, in which consumption ceases to be the only way to distinguish oneself and build an identity and that will allow individuals to participate actively in society not only through work, but also through active citizenship, in which deliberation about how to manage collective goods becomes central to our concerns as citizens as well as to our individual and social existence. This new configuration bears a remarkable resemblance to the world that existed prior to Benjamin Constant,[3] one that recognises itself primarily in the values of the ancient Greeks: moderation, the golden mean, limitations, the refusal of *hybris* (immoderation) and the lack of self-control, and which believes in the superiority of the immovable over the movable, stability over flux, and contemplation over action. It seeks to make interest, engagement, and even a passion for collective and public affairs, as well as for quality work and deliberation, central not only to our preoccupations, but also to the way in which we organise our time. It invites us to focus on the inherent pleasure of such activities and the process of doing them, rather than their results: as Aristotle recognised, life is action, not production. It is because this truth was overlooked and work time was reduced with no effort to reassess the value of other uses of time and other activities that this policy had the results that it did.[4] This is the kind of world and these are the kinds of values whose eclipse in modern times Hannah Arendt lamented. A preference for action, practice, care for the self, the ability to restrain oneself, and sustainability: these are the "ancient" values required to implement the agenda proposed by Jackson, Cassiers, and others (for example, Méda, 2013) – an agenda that seems inevitable. Can these values be "acclimatised" to the modern world? Is it possible to choose among the values and lifestyles advocated by the Greek philosophers, but only those that are compatible with our own, while rejecting other values, particularly those upon which Greece's fine democracy rested – such as slavery and the limitation of the right to participate in public deliberations to a very limited number of citizens? Is it possible to return to such values after so many centuries during which they were systematically called into question? Can we acclimatise them again to a world that would still hold on to modernity's most valuable contributions? Are we capable of inventing, in order to support the project of prosperity without growth, a form of political and social organisation and a conception of human nature that is radically different from what the eighteenth century imagined? In my view, this is why the current economic crisis and particularly growing awareness of the impending ecological crisis provides us with a unique opportunity: we cannot continue this way, but the efforts that are demanded of us as individuals and as a society require a radical restructuring of our social organisation, our values, and our form of government. The great interest of the present volume is, in my view, the essential contribution it makes to this question.

Notes

1 Université de Paris-Dauphine and Collège d'études mondiales (France). For further information see author's biography at the front of this volume.
2 This quote, based on the French edition of Dumont's book (1977a), appears only incompletely in the book's English translation (1977b). The above quote is based on the latter, where sentences equivalent to those found in the French version appear; where they do not, the words are those of the present translator.
3 Benjamin Constant (1767–1830) was a French liberal political philosopher who, in his essay entitled "The Liberty of Ancients Compared with that of Moderns", contrasted the individualistic and commercial liberty demanded by modern societies to the civic-minded liberty prevalent in ancient Greece and Rome.
4 In 1998 and 2000, France adopted a series of laws aimed at reducing the work week to thirty-five hours. They were justified partly on the grounds that they would encourage work-sharing (for a presentation, see Méda, in Coote and Franklin, 2013).

Bibliography

Arendt Hannah (1958), *The Human Condition.* Chicago and London: University of Chicago Press.

Cassiers Isabelle and Delain Catherine (2006), La croissance ne fait pas le bonheur: les économistes le savent-ils? *Regards économiques* 38: 1–14.

Coote Anna and Franklin Jane (2013), *Time on Our Side. Why we all need a shorter working week.* London: New Economic Foundation.

Dumont Louis (1977a), *Homo æqualis*. Paris: Gallimard.

Dumont Louis (1977b), *From Mandeville to Marx: The Genesis and Triumph of Economic Ideology.* Chicago and London: University of Chicago Press.

Gadrey Jean and Jany-Catrice Florence (2005), *Les Nouveaux Indicateurs de richesse.* Paris: La Découverte.

Jackson Tim (2009), *Prosperity without Growth. Economics for a finite Planet.* Oxon and New York: Earthscan.

Méda Dominique (1999), *Qu'est-ce que la richesse?* Paris: Aubier/Flammarion.

Méda Dominique (2010), *Le Travail. Une valeur en voie de disparition?* Paris: Flammarion.

Méda Dominique (2013), *La Mystique de la croissance. Comment s'en libérer.* Paris: Flammarion.

Rifkin Jeremy (1996), *The End of Work. The Decline of the Global Labor Force and the Down of the Post-Market Era.* New York: Putnam and Tarcher.

Smith Adam ([1776] 1982), *An Inquiry Into the Nature and Causes of the Wealth of Nations.* Indianapolis: Liberty Fund.

Stiglitz Joseph, Sen Amartya, and Fitoussi Jean-Paul (2010), *Mismeasuring our lives. Why GDP doesn't add up.* The Report by the Commission on the Measurement of Economic Performance and Social Progress. New York/London: New Press.

Vielle Pascale, Pochet Philippe, and Cassiers Isabelle (2005), *L'État social actif: vers un changement de paradigme?* Bruxelles: PIE-Peter Lang.

Viveret Patrick (2003), *Reconsidérer la richesse.* La Tour d'Aigues: l'Aube.

Introduction

Isabelle Cassiers[1]

What is prosperity? Its ambiguous meaning in everyday language is precisely what makes this question an interesting one. The term is generally defined on two levels, that of *being*, and that of *having*. The *Oxford English Dictionary* describes prosperity as "the condition of being prosperous, successful or thriving; good fortune, success, well-being". On the level of being, prosperity connotes a temporal state of wellness, happiness, luck, even joy; its contrary on this level is misfortune or unhappiness. Prosperity on the level of having designates increased wealth, an advance toward abundance, affluence, or even opulence; its contrary here is hardship or failure. On this level, it is correlated with economic activity and its growth, expansion, and progress, even to the point of a frenzied pursuit of riches and possessions. Just a few centuries ago, the word prosperity referred mainly to the level of being, but over time the two levels became deeply intertwined.

These two intertwined meanings raise a question: prosperity comes from the Latin *prosperus*, which means, "to cause (a thing) to succeed, to render fortunate". Has our continuous striving toward the accumulation of wealth over the past decades, or perhaps even the past centuries, caused us to lose sight of what it might mean to be fortunate on the level of being? Has the eclipse of one kind of prosperity by the other caused, at least in part, some of the difficulties our civilisation faces today? Examining how we as a society have assimilated "flourishing" to "increasing wealth" might indeed help us to understand the many-layered crisis we are currently traversing. This crisis has thrown into sharp relief a shared and growing awareness that the orientation of our social systems has engendered a number of problems and challenges. These problems and challenges have become manifest in many ways, and are rooted in practices and in ways of thinking that can only be overcome if they are thoroughly and broadly understood.

The ills from which the twenty-first century is already suffering are myriad: issues from climate change to the depletion of natural resources to the extinction of species call our development model into profound question. The scale of inequalities and the scope of poverty remind us that the accumulation of wealth does not resolve the problem of its distribution. The privileged among our populations are haunted by questions of meaning: where are we going? Can material wealth make a person happy? Are our cities, workplaces, and homes good places to live? If abundance holds such promise, why are we dogged with a vague but pervasive sense of unease? Can all individuals thrive when a society ploughs its whole effort into material progress, efficiency, and financial profit? For the most part, these are not new questions. They have, however, taken on unprecedented significance and even urgency as globalisation exacerbates and universalises them, and as it becomes clear that traditional approaches cannot offer a satisfactory response. In this sense, redefining prosperity – that is, examining once again what it means to "thrive" and acting accordingly – is a pressing, essential, and complex task.

This book emerged from the asking of these questions. Some twenty scholars, mainly but not exclusively academics from diverse fields – philosophy, economics, economic history, sociology, political science, law, environmental science, agricultural sciences, biology, and medicine – came together monthly to share their questions and their knowledge with one another, agreeing they would each have the right to fundamentally question any and all approaches. When the first meetings began, in 2006, identifying capitalism as a possible source of the ills mentioned above still sounded like subversive discourse. Two years later, one of the worst economic crises the system has ever seen opened the floor to innumerable questions about the desirability of capitalism and what it might mean to push beyond it.

Our first task was to wipe clean our common conceptual slate by defining what exactly should be discussed – happiness, well-being, progress, quality of life, a good or just life, etc. This was in itself a long task, since every discipline brings its own concepts and lines of reasoning to the table, and each one interrogates and intersects with other fields or disciplinary methods in different ways. Ultimately, we chose prosperity, which was flagged as an issue and brought into the media spotlight in 2003 by Tim Jackson, the author of a report for the UK Sustainable Development Commission called *Redefining Prosperity*. There were two reasons for this: first, it is an open concept, whose ambiguity is explained above; and second, it designates a social issue, whereas concepts such as well-being or happiness mostly bear on the individual. This second reason seemed all the more compelling because the excesses of the individualist perspective, both in terms of human behaviour and in the axiomatic terms of certain theories, seemed to us to be one possible cause of the world's current ills.

A multi-disciplinary approach was indispensable for several reasons. First, it was necessary to illuminate the philosophical and historical origins of our current definition of prosperity: although it is really in the past sixty years that the word came to be defined in terms of material possessions above all else, our society has been implicitly appropriating this definition over the past three centuries. Beyond that, this approach made it possible to identify the complex processes that gave rise to the problems we face today; to elucidate the ways in which our contemporary environmental, social, nutritional, economic, political, and cultural crises are interconnected; and to explore why a half-century of economic growth has neither increased life satisfaction in the West nor vanquished world poverty. Having discussed these questions, we could begin the search for possible escape routes; for paths to explore to ensure that our development moves toward the fundamental values expressed by the world's populations; for proposed changes to the way we live, behave, and organise society and public action – changes that actually respond, in an equitable way, to our deepest aspirations.

It seemed crucial to us to do more than simply denounce the ills currently afflicting our societies, though it remains necessary to understand and analyse their origins. While the economic crisis of 2008 bolstered their legitimacy, we believe that the signs of a sea change could be perceived long before that time, both in the aspirations to "something else" being expressed by an increasing portion of the population and in the emergence of alternative practices. Ultimately, this raises the question of whether one role of the scholar is to make such harbingers of change intelligible, to reveal an overall coherence that might, over the long term, unify and reinforce a set of reflections and experiences that began in a local and even marginal way.

Working with this material, it seemed essential to acknowledge that any scholar examining a subject such as prosperity inevitably does so from a specific critical standpoint; there is, in our opinion, no such thing as a "neutral" academic or expert. Researchers examine their subjects through the lens of their convictions, their cultural heritage and their postulates, and we believe it is important to acknowledge its existence. An expert who is unaware of the irreducibly normative facet of her analyses may do great harm, usurping the rightful place of the Other by projecting her own choices onto him. Our group, having arrived at a set of values we saw as basic starting points, and having agreed to work in full acknowledgement of our lack of neutrality, was able to agree to disagree in the most constructive of ways. As a result, the chapters that follow are the fruit of a cross-fertilisation process in which each contributor helped the ideas of the others to grow and flourish, even when those ideas diverged from one another. And, as all of our thinking grew from the common ground we identified at the outset, the book's general conclusions are a faithful reflection of all of our work.

The subjects discussed in this book emerged as a function of the way we worked together; rather than selecting from an abstract list of ideas, our group agreed upon topics that flowed naturally from the combined knowledge of the scholars who were willing and able to take part in a regular discussion group; in this way, the topics also emerged as a function of our geographic proximity to one another. The order in which the chapters appear may be seen as arbitrary, in the sense that each author has examined the question of prosperity from his own field and his own perspective, and has followed the particular path of his study to a set of possibilities for change. At the same time, the chapters are laid out along a specific thread, which we describe below for the reader who wishes to follow it.

The first three chapters stress the importance of groundwork in the definition of prosperity, and the manner in which that definition takes root. In the first chapter, Dominique Méda chronicles the evolution of our identification of prosperity with the abundance of material goods, tracing it back to the seventeenth and eighteenth centuries, when the accumulation of wealth, both individual and collective, began to be seen as a legitimate pursuit, and then forward to the present. She concludes by examining possibilities for prosperity without growth. Isabelle Cassiers and Géraldine Thiry offer a second historical perspective, looking back on the accounting conventions from which the idea of GDP emerged. In this light, they discuss the impossibility of maintaining social compromise based on the goal of economic growth, and explore what is at stake in today's vast debate over alternative wealth indicators. In the third chapter, Stéphane Leyens explores the intrinsically normative nature of the concept of prosperity. He asks whether, in today's highly diverse and globalised world, it is actually reasonable to hope to define prosperity in a way that fits such a vast range of value systems. In the tradition of Amartya Sen, he sketches out several possibilities for an inter-cultural (re)definition of prosperity.

In the four chapters that follow, the theme of prosperity is considered from four specific points of view essential to critical thinking about the problem at hand: consumption, labour, food, and environment. Jean De Munck begins this second phase of our investigation by discussing consumerism, considered as a way of life that is collectively produced and reproduced. He offers a critique of consumerism from three angles, that of justice, that of culture, and that of ecology, and explores the links among them. The central issue of labour is then taken up by Thomas Périlleux and Julien Charles, whose chapter is dedicated to "the experience of living work". They interpret trouble in the workplace in terms of "pathologies of commitment" and contrast these with an examination of the conditions of "prosperous work". From there, we turn to the question of food: Gaëtan Vanloqueren and Philippe Baret observe the impossibility of sustaining contemporary industrial agriculture and show how technological barriers constrain the potentially rich diversity of possible innovations. In the final chapter of this section, Tom Bauler and Edwin Zaccai discuss the environment from two main angles: first, they recall the coexistence of three alternative levels of interpretation when it comes to the relations between economic growth and the environment. They then examine environmental governance, its capacity to respond to the problems identified in this domain and the leverage that such governance might produce in favour of an overall redefinition of prosperity.

A sensitive question emerges from these pages, to which the two final chapters of the book attempt to offer a clear answer: what are the political conditions necessary to redefine prosperity? To this end, Laurent de Briey examines the causes behind the weakening of the state, which has reduced politics to the model of governance. In response to this reductive way of thinking he proposes a renewal in the meaning ascribed to politics, which he argues should offer the power to imagine a prosperity that takes into account the affirmation of collectively promoted values. Christian Arnsperger pursues the theme of collective action and its many facets, in particular with regard to transition. He considers how the diversification of lifestyles within the current system might be organised, and, more specifically, how to encourage lifestyles that are ecologically and anthropologically sustainable. Rather than taking green capitalism as the only possible model, he explores what it would mean to live with a full spectrum of post-capitalist options.

As we mentioned above, the themes discussed in this work were all selected based on the areas of expertise of the members of our research group; in other words, we do not claim to have covered every facet of a full redefinition of prosperity. This book is firmly rooted in a "Northern-hemisphere" perspective; though fully aware that the issue at hand is global in nature, we have nevertheless approached it as it has emerged in the wealthy countries in which we live. A "Southern-hemisphere" perspective would undoubtedly fill the pages of a second volume. Other themes mentioned in passing here merit chapters of their own, including poverty; various forms of inequality (particularly gender); the organisation of the health system; demographic pressure and migratory movements (and therefore of territories); the positioning of stakeholders, particularly in the realm of labour and management; the role of markets and financial entities and the manner in which they limit the exercise of democratic power; the role of the media and their emancipatory function – or, conversely, their responsibility in the confusion of desires and needs; education, culture, and the risks associated with formatting thought. We hope these silences – or half-silences, since each of these issues appears between the lines of this book – will be understood as an invitation to pursue and extend our line of thinking.

A number of themes mentioned in the preceding paragraph were discussion topics in our meetings, and the conversation among the contributors to this book was considerably enriched by the presence of others, academics and non-academics alike. We would like to express our gratitude to them for their knowledge, ideas, and expertise. As this manuscript goes to press, we would like to extend particular thanks to Anne-Françoise Bray, Anne-Hélène Pilon, and Céline Polain, who, with infinite patience, proofread our texts line by line and prepared them for publication, and to Pierre Reman (Université catholique de Louvain), who made possible this painstaking achievement. We also wish to thank the translators of the different chapters of this book, notably Michael Behrent and Miranda Richmond Mouillot, who worked hard to ensure the quality of the English version, as well as the Institute for the Analysis of Change in Contemporary and Historical Societies (IACCHOS, Université catholique de Louvain) and the Institut de recherche interdisciplinaire en sciences sociales (IRISSO, Université de Paris-Dauphine) who offered financial support for the translation. And last but not least, we would like to thank everyone who, through their presence behind the scenes, in word and in deed, inspired and supported the fifteen authors of this book – we offer it now as a warm expression of our deep gratitude.

Note

1 Université catholique de Louvain and Belgian National Fund for Scientific Research. For further information see author's biography at the front of this volume.

1 Can prosperity be disentangled from growth?

Dominique Méda[1]

As the dictionary tells us, the word "prosperity" took on quite early (in the twelfth century) what is still a component of its modern meaning: "the state of being prosperous, a happy situation". It comes, moreover, from the Latin *prosperare* (*pro-sperare*), which means to make happy, cause to succeed, achieve success, and which encompasses the idea of continuity, of projection into a situation likely to improve or which one hopes will continue. The dictionary tells us that the economic connotation, a condition of plenty, increased wealth was a much later arrival, making its appearance, or so it would seem, in 1751, i.e. at a time when political economy was on the way to establishing itself. From my own point of view, the foremost question in fact is: what was the path that led from one definition to the other? How did a "happy situation that is likely to continue" come to be equated with "increased wealth" and a "condition of plenty"? How was it that our society's progress, wealth, and prosperity came to be reduced to the abundance of the material goods that it had acquired? We must follow a complex etymological trail if we are to understand not only how "prosperity" came to be identified with "plenty" but also how, in the twentieth century, the growth of GDP has come to be regarded as the primary cause of national progress and performance. Only by answering this question will we be able to step back from this assimilation and ask the question that really matters today: is prosperity without growth possible?

This essay is based on the author's previous studies in the history of ideas, which sought to trace a genealogy of concepts relating to work (Méda, 1995) and wealth (Méda, 1999, 2009). The first part goes back over the ideological upheaval of the eighteenth century, with the legitimisation of individual and collective enrichment and the spread of the idea that they create the conditions of prosperity. The second part endeavours to describe the conventions and instruments to be used by nations to measure their prosperity with ever-increasing precision – the better to emphasise their power. The last part, after evoking the criticisms levelled at these conventions, considers the possibility of severing the link between prosperity and growth.

1 Individual enrichment as the basis of the prosperity of nations

The eighteenth century experienced the pinnacle of the radical transformation that Albert Hirschman (1977) described as an astounding upheaval of the moral and ideological order, which brought in its wake widespread approval of the desire for enrichment together with the activities symptomising this desire, and in a very short time. Indeed, the Aristotelian and medieval condemnation of chrematistics abruptly gave way to the legitimisation of individual and collective enrichment, which henceforth became society's primary purpose.

The end of the repudiation of chrematistics

Let us recall a word proposed by Aristotle in his *Politics* (1998: I, 9) to make a radical distinction between economics and chrematistics, or rather between the two branches of the art of acquisition, one natural, the other unnatural. Economics is the natural branch. It is the art of administering the estate, the household or the city and consists in acquiring the resources required by the community. Barter and small trade are permitted, provided they are subordinated to subsistence and communal autonomy and have as their purpose the community's well-being. The unnatural branch is chrematistics. Because it is the art of finding the sources and methods of exchange designed to ensure the maximum profit, this mode of acquisition is responsible, according to Aristotle, for the opinion that wealth and ownership can be limitless. "[W]ealth acquisition [chrematistics] is concerned primarily with money, and its task is to be able to find sources from which a pile of money will come" (1998: 16). Consequently, money is the principle and the source of commerce. Chrematistics is only concerned with exchange value, not use value, and the wealth arising from chrematistics is undeniably "limitless". It corresponds to the state of mind of those who are content simply to live, rather than to "live properly". The problem is that this extreme, limitlessness activity and this inability to set limits discourages us from living "properly". As we know, medieval and notably thomistic thought maintained this mistrust of trade and barter, whose primary aim is the accumulation of wealth.

The eighteenth century witnessed the legitimation of individual enrichment. Max Weber was among those who best described this change of attitude, evoking the words of Benjamin Franklin from the middle of the eighteenth century, on which the author dwelt at some length in his *Protestant Ethic and Spirit of Capitalism*:

> Remember that *time* is money. He that can earn ten shillings a day by his labour, and goes abroad, or sits idle, one half of that day, though he spends but sixpence during his diversion or idleness, ought not to reckon that the only expense; he has really spent, rather thrown away, five shillings, besides (…). Remember that money is of the prolific, generating nature. Money can

> beget money, and its offspring can beget more, and so on. Five shillings turned is six, turned again it is seven and three pence, and so on, till it becomes a hundred pounds. The more there is of it, the more it produces every turning, so that the profits rise quicker and quicker. He that kills a breeding sow, destroys all her offspring to the thousandth generation. He that murders a crown, destroys all that it might have produced, even scores of pounds.
>
> (Weber, 1992: 48–49)

As Weber says, what Franklin expresses is an *ethos*: "this ethic… is above all completely devoid of any eudaemonistic, not to say hedonistic, admixture".[2] Here, the *summum bonum* may be expressed thus:

> the earning of more and more money, combined with the strict avoidance of all spontaneous enjoyment of life.… [Money] is thought of so purely as an end in itself, that from the point of view of the happiness of, or utility to, the single individual, it appears entirely transcendental and absolutely irrational… Economic acquisition is no longer subordinated to man as the means for the satisfaction of his material needs. This reversal of what we should call the natural state of things, so irrational from a naive point of view, is evidently as definitely a leading principle of capitalism and it is foreign to all peoples not under capitalistic influence.
>
> (Weber, 1992: 53)

Individual enrichment, the key to collective enrichment

This initial reversal is closely linked to another. If individual enrichment is legitimate, it is doubtless, as Weber explains, because for some it has become the means of expressing their "choice", in addition to the fact that it is the key to collective enrichment. At any rate, that is precisely what the burgeoning discipline of political economics strove to demonstrate. During the first half of the eighteenth century, this idea, which appeared in the *Fable of the Bees [Fable des Abeilles]* (luxury and the wish to see all one's desires fulfilled, particularly those born of *Pride*, are good because they lead to the greatest possible production) went largely unheeded and was severely condemned. As early as 1734 it was popularised by Melon in his *Political Essay on Commerce*, and then taken up by Voltaire (2010), who made himself its herald in the "Luxury Debate".[3] This idea flourished and, in the second half of the eighteenth century, became the new *doxa*. Thus in 1771, a book by Georges-Marie Butel-Dumont was published, entitled *Theory of Luxury, or Treatise in which the author attempts to show that luxury is not only a useful tool but one indispensably necessary to the prosperity of nations*. He shows that a taste for luxury is inherent in man and that without it societies would not flourish and would not even exist. "Attitudes towards luxury, says the author, can have serious consequences affecting the prosperity of nations" (Butel-Dumont, 1771: VII). And if, he goes on to say, nearly everyone condemns luxury at the time when he is writing and if only those with some experience of political economics or public affairs know that luxury is good for national prosperity, then popularising this idea and emphasising its cogency is an essential task that must be undertaken.

Chapter IV of the same work evinces an unfailing utilitarianism, used to demonstrate the equivalence between private enjoyment and public prosperity:

> happiness rests on positive bases and in no way depends on opinion. It lies in the extent of that enjoyment. The happiness of a nation only exists through the happiness of the individuals it comprises. The more means of enjoyment the individuals acquire, the happier they will be and the more the state of which they are a part acquires wealth and resources of every kind, in a word, power. As a necessary consequence, the sacred maxim of good government should be to encourage anything that tends to increase the enjoyment of its subjects, not only because their happiness depends on it and the government should seek to ensure their greatest happiness, but also because anything that increases the power of the subjects also increases the power of the nations.
>
> (Butel-Dumont, 1771: 72)

For a nation to enjoy full and lasting prosperity, the author tells us, it must be vast: because

> the need to provide life's needs, which are difficult to satisfy in a large society, spurs on the mind and speeds up production, and the more societies there are, the greater production will always be, because since competition in every aspect is more intense, the greater the effort required to fulfil people's desires.
>
> (1771: 18)

Where does prosperity come from? From the ability of a large state to encourage production that exceeds the satisfaction of its needs and thus increasingly intense consumption: if the government allows trade to increase freely, then the ensuing consumption and enjoyment will be a continual encouragement to more and more production – and thus ever greater prosperity; "hence sustained emulation; hence an abundant production of substances and forms; hence a large population. The concatenation of these effects creates wealth, strength, in a word, the lasting felicity of an empire" (1771: 41).

Adam Smith does not try to justify luxury; on the other hand, he feels no need to repudiate what now appears to be an obvious fact: men have been put in society to satisfy their needs and society's primary (not to say sole) task is to increase the number of things both necessary and useful to life and to pursue abundance so that it spreads through all of society: "This great multiplication of products in all the different arts and trades, resulting from the division of labour, is what, in a well governed society, creates this general wealth which reaches the lowest classes of the people". Thus society is not the product of a contract or a debate in which rights and responsibilities (and words) have been weighed. It is not a community of citizens unified by a political relationship whose intensity has to be constantly verified and maintained. It is an association of developed individuals, fully constituted even before they enter society, and who decide that their needs can be best satisfied through trading and exchanging. As Louis Dumont wrote (1977), speaking of Mandeville, and in fact the whole tradition that he pioneered:

> Mandeville focuses on gain, wealth, material prosperity, as the core of social life. We can look at the *Fable,* and especially the poem itself, as dealing throughout with this change in primacy: morality fits (perhaps) the small and stagnant society (of yesterday), not the large and powerful society (economy) of today.
>
> (Dumont, 1977: 76–77)

Once this radical transformation was complete, society appeared to be primarily governed by – and even founded on – the economic bond between individuals. In both Voltaire and Smith, we find the fundamental idea that commerce pacifies, that it encourages, even forces individuals to cooperate: cooperation in work and in the task of production, cooperation built on exchange. Later repudiated by Durkheim, the prevailing ideology at the close of this stage was that the bond that really unites individuals – individuals in possession of all their faculties and attributes – is based on exchange, is economic in nature, and that the social bond, far from being of a political nature, as Rousseau believed, is first and foremost economic. Society is not this entity, this whole that is greater than the parts and in any case different from them and not reducible to them, which is born of a decision and an assent which have to be constantly renewed – in democratic actions in which free speech is important. Society is not a political community constituted by the common will of the citizens. It is an association of individuals who exchange goods and services and who have absolutely no need to talk about or debate the ends they wish to pursue. Society was reduced to economics. At the end of the eighteenth century, the reversal was complete. Not only was economics somehow confused with chrematistics, economics itself had ceased to be the art of managing resources for a community seeking to be independent, becoming the science of wealth acquisition for the nation as a whole, aimed at systematically increasing prosperity. Meanwhile, politics, too, had become entirely subservient to economics, reduced to economics, and existing only to serve it.

According to Mandeville, Melon, and Voltaire, government must, in effect, act shrewdly to maintain competition, create new needs, and act in such a way that emulation results in constant increases in production. Economics – or rather the science of finding the best means of achieving the highest possible production – was now the queen of the sciences. Politics *qua* art of collective deliberation on the conditions of living appropriately among equals, and even among friends – a pre-eminent concept from the Greeks to Rousseau – was eradicated and replaced by economics *qua* art of acquiring wealth. The state now resembled a company in which the noblest and most worthy task was to work, produce, and get rich, for it was here that the social bond would be most intense. The well-being of the individual depends essentially on the well-being of the nation, hence on the abundance and even the enormity of production. The greater the number of objects produced and/or acquired, the greater the general well-being and prosperity: the level of production became the main collective task on which everything else collective well-being, individual well-being depended. The consumption of new products was in itself a pleasure and was, moreover, the source of many benefits, both individual and social: civility, harmonious relations, and intellectual growth. Voltaire, Melon, and Smith agreed: one of the essential benefits to be expected from the increased general prosperity was, perhaps even more than increased material comfort, the strengthening of social exchanges and the social bond, which was now self-regulated or self-maintained with no need for any intervention of a political nature. The greatest prosperity was also *the key to a free, democratic* society. There could be no progress under despotism. With the division of labour, however, there could be. In any case, one thing is clear about this moment: the multiple nature of the concept of prosperity, still extant in the seventeenth century, gave way to a single definition: the increase in the quantities of goods produced and consumed.

The end of the natural orders, work, and prosperity

As we know, to explain this upheaval Hirschman applied the principle of compensatory passion: to counterbalance the destructive passions marking the seventeenth century, the appeal would gradually have shifted to individual interest, egoism, increasingly seen as the most effective bastion against violence. Hence, too, the redemption of commerce, which was previously held in contempt but was now suddenly seen as benevolent and uniquely suited to counterbalance the state's temptation to seize all power. Insofar as it sought to increase the general prosperity, economic activity would have thus been a means of depriving political power of part of the place it would otherwise have occupied. But there is room for other explanations (Méda, 1995, 1999). The seventeenth century saw the disintegration of all natural orders. With Newton, the geocentric conception of the world was rejected: man was now the centre of the world. The seventeenth century also witnessed the end of natural communities, of *Universitas*, the social, natural, hierarchised community whose unity was organic and in which each had his or her place. It was also the century in which society found its legitimacy and its basis in human will and not in divine authority (Hobbes). Thus the social order was not a natural order. It was arbitrary. Accordingly, a means had to be found of holding together individuals who, in the pre-social state, fought one another relentlessly in a permanent state of war; of establishing rules upon which to base a stable social order not under constant threat. These rules would be based on *work*, which would measure each person's contribution to production and make it possible to exactly calculate not only the remuneration due to him or her, but also and more generally the relations on which the entire social order would be based.

The social body is born of a contract, a convention. This was the most widely shared belief among the political authors of the eighteenth century. This contract, however, could be found in numerous versions and two major interpretations rivalled with one another: an "economic" version and a "political" version. They both proposed a principle intended to unify the disordered multiplicity of individuals in a state of nature. Both had recourse to a form of contract. But in one case, that of the political contract – as imagined by Rousseau, for example – the contract is the act whereby political authority is constituted and by means of which the body politic is unified. In the other case, the contract defines the conditions of the exchange and sets the laws of equivalence between two magnitudes. In the first of these cases, the contract allows all the individuals to be recognised as a body politic and to establish the rules according to which it will be organised. In the second case, there is no original contract, but rather an infinite number of contracts, most of them in fact implicit, under which exchanges are regulated. For Smith, it is thanks to exchanges that society is created and maintained. It is the multiplicity of exchanges which at any given time constitutes the social link. Everything happens as though the development of the economy depended on the mistrust of individuals: human action is not sufficient to safeguard the social order. Men who discuss together the ends to be pursued and the means of achieving them are not capable of ensuring as stable and sustainable a society as that created by economic exchanges. Possible discord, and hence violence, are a constant threat to its fragile equilibrium. The order sought by men, the order decided on by political debate, in which speech is susceptible to misunderstandings, is too fragile. Better by far, and championed unequivocally by such economic philosophers as Smith, is the stability of an unintentional order (Hayek was to express this more succinctly two centuries later: orders that are not of human making are more solid).

2 Prosperity and power

As Butel-Dumont's writings have made very clear, prosperity has to do with power, and more precisely the power of nations. Vanoli (2002), one of the major French national accounting experts, also showed how the initial estimates of national income were inseparable from national concerns about assessing and exhibiting their power in the eyes of others. At the same time, it was doubtless necessary to display their power and hence to assess it, which explains why prosperity, particularly in the eighteenth century, took the form of quantities able to be added up and point to growth.

An inventory of the factors of prosperity

Malthus is among those writers who give us a better understanding of the link between the manifestation of power and the ability to display growth. In 1820, he published his *Principles of Political Economy*, the first chapter of which is devoted to the question of wealth, and more particularly the question of its definition. He immediately contrasts two definitions of wealth: that of the Physiocrats, who, in his eyes, endowed it with too restricted a meaning; and that of those who gave it too broad a meaning, among them Lord Lauderdale, for whom wealth is "all that man desires as useful or delightful to him". Malthus long disputed this latter definition, for two main reasons: if one were to accept this definition, he argues, on the one hand one would have to draw up an "inventory"; and on the other, the language of the economist would be in total disarray.

Real wealth, Malthus tells us, is not one of those intangible and pleasant things, beliefs, laws, civil liberty, the arts, morals, and so on. One of the main reasons is that it is impossible to evaluate, count, or measure the role and the variables inherent in such "things", which are not quantifiable. Malthus raises the possibility that a diminution of the manufactured and mercantile products may be "balanced, in the opinion of some, by the enjoyment derived from the intellectual attainments, and the various personal qualities and services of the inhabitants of a country", and then goes on to point to the intrinsic difficulty:

> But how is this balance to be ascertained? How is it possible to estimate the degree of wealth derived from these sources? Yet it is quite obvious that we cannot practically apply any discussions respecting the relative increase in the wealth of different nations, without having some means, however rough, of estimating the amount of such increase.

The ability to say whether the wealth of a country has increased or not, to tell whether any such increase in wealth is equivalent to any other increase, requires the ability to demonstrate the increase and thus, on the one hand, there needs to be an "inventory", and on the other hand, the inventory must be composed of quantities whose increases, and even changes, are measurable.

Moreover, economic science must be able to play a central role in the evaluation of such wealth; indeed, it must be *the* science applied to this evaluation. This is a further reason why that which constitutes wealth, or prosperity, should be quantifiable. But we have come full circle: for it to be compared to the wealth of others as well as over time, the wealth of a country, which constitutes its prosperity and hence its power, must be "countable". But the only things that can be counted are quantities, structured and measurable realities. Thus the only valid definition of wealth, Malthus asserts, is that which is calculable and quantifiable:

> If therefore, with M. Say, we wish to make of political economy a positive science based on experience and capable of giving exact results, the greatest care must be taken to embrace in the definition of its principal term only those objects whose increase or diminution can be measured; and the most natural and the most useful line to draw distinctly is that which separates material from immaterial objects.

One can see at work here the extraordinary power taken unto himself by the economist: that of giving a definition of wealth deduced entirely as the result of an external need to exhibit his power and save the economy; of giving a definition that in no way derives from collective discussion, from exchanges with other disciplines, other people, other points of view, and which on the one hand consists in excluding from what constitutes the wealth of a society everything that cannot be measured, and on the other hand, assimilating wealth, objects capable of increase and material objects. With a wave of the magic wand and pretexting that it is impossible to put them down as additional quantities, the factors of wealth and prosperity other than the material factors are excluded. Another wave of the wand, and the "democratic" moment of quantification is forgotten. Indeed, it will be remembered that, as Desrosières made clear, quantification consists of two moments: agreeing and measuring. "The verb 'quantify', in its active form", he writes, "presupposes the elaboration and exposition of a series of preliminary equivalences involving comparisons, negotiations, translations, records, codes, reproducible codified procedures and calculations enabling expression in numbers" (Desrosières, 2008: 9–10).

Thus this argument leads to the idea that a society's prosperity depends mainly on the material objects it produces or acquires. Real wealth, quite explicitly, is what can be counted and what fulfils the primary needs of the individuals. These are the goods which simply enable people to live, satisfy their basic needs, even improve the material conditions of their lives. Malthus recognises that there are certainly other sources of happiness, other factors of prosperity (such as the works of Newton or Shakespeare), as well as other needs; but their satisfaction, either because it is more personal or because it is of secondary importance, and above all because it is immaterial, cannot in any way be counted or measured and has to be recognised or considered by other means.

> To assess the value of Newton's discoveries or of the enjoyment derived from the works of Shakespeare or Milton in terms of the price their works fetched would indeed be very paltry measure of the amount of glory and pleasure enjoyed for their country;

and it would be no less crude and absurd to evaluate the benefits England derived from the Glorious Revolution of 1688 in terms of the debits and credits attaching to its accomplishment. Therefore one must consider them as belonging to another order, refuse to put a price on them, to count them.

Let us remember that in the mid-nineteenth century, the idea that a nation's prosperity depended first and foremost on the quantity of material objects produced or acquired became fairly widespread. The systems used to formalise this idea and give concrete expression to the fact that national prosperity was the sum of the goods and services produced and acquired were introduced a century later.

Corporate and national accounting systems

The analyses devoted by Max Weber to the advent of capitalism in several of his works arguably provides us with a better understanding than any other source of how the obsession with calculability and the concentration on increases in quantities and then prices gradually impoverished the original concept of prosperity and reduced the plurality of the factors favouring growth, health, and happiness to an extremely univocal notion of prosperity. Weber says that apart from "free" work, the growth of Western capitalism was based on two other factors: on the one hand, the separation of the household from the business enterprise; and on the other hand, rational accounting methods. In certain places in his works, Weber goes so far as to say that it is in fact calculability, the ability to calculate so as to exhibit an increase, which lies at the heart of capitalism: rationalisation "on the basis of rigorous calculation" is "one of the fundamental characteristics of an individualistic capitalistic economy" (Weber, 1992: 76).

Seeking to explain the absolute singularity of Western capitalism and distinguish it from the greed or the thirst for acquisition, Weber affirmed that the thirst for acquisition, the profit motive, the quest for money, for the greatest possible amount of money, had, in themselves, nothing to do with capitalism and that the lust for limitless gain in no way implied capitalism, much less the "spirit" of capitalism: "The important fact", he says,

> is always that a calculation of capital in terms of money is made, whether by modern book-keeping methods or in any other way, however primitive and crude. Everything is done in terms of balances: at the beginning of the enterprise is an initial balance, before every individual decision a calculation to ascertain its probable profitableness, and at the end a final balance to ascertain how much profit has been made.
>
> (Weber, 1992: 18)

What counts is that everything can be reduced to a unit of measurement, that everything can be evaluated and that a profit, a balance can finally be announced. It was during the twentieth century that this obsession and these instruments (private ones, those of the entrepreneur described by Max Weber) became public, applied to the nations themselves and the object of an implacable rationalisation: it was that period which saw the introduction of the accounting conventions that definitively assimilated prosperity and increased production.

The French national accounting system was developed between 1938 and 1952. It was the work of a few individuals of whom François Fourquet drew a picture in *The Accounts of Power*. The system was entirely conceived, he showed, as a response – and an antidote – to the so-called "Malthusianism" of pre-war France, Malthusianism and over-cautiousness which, according to our reformers, led to a sort of decline, of decadence, and finally to humiliation: "The historians", writes Fourquet,

> have almost all detested the Malthusian desire for a smaller, ageing France for a century or more; and whether they be patriots or internationalists (or both), they have worked to ensure the position of France as a great power, modern and vigorous.

How is the national accounting system an antidote to Malthusianism (in the popular interpretation of this term)? In that in its very structure it underlines the decisive role of the state, public expenditure, the Keynesian multiplier and above all growth. The French national accounting system is entirely designed, just as Malthus wished, to calculate from year to the next, the increase in the nation's wealth, that is to say in national production. One has to make a parallel between Malthus's text and his conclusion, in the sense in which it is formulated in terms of material resources, and the concept of production lying at the heart of the national accounting system. What interested the men who implemented the system was indeed the mechanism of growth: "What in the thirties scandalised Gruson and Denizet, was not the upset per se, but ignorance and the inability to climb out of the depression". The growth of what? The growth of production. Curiously enough, its content seemed to interest them less than the general dynamic of growth. It was the actual movement of increase, the phenomenon of increased production, which seemed more than anything else to fascinate the inventors of the national accounting system, just as the productive power of work had fascinated Smith in 1776.

But what is production? In France (initial accounting practices vary from country to country), it was constituted by agreement, between 1945 and 1956, of the production of exchanged, i.e. mercantile, goods and services. Today, it is defined as the socially organised economic activity which consists in creating goods and services usually exchanged on the market and/or obtained from the factors of production exchanged on the market, i.e. it includes, since 1976, non-mercantile services. Paradoxically, this is the same belief, in which wealth and the production of goods are assimilated, which inspired Malthus and those who created the national system of accounting. In both cases, the focus is on the elements of reproduction of the material conditions of life. For Smith, and fifty years later for Malthus, this meant identifying the real sources of prosperity so as to put that prosperity within reach of all the citizens of the nation.

The system introduced in 1945 played the role that the economists of the eighteenth and nineteenth centuries intended that economics should play: to identify precisely the sources of wealth and the circuits taken by wealth to generate abundance. It is understandable that after the ruin wrought by the war and faced by the immense task of reconstruction, the need was felt for a means whereby essential production could be rapidly resumed, the production of those things that satisfied people's basic needs: housing, food, clothes, etc. Understandable, too, that all the attention of the Inventors of the national accounting system was focused on the state and its task of encouraging private initiatives. The specific difference between the concept of productive power in the eighteenth or nineteenth century and that dating from the implementation of the accounting system is rooted in the role of the state: in the eighteenth century, the state was a burden, the very symbol of uselessness and unproductiveness. For Smith, "the role of the 'sovereign' should be reduced to a minimum". In classic political economy, "the state is coextensive with the wealth of nations". As for the inventors of the national accounting system, they had read Keynes and had drawn from their analysis of the thirties one conviction: the role of the state is not to balance – hesitantly – public finances. It is to inspire the entire national system of production with a positive dynamic, to encourage and support private producers and to increase their power and their actions. Vanoli confirms this:

> the birth of national accounting is historically linked to the crisis, Keynesian macroeconomics and the extended role of the state, a state strengthened as a result of the war and then further strengthened by the post-war policies of reconstruction, growth and social welfare.

The national accounting system, a convention *par excellence*, indirectly illustrates the fact that at the time when a battered France emerged from the war, real wealth could only be identified with the greatest possible production of basic goods enabling the reconstruction of the country and intended to satisfy basic needs. Services were sparingly integrated into what in 1945 was seen as genuinely resulting from production.

National prosperity, the sum total of individual prosperity

The inventors of the French national accounting system reduced their scope, like Smith and Malthus, to only a very small part of reality (production), but, moreover, conceived it very narrowly (all mercantile goods and services), without explaining the choices governing their decisions or the conventions by which they were guided. But two things stand out: first, national production is only a huge added value. GDP is the sum total of the values added together by the basic units; it is an aggregative concept which reveals the extent to which the macro and micro levels are linked, and illustrates the fact that the same reasoning now prevails at all levels. At all levels, it is important to obtain an added value, calculate the difference between two monetary magnitudes, and show a positive balance. Each positive balance generated by each unit increases the overall balance representing the wealth of society, which is plainly the sum of individual wealth. And national accounting is clearly the system that makes it possible to calculate, in the same way as corporate accounting is required if capitalism is to work, the increase in the nation's wealth from one year to another. And even though the economists and the accountants proclaim that GDP is in no way an indicator of well-being but is limited to measuring production or the national income, the everyday use made of GDP and the logic which decrees that whatever cannot be counted will end up being forgotten and thus irrelevant speak for themselves.

Second, the nineteenth century saw another, absolutely major, change which completed the reduction of economics to chrematistics and made national prosperity the sum total of individual prosperity, seen as the satisfaction of no matter what individuals want, such as consumer indulgences between which no distinction is made, so long as they represent the acquisition of a product or service placed on the market. The revolution that Voltaire hoped and prayed for, that non-essentials would be seen as very necessary in order to permanently sustain the grandeur of the state, with emulation used as an incentive to increase general prosperity, was made possible by the new concept of value embraced by the marginalist economists: value no longer comes from work but from rarity, utility no longer has anything to do with the satisfaction of essential needs but with the satisfaction of desire, any individual desire. The satisfaction of any individual desire generates utility and must therefore be entered on the credit side of the national ledger. The more the individual acquisitions and indulgences increase, the greater the national wealth. Thus our accounting convention takes note of the marginalist revolution: everything that is useful in the eyes of a single individual, no matter whether "useful" means necessary or non-essential, is recorded positively in the aggregate supposedly representing national wealth and prosperity, GDP.

It is astonishing that national accounting, inspired as it was by Keynesianism and Marxism and centred around production and material resources, should nevertheless have adopted their vision so zealously. Everything happens as though our contemporary national accounting were a jumble of macroeconomic reasoning on the subject of production and the entire neoclassical conception of utility, as though that conception had simply been transported bag and baggage into a realm in which production is simply better modelled and considered from every angle. That is why wealth is organised, in the conception of national accounting, from the point of view of the individual: there is wealth only where there is production, and by definition only if the product is put on the market and purchased by someone. Thus national accounting is solely a two-dimensional reflection of the market. It approves all consumption, all acquisitions of any product or service that satisfies no matter what desire, since what counts is the fact of being put on the market and then bought. National wealth consists only of the goods and services produced and the sum total of individual enrichment.

Prosperity without growth

The other two questions bear directly on the links between growth and prosperity and not the conventions used to represent it. The first is that it now seems increasingly probable that, far from being the condition *sine qua non* of prosperity (in the sense of sustainable well-being), economic growth will, to the contrary, precipitate its decline. The information gathered by Tim Jackson, first for the British Government's Commission for Sustainable Development and then in his book *Prosperity without Growth,* shows that continuing to produce and consume goods and services in the same proportions as today, with a world population which by 2050 will reach nine billion people hoping to achieve the standard of living currently enjoyed in the West, is simply not ecologically sustainable. Jackson shows on the one hand that current economic growth is incompatible with the normal conditions of habitability of our planet; and on the other hand that the present response to this realisation – "clean" or "green" growth – i.e. the possibility of continuing to have economic growth while avoiding the destructive impact on the environment ("decoupling") is an illusion. A third point: the fact that growth would go hand in hand with – and even generate increasingly greater – well-being and would thus be the condition *sine qua non* of a prosperity conceived as sustainable well-being. In opposition to studies showing that increased income is always correlated with increased satisfaction and growing well-being (Clark and Senik, 2007), or that there are strong correlations between growth levels and social indicators (OECD, 2007), other studies, including those of Gadrey (2010) and Jackson show on the contrary that the benefits of growth decrease beyond a certain level of per capita income and thus that life expectancy, quality of life, and levels of education cease to increase with growth. Conversely, Jackson develops an argument bordering on the philosophical and the psychological to explain that the consumption of ever-increasing quantities of material goods is antithetical to prosperity and that on the contrary prosperity must be taken to mean, in the sense of Amartya Sen, the full development of individual capacities.

Jackson in fact distinguishes between three meanings of the word "prosperity": prosperity as wealth; prosperity as utility; and prosperity as capacities for development. After assembling a certain number of arguments indicating that the first two interpretations of the word are anachronistic, Jackson opts for the third meaning as being more relevant to the present situation (limited resources and a growing world population), and makes a point of saying that the list of central capabilities must be negotiated in open dialogue. Jackson's argument is altogether extremely stimulating insofar as he aims to accommodate a number of theories concerning (individual) happiness and the present, radically new situation and turn them into theories of collective sustainable well-being. This poses huge questions, which it is impossible even to suggest in the context of this article, on the revolution necessitated by the adoption of such a theory.

Moreover, it has a certain heuristic interest insofar as it enables us to understand the place occupied by growth in our social edifice and the safeguards that need to be established if we should ever dispense with it. In any case, it obliges us to reinvent new "conventions of wealth and prosperity" which it will not be possible to establish without collective deliberation of a radically new nature. So we should turn back, to the heart of the eighteenth century, *before* the time when the Voltairian conception of prosperity triumphed, *before* "prosperity" took on its new meaning, *before* it became assimilated to the accumulation of quantities of material goods, *before* the "Luxury Debate", to the conception that was historically eclipsed, in the West at least. And so we arrive at Rousseau, the man who argued against the development of luxury and of commerce, a destroyer of morality and of the democratic community, and insisted on the importance of political deliberation in the public arena, frugal prosperity as opposed to worldly inessentials, limits on accumulation, the importance of political discourse against all-pervading consumption. This is assuredly the path we need to rediscover today.

Notes

1 Université de Paris-Dauphine and Collège d'études mondiales (France). For further information see author's biography at the front of this volume.
2 Eudemonism (from the Greek *eudaimonia*, "happiness") is the doctrine according to which happiness is the purpose of human life. Hedonism is the doctrine according to which the pursuit of happiness and the avoidance of pain are the purpose of our existence (Author's note).
3 In his *Lettres philosophiques*, Voltaire champions the idea that commerce is the surest road to prosperity. Commerce enables surplus to be traded (which Voltaire reminds us is very necessary) and contributes to the grandeur of the State. For Rousseau, luxury and commerce corrupt morals and bring about the ruin of the body politic.

Bibliography

Aristotle ([350 BC] 1998), *Politics.* Indianapolis: Hackett.

Butel-Dumont Georges-Marie (1771), *Théorie du luxe, ou Traité dans lequel on entreprend d'établir que le luxe est un ressort, non seulement utile, mais même indispensablement nécessaire à la prospérité des Etats.* Londres: J.F. Bastien. Available at: www.archive.org

Cassiers Isabelle and Delain Catherine (2006), La croissance ne fait pas le bonheur, les économistes le savent-ils? *Regards économiques* 38: 1–14.

Clark Andrew and Senik Claudia (2007), La croissance rend-elle heureux? La réponse des données subjectives, *Working Paper Paris School of Economics* 6: 1–26.

Clark John Bates (1907), *Essentials of Economic Theory.* New York: The Macmillan Company.

Desrosières Alain (2008), *Pour une sociologie historique de la quantification.* Paris: Presses de l'École des Mines.

Dumont Louis (1977), *From Mandeville to Marx: The Genesis and Triumph of Economic Ideology.* Chicago: University of Chicago Press.

Fourquet François (1981), *Les Comptes de la puissance. Histoire politique de la comptabilité nationale et du plan.* Paris: Encres.

Gadrey Jean (2010), *Adieu à la croissance.* Paris: Les Petis matins/Alternatives économiques.

Gadrey Jean and Jany-Catrice Florence (2005), *Les nouveaux indicateurs de richesse.* Paris: La Découverte.

Goux Jean-Jacques (1995), L'utilité: équivoque et demoralisation, *Revue du Mauss* 6: 106–124.

Hirschman Albert O. (1977), *The Passions and the Interests: Political Arguments for Capitalism before its Triumph.* Princeton: Princeton University Press.

Jackson Tim (2009), *Prosperity without Growth: Economics for a finite Planete*. London: Earthscan Publications Ltd.

Malthus Thomas (2008), *An Essay on the Principle of Population.* Oxford: Oxford University Press.

Mandeville Bernard ([1974] 1988), *The Fable of the Bees, or Private Vices, Publick Benefits* (2 vols). Indianapolis: Liberty Fund.

Marx Karl (1967), *Œuvres*. Paris: Gallimard.

McCulloch John Ramsey (1825), *Principes d'économie politique*. Paris: Guillaumin.

Méda Dominique (1995), *Le Travail. Une valeur en voie de disparition?* Paris: Aubier.

Méda Dominique (1999), *Qu'est-ce que la richesse?* Paris: Aubier/Flammarion.

Méda Dominique (2009), Quel progrès faut-il mesurer? *Esprit* 6: 86–118.
Méda Dominique (2013), *La Mystique de la croissance. Comment s'en libérer*. Paris: Flammarion.
Melon Jean-François (1734), *Essai politique sur le commerce*. Amsterdam: François Changuion. Available at: http://books.google.be.
OCDE (2007), *Panorama de la société*. Paris: OCDE.
Perret Bernard (2002), *Indicateurs sociaux, état des lieux et perspectives*, Rapport au Conseil de l'Emploi, des Revenus et de la Cohésion Sociale, janvier.
Say Jean-Baptiste (1840), *Cours complet d'économie politique*. Paris: Guillaumin.
Smith Adam ([1776] 1981–1982), *An Inquiry Into the Nature and Causes of the Wealth of Nations* (2 vols). Indianapolis: Liberty Fund.
Stiglitz Joseph, Sen Amartya, and Fitoussi Jean-Paul (2009), *Report of the Commission on the Measurement of Economic Performance and Social Progress*. Available at: www.stiglitz-sen-fitoussi.fr/documents/rapport_anglais.pdf.
Vanoli André (2002), *Une histoire de la comptabilité nationale*. Paris: La Découverte.
Voltaire ([1764] 2010), *Dictionnaire philosophique*. Paris: GF.
Walras Léon (1926), *Éléments d'économie politique pure ou théorie de la richesse sociale*. Paris/Lausanne: Pichon/Durans-Auzias/Rouge.
Weber Max ([1905] 1992), *The Protestant Ethic and the Spirit of Capitalism*. London: Routledge.

2 A high-stakes shift

Turning the tide from GDP to new prosperity indicators

Isabelle Cassiers[1] *and Géraldine Thiry*[2]

For more than half a century, Gross Domestic Product (GDP) has been considered the main indicator of economic and social progress. Its existence, its visibility and its popularity have all led to its overuse, and even abuse: economic growth – that is, higher GDP – is almost constantly conflated with improved well-being. Today, though, GDP's hegemonic reign as a wealth indicator is being challenged. Its limits, as well as possible ways of overcoming these limits, are currently a matter of widespread reflection. This debate may be located within an already lengthy tradition of academic research; it has gathered momentum as numerous citizen-sector organisations express unease over the traditional "going for growth" paradigm and gained profile as it is discussed and examined by large institutions such as the UNDP, UNEP, OECD, European institutions, German Council of Economic Experts or the French Council of Economic Analysis, as well as Nobel prize winners such as Joseph Stiglitz or Amartya Sen (Stiglitz *et al.*, 2009).

The stakes in this debate are very high if seen from the now broadly accepted perspective that the indicators we choose affect our reality. The very process of quantification is not neutral:

> Quantification, understood as the totality of socially accepted conventions and of measurements, creates a new way of thinking, representing, expressing the world and acting on it. [...] Statistics, and, more generally, all forms of quantification (for example, probability or accounting), reconfigure and transform the world; by their very existence, by their propagation and by their use in argument, whether scientific, political or journalistic.
>
> (Desrosières, 2008: 11)[3]

To re-fashion the indicators we use to gauge prosperity is, potentially, to change the way we represent the world, to redefine our ends and reinvent the means we use to pursue them. By doing so, we are not adding a room or demolishing a tower in some castle in the air: such transformations imply complex changes to our economic, social, political, and ideological systems.

In this chapter, we argue that the debate over new prosperity indicators signals a turning point in history, and as such deserves close attention. We shall demonstrate this in four steps. First we recall how GDP emerged from a specific historical context, in which national accounting was established as a tool of economic policy, rooted in post-war social compromises. While this historical context explains the accounting conventions of the era, the changed world in which we now live has made these conventions seem uncomfortably circumscribed.

If the post-war generation saw the growth of market activity as a central source of well-being and GDP as an indicator of progress, the challenges we face in the twenty-first century have made the quantification of "progress", "well-being", and "prosperity" more complex. In the second step in our argument, therefore, we introduce three major issues specific to our era which justify the search for alternative indicators: first, the growing importance of social goals to which economic growth cannot respond in a fully satisfactory way; second, the disconnect between economic growth and subjective evaluations of life satisfaction; and, finally, the urgent and complex problem of the environment.

As awareness of these new challenges has grown over the decades, numerous highly creative approaches have emerged, producing a host of quantified indicators that might complement or replace GDP. The third section will therefore present a concise overview of existing indicators designed to that end, categorised according to the three issues identified above, and then outline the main questions each indicator would raise with its use. These questions are either explicitly axiological; that is, they have to do with the values implicit in these indicators, or may seem purely formal in that they have to do with the choice of units of measurement, or methods of aggregation. But our examination will show that methodological and normative questions are inextricably linked.

The fourth and final step in our argument will explore the fundamental concerns that underpin this debate. We will flesh out the hypothesis that our societies are at an historical turning point that will give rise to new compromises not yet fully understood by those involved. In this respect, our current situation may be compared to the period preceding the development of national accounting and the Fordist growth regime. Given the far-ranging effects of the introduction of GDP as an indicator, could new prosperity indicators act as a catalyst to precipitate the sea change? What forces are resisting this impending change? What principles are emerging to maintain coherence? We will also explore the dangers of "governance by indicator", which has been gaining currency over the past twenty years, and which is motivated by the (debatable) line of reasoning that would regulate human relations using managerial standards and judge all activity, directly or indirectly, by criteria of performance, efficiency or profitability. Seen in this light, the stakes are very clear: we must distinguish between new prosperity indicators that essentially perpetuate the system they (rhetorically) claim to supersede and those that truly offer an alternative. This question has a political dimension: will new indicators help to propagate a debatable principle of governance or will they be a Trojan horse that cracks the citadel of managerial reason?

1 The specific historical context of GDP[4]

Gross Domestic Product, commonly known as GDP, is the total monetary value of all the finished goods and services produced (and inventoried) by an entity (generally a State) in a given period (generally a year). It is thus a comprehensive evaluation of monetary flow. National accounting may record activity in three different ways, whose totals are equivalent: production, income, and expenditure. In this way, GDP is a concept that can be represented by a number, and when this number increases from one year to the next, that increase, minus inflation, is called "economic growth". These data are obtained through specific accounting conventions, which, like all conventions, are subject to debate, in that they are ways of simplifying reality in order to better understand it.

National accounting was established in the wake of the Second World War, and the conventions it adopted reflected the beliefs and knowledge of that time, as well as the state of labour relations and political compromises. Several factors determined the way national accounting was established: the aftermath of recession and war; labour-management and social welfare agreements; the growing dominance of the United States; the two opposing models of market economy and planned economy; the Keynesian revolution; the consolidation of the role of the nation-state; the expansion of social security. Presenting these elements sequentially inevitably produces a somewhat arbitrary and reductive account; nevertheless, the brief review offered below will demonstrate the coherence of the system they helped to form.

In Europe, the Great Depression and the four years of war that followed brought massive unemployment, wrought havoc on the economy and inflicted significant hardship on the majority of the population. Europeans emerged from this era with a strong desire for material well-being. The labour-management pacts forged at that time reflected the idea that workers would play an integral part in the pursuit of increased productivity, and that employers would share the benefit of that increased productivity between salaries and profit. Economic growth was thus fashioned as the cornerstone of social concord.

The United States, which had become the leading Western power, provided aid for European reconstruction through the Marshall Plan, which came with a certain number of conditions. First, in opposition to the satellite countries of the USSR, countries that accepted Marshall plan aid had to adopt market economy principles, and justify the aid they received with quantifiable data. In 1950, the OEEC, an institution created alongside the Marshall Plan (and the predecessor of the OECD), published a standardised accounting system that would serve as the model for national accounting in the West.

National accounting was explicitly designed as the tool of an economic policy, whose main goals included controlling growth. The Great Depression had led to a general consensus that markets could not spontaneously create full employment, while the war and the imperatives of post-war reconstruction created a de facto increase in public interventionism. In this context, the work of J.M. Keynes was taken as a theoretical foundation for re-conceptualising the role of the State. At the same time, socialist unions and public opinion influenced by the model prevailing in the East both exerted pressure to push the market economy towards a "mixed-economy" in which the market was still the driving force but in which the State intervened to curb its excesses and compensate for its deficiencies. It was thus generally acknowledged that, even in a market economy, it was incumbent upon the State to steer economic activity, at least to some degree. Steering requires a dashboard, and business accounting provided the blueprint for that dashboard. Or, to use another simile, national production was the central conduit linking businesses to consumers, passing, where necessary, through the State; a circulatory system in which currency was the lifeblood. This choice arose from a specific historical context: to the east, planned economies were establishing another accounting system to meet needs in the absence of a market.

The role of the Nation-State, with its centralised powers, was strengthened in other ways, as well. Representatives of these States came together to create major international organisations such as the UN, the IMF, and the World Bank, and international agreements such as Bretton Woods. The international monetary system fashioned through this process granted States a great deal of autonomy in the implementation of national economic policies. This new understanding of the State is known by a variety of names: the Keynesian State, in reference to its embrace of growth-oriented economic policy; the Social Welfare State, in reference to the labour conventions that arose in concert with it, bringing with them a battery of social protection and wealth-redistribution mechanisms; and in reference to its role as a buffer against life's uncertainties (for individuals) and economic downturns (for businesses).

These different elements combined to form a system dependant on the growth of monetary flow, which was necessary to prevent social unrest, to justify the role of union representatives, to support the expansion of the Welfare State through tax revenues, and, on the international level, for the symbolic power of the Nation-State.

In the three decades that followed the end of the Second World War, the standard of living rose considerably, inequalities shrank and the middle class grew across Western Europe. An increasing portion of the population entered the ranks of the "average citizen", whose incomes were reasonably represented by GDP per capita. During this "golden age", most were convinced – or allowed themselves to be convinced – that the goal of continuous revenue growth was possible and desirable. In economic theory, the development of growth models that relied on mathematical instruments justified the existing system while increasing the need for standardised accounting. Research focused more on refining econometric models than on the underlying theoretical principles that tied well-being to revenue growth, much less on the ecological limits to permanent growth, which were then still barely perceptible.

Few were the voices warning of *The Limits to Growth* (Meadows *et al.*, 1972). A handful of people cautioned that infinite growth in a finite world was impossible (Georgescu-Roegen, 1971) and denounced as absurd the idea of a society whose sole objective was to accumulate material goods (Illich, 1973). These warning calls were met with favour by a minority of the population (student movements, alternative lifestyle movements, and the self-management movement), but were stifled when the West was hit by the economic crisis of 1973, which moved the reasoning of every actor in the economy back to square one: businesses sought to shore up profits; unions fought wage decreases; individuals set aside alternative aspirations and focused on staying employed. The State, unable to galvanise the economy or support its social policies without maintaining its tax base, pursued the growth of monetary flow. Over the next thirty years, State governments, encouraged by major institutions such as the IMF and the OECD, strove mightily to increase GDP. This occurred even as the problematic nature of this pursuit became more clearly apparent – strains on the environment became acute; growing inequalities weakened the legitimacy of the process; certain factors determinant of quality of life were destroyed with increasing wantonness.

2 The indicator falls behind: GDP in today's context

Circumstances have changed profoundly since the thirty years of growth that followed the end of the Second World War. If the post-war generation saw market growth as crucial to well-being and read GDP as an indicator of progress, today's perspective has been complicated considerably.

First, the goal of economic growth was dissociated from that of the equal distribution of the wealth it generated as economic policy began to shift at the end of the 1970s, starting with Reagan and Thatcher in the United States and in England and then spreading to most countries in Western Europe.[5] The thirty-year period that followed the end of the Second World War was characterised by decreased inequality (thanks to progressive taxation and the expansion of social welfare programmes), allowing most members of society to identify as "average citizens". Beginning in the 1980s, however, the income spread increased, creating a dissonance between the image conveyed by official figures (GDP per capita) and the reality experienced by most individuals. Within the OECD, the income of the richest 10 per cent is, on average, now nine times greater than that of the poorest 10 per cent. The past twenty years have been marked by a significant rise in income inequality and relative poverty. Over three-quarters of OECD countries have been affected. The Gini coefficient, calculated using OECD averages, increased by 10 per cent (from 0.29 to 0.32) between the mid-1980s and the end of the 2000s (OECD, 2011a).

These trends have begun to cast doubt on the idea that economic growth is inherently beneficial to social progress. Numerous academic studies have questioned the theoretical and empirical foundations underlying the assumption of a causal relationship between growth and the reduction of inequality and poverty. To argue that growth is a means of increasing the "economic pie" to be shared is to postpone indefinitely the difficult question of redistribution. As Amartya Sen observed in the 1970s, the fact that GDP per capita fails to include any consideration of redistribution is enough to disqualify its use as a measure of well-being (van den Bergh, 2009).

The rise of inequality was accompanied by a resurgence of the poverty, exclusion and social ills growth was believed to have attenuated. Increased per capita GDP and the health of societies no longer advanced hand-in-hand. Development as it has been pursued over the past thirty-five years has failed to overcome unemployment while increasing job insecurity and workplace stress, and has encouraged consumer behaviour that leads to obesity, cardio-vascular diseases, and cancer. This frenzied pursuit of material possessions has failed to address the problems tormenting teenagers (suicides are increasing) and families (family instability and single-parent homes are on the rise).

These observations partly explain why subjective measurements of life satisfaction are largely stagnant and sometimes diminishing, while GDP is still on the rise. Easterlin (1974) was the first to highlight this paradox, which has since been amply demonstrated and discussed. In most Western countries, real GDP per capita has nearly doubled since 1973, with no significant increase in life satisfaction.[6] In addition to those noted above, other factors may explain this phenomenon, such as the relativity of any measure of well-being. Because individual and collective aspirations are constantly compared to the achievements of others (through mimesis) and scaled up (due to habituation), economic growth can never completely fulfil them (Cassiers and Delain, 2006; van den Bergh, 2009; Layard, 2011; Clark *et al.*, 2008). As observed life satisfaction stagnates in almost all rich countries, questions emerge about the goals of our development model and whether it actually serves the well-being of all. Is this stated goal merely a false pretext to increase market activity – in other words, the activity registered by GDP accounting?

This question has taken on new urgency now that human activity has begun to endanger other living species to the point of threatening a large number with extinction, now that it has eaten away at the resources that will be handed on to future generations. Environmental concerns become more pressing with every passing day. Rockström *et al.* (2009) have detailed the scope of these threats in nine different fields; among them, biodiversity, the nitrogen cycle, and climate are the most imperilled. In terms of renewable resources, humanity's ecological footprint ceased to be sustainable in 1976, and currently exceeds the earth's capacity to sustain it by some 50 per cent (Global Footprint Network, 2012). The relationship between per capita GDP and environmental damage remains controversial. Some argue that the former will initially cause the latter to increase but that green technologies will ultimately reverse this trend (OECD, 2011b), an optimistic perspective that has been challenged with increasing vigour: numerous recent works (for example, Jackson, 2009; Costanza *et al.*, 2012) distinguish between relative decoupling (pressure on the environment *growing less rapidly* than GDP) and absolute decoupling (environmental pressure *decreasing* despite continued economic growth). The latter appears to be impossible within our current state of knowledge.

The three issues outlined above – redistribution and social progress, life satisfaction, the environment – are of such magnitude that an indicator intended to represent the goals of a society cannot ignore them. However, as an abundant literature has reminded us in recent years, GDP takes them into account with difficulty, or not at all (see in particular Gadrey and Jany-Catrice, 2006; Méda, 2008; Stiglitz *et al.*, 2010; van den Bergh, 2009, 2012; Cassiers and Thiry, 2009). This is the case for several reasons: first, GDP entirely disregards the question of the redistribution of wealth within society. Second, national accounts record and evaluate activity according to conventions which alternative criteria may have rendered inadequate (for example, remunerated and volunteer work are treated as totally different) and do not properly account for outcomes in terms of social progress, well-being or life satisfaction. Finally, by booking only flows (as opposed to stocks) and by neglecting to account for the depreciation of natural resources, GDP is functionally blind to environmental problems. With this in mind, and given the realities we currently face, continuing to pursue GDP growth as an absolute end as we have in the past seems increasingly irrational.

This, then, is the quandary we face today: the problems cited above are common knowledge. In some cases, they have even been quantified: as discussed below in section three, numerous indicators have been invented over the years to measure the scale of these problems, to raise awareness about them, and to provide social and environmental policy tools to address them. And yet none of these alternative or supplementary indicators has succeeded in replacing GDP, or at least putting its significance into perspective. Despite its weaknesses, despite its inability to faithfully reflect the end goals of development considered from a contemporary perspective, GDP has retained its supremacy. We will discuss possible reasons for this puzzling state of affairs further on, in section four.

3 A multitude of indicators, methods, actors, and values

Creative responses to the inadequacies of GDP have produced a wide range of indicators used in a wide range of fields, including social progress, well-being, and the environment. These indicators express an equally wide range of visions and interests, as they are being promoted by a vast array of institutions, including major international organisations like the UN, the OECD, the EU, or the World Bank; not-for-profit organisations such as the World Wildlife Fund; and community and academic organisations. Their aims differ broadly, as well; for example, they may be designed for informational purposes, to assess or guide policies or to establish goals. These different goals require different levels of abstraction and aggregation: while the rate of obesity or the rate of natural resource extraction are more or less raw measures of major social phenomena, indicators such as the Index of Economic Well-Being (IEWB) or the Genuine Progress Indicator (GPI) seek to capture complex phenomena that are multidimensional in nature. Such phenomena may also be quantified using scoreboards, such as the set of indicators the Belgian Federal Planning Bureau uses to measure sustainable development, or by using aggregate indicators. These may either be hybrid – weighted averages of diverse variables such as the UNDP's Human Development Index (HDI) – or may be calculated from a single unit, as is the case with financial indicators such as Adjusted Net Savings (ANS) or the

Inclusive Wealth Index (IWI), or indicators that use physical units of measurement, such as the Ecological Footprint (EF).

The goal of this chapter is not to provide an exhaustive index of this cornucopia[7]; rather, we shall focus on a few indicators that, due to the motivations behind them, their design, or those promoting them, promise to address, at least partially, the failure of GDP to account for redistribution, social progress, subjective well-being, and the environment. We will then examine some of the problems associated with these indicators, which, though they appear at first glance to be methodological in nature, show upon further examination the extent to which values are implicit in measurement.[8]

A multitude of indicators

Numerous indicators have been used to attempt to address the gap between social progress and growth of GDP. Whether they are scoreboards or aggregate indicators, they take into account a range of sub-dimensions, including inequality, poverty, employment and work, income, health, education, housing, and justice. The HDI, which adds life expectancy and education to real income per capita, is probably the most emblematic of these attempts to consider *outcomes* rather than monetised production. But the high-profile global success of the HDI should not overshadow the plethora of lesser-known initiatives from which it emerged, most of which came from academic institutions and citizen-sector organisations. The Index of Social Heath (ISH), for example, was designed by American sociologists to supplement the State of the Nation report presented annually to the US Congress, which included only economic and financial indicators. More recent initiatives around the world include the BIP-40 (the *Baromètre des Inégalités et de la Pauvreté,* an indicator of inequality and poverty) and the ISS (*Indice régional de santé sociale*, or regional community health indicator) in France, Buen Vivir in Equador and the New Zeeland Social Report.

In another category, indicators have been designed to address the gap between GDP and well-being, seeking to reflect the way people feel, either collectively or individually, in a systematic manner. Some collective indicators are based on consultative or deliberative processes, and address both objective and subjective aspects of well-being, such as the American Community Indicators movement, the Canadian Index of Well-Being or the British "Measuring National Well-Being" programme. By the same token, Bhutan, having conducted a series of investigations and debates on how to define and measure them, evaluates societal conditions necessary for happiness through a Gross National Happiness Index (Ura *et al.*, 2012). On the individual level, these indicators generally take the form of surveys, and chiefly examine subjective aspects of well-being; examples include the Happy Life-Expectancy index, the Satisfaction With Life Index and the Eurobarometer of Life Satisfaction. As we shall see below, while these indicators are illuminating, their methodologies have been critiqued and they should be used with caution.

The urgent nature of the ecological problems we face has also sparked numerous initiatives. The Ecological Footprint mentioned above has probably received the most media attention, thanks in large part to a global campaign by the World Wildlife Fund. It expresses the impact of human activity – both consumption and waste production – on renewable resources in terms of global hectares. Like other "footprint" measurements (water, carbon, etc.), the Ecological Footprint is designed as a warning signal that conveys the urgent necessity of adapting human behaviour to the physical constraints of the planet. Another approach, which more closely resembles traditional accounting methods, and has been embraced by major international institutions, consists of "greening" traditional economic indicators. The OECD's recent work on green growth is an example of this (2011b); as is the World Bank's Adjusted Net Savings index, which measures the net creation or destruction of wealth in monetary terms, giving equal status to natural, physical, and human capital. Across the world, government statistics and census offices have shown interest in developing supplementary accounting systems; for example, the National Accounting Matrix with Environmental Accounts (NAMEA) in the Netherlands.

As social progress, subjective well-being, and respect for the environment are arguably highly interconnected considerations, certain authors have chosen to bundle some or all of them into a single indicator. The Index of Economic Well-Being (IEWB) is a good example: based on the premise that a society's well-being depends on many factors, monetary and non-monetary alike, it measures consumption, the accumulation of various resources, inequalities and economic security. The Index of Sustainable Economic Welfare (ISEW) also embraces diverse aspects of well-being (consumption, environment, inequalities, etc.) but has opted to monetise all of its measurements. Conversely, the Happy Planet Index (HPI) – a recent attempt to gauge ecological and social conditions as well as subjective well-being – is an entirely non-monetary indicator. Following the example of the HPI, the Sustainable Society Index (SSI) assesses personal development, social equilibrium, the environment, and sustainability in one hybrid index, as does the OECD's Better Life Index, which has innovated by letting its users weight the elements in the index themselves. The UNDP has also begun considering the possibility of including environmental considerations in the HDI (UNDP, 2013).

Each of these indicators highlights, in its own way, factors that must be taken into account when measuring prosperity, and in this sense they are all stepping stones on the path that leads beyond GDP. None of them, however, has yet succeeded in replacing GDP. Their very diversity may be at fault, since the actors promoting them are sometimes at odds with one another, as their objectives and values are not always compatible (see Thiry *et al.*, 2013). These differences are apparent in the choices they make about quantification.

Quantifying prosperity: methods reflect values

"What counts?" The components we choose for a given indicator are a reflection of what we value, and require us to confront many different worldviews from the outset. But who is the "we" assigning the value? Considering the multitude of different ideas of prosperity, Amartya Sen suggests that *access* to sources of emancipation and quality of life should be the priority, and that actors should be left to choose the form these take, according to their particular situations. Nussbaum, by contrast, suggests a list of "fundamental entitlements" that includes bodily integrity, the capability to form one's own idea of what a good life is and control over one's environment.

In addition to the questions of "what counts" and "who decides", the question of "how to count" arises at different levels: the choice of subjective or objective measurements; the form of indicator; the choice of weighting; and the advantages and disadvantages of monetisation – these key examples deserve further examination.

Should well-being be approached as entirely subjective, as a function of objective characteristics, or as a mixture of the two? While objective preconditions for quality of life are no guarantee of individual happiness, accounting for subjective perspectives alone is not sufficient to address inherently collective questions such as social relations or the environment. Mixing objective variables and subjective data is not easy, however. The latter, based on surveys, are not always temporally or geographically comparable. Life satisfaction in Mali and life satisfaction in Norway do not speak to the same reality. Moreover, responses to the question "overall, do you feel happy?" can vary greatly depending on phase of life.

The question of format is equally germane: is a single figure better than a scoreboard? The precision offered by a scoreboard of distinct indicators can serve to develop targeted policies, while the simplicity of a single-figure indicator is a better tool for political mobilisation. Certain voices in the current debate over format have criticised single figures for being difficult to interpret, as they cover so many diverse dimensions. It has been suggested that the multiple dimensions of prosperity should be treated separately. But the choice to separate the various dimensions can never be only a matter of intelligibility and use; it reflects and feeds a whole set of conceptions about the world. The work of the Stiglitz Commission is a good example (Stiglitz *et al.*, 2009) of this: the Commission examined the expansion of national accounting to include a measurement of quality of life and the measurement of sustainable development as separate questions, without addressing how they might be connected to and delineated from one another. In this way, they sidestepped any contradictions that might have arisen from such a comparison: for instance, how to reconcile individual preferences in the present (the pleasure of driving a SUV), the current collective good (mounting congestion in cities as many different kinds of self-interest collide) and the well-being of future generations (threatened by CO_2 emissions)? If indicators influence reality, then building them without considering how these questions interact will, in the end, prevent us from thinking about and living the social and the ecological as integral to quality of life (Cassiers and Thiry, 2009).

Single figure indicators, by their nature, require weighting, which is generally critiqued as an arbitrary practice. In response to this accusation, some have proposed weighting that is transparent and adaptable to specific situations, as does the IEWB. Others, influenced by national accounting, use market prices to weight an indicator's dimensions, as is the case with the ANS. However, monetisation resolves the problem of arbitrariness in appearance alone[9]: the reality of imperfect markets means that monetisation is never neutral.

This is true for several reasons: first of all, some goods and services are not traded on the market, so monetising them is just as arbitrary as weighting them would be. This raises the question of the limits of monetisation: can everything be assigned a market value? In ecological terms, monetising the environment raises an important question about humanity's relationship with nature, in that assigning a market price to parts of nature reduces them to commodities, establishing an instrumental relationship to the world.

Furthermore, market price is not always the most appropriate way to evaluate goods that *are* traded on the market. Does a rise in price reflect better quality, or inflation? Moreover, market prices do not take externalities into account. Market prices do not include the harmful collective effects that production and/or consumption might generate. Some have proposed using external or social cost as a response to this problem, but critics have objected that this raises its own set of questions: for example, what does loss of biodiversity cost? Answering that question supposes that the current and future impact of production on biodiversity have already been identified – which is not the case.

Assigning monetary value is in this way a fundamentally axiological exercise. Monetary indicators make the market the prime determinant of value, while non-monetary indicators allow value to be determined elsewhere, be that in the life experiences of individuals or in the finite nature of the ecosystem. Adopting market prices as the accounting unit for an indicator that claims to reflect prosperity better than GDP allows supply and demand – driven by the maximisation of profit and utility – to determine value. Is prosperity redefined on this basis capable of transcending a materialist conception of prosperity?

A brief inquiry into what appear to be purely methodological questions about indicators – the fields covered, objective and/or subjective approaches, form, aggregation, weighting, and units of account – reveals that worldview is implicit in any choice of measurement. The search for a new prosperity indicator is thus an opportunity to strive for agreement on the goals of our development.

4 Beyond GDP: what is at stake?

This leaves us in a highly contradictory position: the limitations of GDP are increasingly obvious; alternative indicators exist and are being promoted by numerous actors; and yet the ascendancy of GDP remains. The debate has begun, however, and it will progress; the direction it takes may help shape future development models.

The lack of consensus on an alternative to GDP, either in the form of a single indicator or a scoreboard, is a reflection of our society's uncertainties; the self-reflection currently under way in some way resembles the thought processes preceding the emergence of national accounting. It is possible that a new social compromise is already emerging, in ways not yet intelligible to its participants, whose orientation is still open to change. Those concerned by this process are numerous, and so are their end goals, which may be quantified in many ways that are more or less in line with their initial intentions. The quantification process is a proving ground, and as such, should be approached with caution, since inappropriate methodological choices can easily deflect indicators from the ends they were intended to serve.

This risk is amplified by the historical context in which these debates are taking place. Indicators have the potential to play a key role in the redefinition of prosperity, and yet they are also cogs in a system of governance that seems to be contributing to the very problems this redefinition seeks to overcome. Among available indicators it is therefore important to identify those capable of effecting deep changes and to unmask those merely offering a whitewash solution.

Society in transition, coherence emergent

As we have said before, the current context recalls in many ways the period of reflection preceding the establishment of national accounting and the social compromises of the 1940s, which coalesced around the principle of economic growth. The variety of indicators available today is symptomatic of a fragmentation of systems of action and value, as if the whole of socio-economic reality were once again under construction. Just like GDP in its time, the indicator (or set of indicators) that emerges from this search may lead to new social compromises and contribute to redefining prosperity.

At this point, the various elements in play have yet to cohere around a single principle strong enough to play the role exercised by economic growth in the thirty years that followed the Second World War. The only consensus right now is a negative one: it seems increasingly obvious that growth in its current form is unsustainable, even to its most fervent defenders. Based as it is on over-indebtedness (private and public), it is an incubator of cyclic social and economic crises, making it inherently unstable. In the current context of extreme competitiveness, it is no longer synonymous with social and geo-political peace. Adding the pressure it puts on the planet's finite resources, it seems downright suicidal.

Observing the limits of growth and its measurements is the common ground shared by alternatives to GDP, but it is not sufficient to produce a common project, to which there remain several impediments. First, the issues being contested are so different from one another that it is difficult to unite them in a single system of action and analysis, as Keynesianism was able to do within Fordism. Moreover, the debate's participants have disparate, even antagonistic, goals. Finally, historical events have left contemporary society at a kind of impasse – despite the numerous critiques levelled against it, GDP remains an indispensable point of reference for many: governments use growth forecasts to determine structural investments; social security financing depends on revenue growth; private investors are sensitive to business climate, which is tied to GDP; individual savings decisions are influenced by the overall economic climate; GDP determines the mood – optimistic or pessimistic – of financial institutions; finally, it is still generally accepted that insufficient growth causes economic instability and higher unemployment (Lachaize and Morel, 2013). It is therefore not surprising to observe that the indicators most likely to be adopted in the near future are those whose methodology and use are in line with the perspective and goal of GDP growth (Thiry *et al.*, 2013).

Moving beyond the dominance of GDP involves more than debating alternative measures. It requires becoming aware, through these alternatives, that times are changing; it demands also that new values be used to reach new compromises. Today's debates rightly remind us that our measuring tools are not natural law, but rather the product of historically and geographically situated conventions. These debates have also brought new participants to the table, whose proposed indicators translate into political and axiological demands; in this way, they are helping us to collectively redefine the goals of our societies.

However, these debates bring certain risks with them. Challenging growth and GDP might lead to a too-hasty adoption of alternative solutions, driven by a sense of urgency about the need for change rather than by considered reflection and debate. Drift from issues of substance (what choices are right for society?) towards methodological questions (what is the best way to weight or aggregate data) is another risk, as it could lead to the dominance of experts' voices in the choice of new measures of prosperity. The power this choice brings with it is not negligible, since the abstract concept of prosperity is so closely linked to the way it is measured: to quantify prosperity is to define it. The respective roles of experts and members of society should thus be clarified. Indicators are built on the bedrock of values, but their highly technical nature often makes them inaccessible to the general public. Thiry *et al.* (2013) have chronicled how difficult it is to make such debates truly democratic.

The Sustainable Society Index (SSI), presented in section three, provides a good example. This indicator was originally (in 2006) composed of twenty-two sub-indicators, all non-monetary. In a review conducted two years later, four sub-indicators were removed (soil quality, waste recycling, Ecological Footprint (EF), and international cooperation) and six added (air quality, energy consumption, material consumption, organic farming, Adjusted Net Savings (ANS), and GDP). While the authors clearly announced the changes, their normative impact went far beyond a simple refinement of measurements. With the addition of ANS and GDP, monetisation, whose implications were examined in section three, was introduced. Moreover, the ANS is rooted in an understanding of sustainability radically different from the one motivating the EF, which has been eliminated from the SSI (Thiry and Cassiers, 2010). Whereas the EF emphasises the ecosystem's physical limits (strong sustainability), the ANS offers a sum of the variations in different kinds of wealth (produced capital, human capital, and natural capital), implying that depletions to natural capital can be made up for by increasing investments in other categories of capital (weak sustainability). Thus, while the SSI changed neither its name, nor the definition of its overall purpose, its values and representations of sustainability were incontestably modified by the change in methodology, and its critical scope significantly reduced.

This example is a reminder of the democratic issues at stake in the debate over indicators. Individuals and groups with diverse interests and goals are grappling with this question; new compromises are being forged; at the same time, it is clear that indicators carry implicit values and can have a long-term influence on the dominant conception of prosperity and how it is mobilised. It is crucial, then, that all participants are able to follow and position themselves within these debates. To this end, the values implicit in the construction of indicators should be made explicit in a systematic fashion.

The risk of misappropriation

The impact of indicators upon society cannot be accurately assessed without taking into account the systems in which they are rooted and which they are helping to fashion. The question of whether they are the instruments of an expanding doctrine of governance is not a neutral one. The nature of such a doctrine must be clearly grasped, since it threatens to stifle the attempts at social innovation emerging from the current debate on indicators. We may shed light on this question by examining the large-scale change in the role of the state and modes of exercising power that took place in our societies after the era of prosperity that followed the end of the Second World War came to a close.

As noted above, economic policy took a new turn at the end of the 1970s, a shift that came hand in hand with a doctrinal shift toward globalisation and financialisation. The rise to power of Reagan and Thatcher threw previous principles of social democracy into question. The re-establishment of free markets reduced the role of labour dialogue and consultation mechanisms. The liberalisation of the movement of capital restricted the nation-State's field of action. State intervention was also called into question. Keynesian macroeconomic regulation, public ownership of companies, the degree of progressive taxation, the scope of social welfare, the strict regulation of the private sector – all these were named as barriers to be dismantled. Government reform was constrained and re-conceptualised to follow a business model: the client-citizen was to receive efficient service from public entities, which were to be evaluated on the basis of their performance. The term "good governance" became widespread as the public equivalent of "good management" in the private sector. States were seen through the lens of competition and were subject to benchmarking. No authority appeared to have the power to effectively impose rules or to coordinate the decision-making processes handed off to the private sphere.

The role of indicators has expanded considerably in this context, both as incentives and as tools for flexible coordination. But indicators mean even more than that: without them, it would be impossible to assess, to compare, and to incite performance-based competition following the imperative of profitability – itself defined in quantitative terms. Indicators assume and impose the comparability and commensurability of things and activities, and their very existence and use in this way helps to propagate the competition-based organisational model.

The power of indicators continues to increase as competition becomes the watchword in areas of life once spared the dictates of productivity. Financing for many institutions of higher learning, for example, has come to depend how well the fields of study they offer score in terms of "return on investment". Practices of social solidarity have also been affected by the principle of profitability and the quantitative evaluation it requires: in the slipstream left as the active welfare State recedes, indicators are now used to assess the costs of an unemployed person, a student or an old age pensioner.

These examples show that indicators, as they are applied to society, are a force reshaping numerous aspects of existence. Indeed, they may almost be seen as the cornerstone of a model in which managerial norms have been transposed onto society as a whole, pervaded by a spirit of competition:

> benchmarking is based on the managerial presupposition that all organisations – public and private, (inter-)State and non-governmental, economic and social – constantly aspire to excel and can only be competitive if they participate in competition, and thus functions by establishing competitive relationships and patterns in non-commercial sectors traditionally regulated by rules of cooperation.
>
> (Bruno, 2010: 42)

Thus, while the need to move beyond GDP has become obvious, the ascension of the doctrine of governance may be impeding this from happening. After all, national accounting has the merit of existing, and of internal coherence. Its compatibility with business accounting has helped push managerial standards beyond their original sphere of influence.

Indicators are not merely indispensable tools in the expansion of the managerial model; they legitimate the application of this model to society:

> any exercise of political power is accompanied by a discourse of legitimation (…). The tenor chosen for this discourse sounds the tone for government action and sets an order of priority for the political problems it intends to solve (…). Some fifteen years ago, "results-based governance" (understood as a performance measurement for State action based on how well it meets numeric targets set by pubic policies) emerged as the new brand of legitimation.
>
> (Ogien, 2010: 5)

Numbers have become the cornerstones of the decision-making process.

A model in which indicators structure decision-making sees human activity through the lens of quantitative rationality; indeed, the ubiquitous use of quantification has helped to de-politicise the political. Quantification has disguised convention and doctrine as a logical axiom. Justifying choices about society by arguing for the need for profitability or quantified performance occludes the political nature of these choices, making them seem impossible to contest on non-numeric grounds.

And yet, this new mode of organisation is contestable, and on many grounds. First, it implicitly sees individual members of society in terms of cost and benefit. Rather than focusing on links between economic progress and the equitable sharing of the fruits of growth, this "new logic considers populations and individuals from the narrower perspective of their contribution and cost to international competition" (Dardot and Laval, 2010: 366). Moreover, this mode of organisation feeds and reinforces the problems attendant on our obsession with growth. It relies on the simultaneous increase in the mobility of capital and the flexibility of labour, which often makes labour more precarious. It heightens inequalities. It poses an active threat to the natural world. Because it is founded on competition, it makes social cohesion difficult. More fundamentally still, it makes the market into a central reference point, reducing the idea of prosperity to fit the narrow framework of competition, in which actors are judged according to their market performance, expressed in monetary terms.

The debate over indicators is society's laboratory, a proving ground for a new definition of prosperity. A unifying principle is being tested there: competition for all, following the imperative of productivity. Given how questionable this principle is, and how difficult it is to challenge – as political choices are justified in technical terms and as the spheres in which legitimate power is exercised are decentralised – we must proceed with clarity, sensibility, and caution.

Our first task is to expose the essentially political nature of a model whose great strength is to appear as a naturally legitimate principle of efficiency rather than as a new form of power. Within this model, indicators facilitate the spread of a "strategy without a strategist", to use Foucault's expression. We are in no way arguing for the existence of a conspiracy; rather,

> what must be pictured here is a logic of practices, often disparate, which puts into play techniques of power (...); little by little, without any single instigator of this "push toward a strategic goal," the multiplication and widespread adoption of all these techniques sets a general course.
>
> (Dardot and Laval, 2010: 276)

It is important to be aware of this strategic pressure so as not to fall into perceiving this mode of organising society as a naturally occurring phenomenon. Revealing the ideological scope and bearing of this managerial system, which ultimately holds no one globally accountable, opens a space for critical thinking.

Our next task is to identify indicators from among those being proposed in the current debate that might be capable of bringing about real change. In other words, indicators grown from the seeds of the system they claim to challenge must be distinguished from those whose conceptual and methodological foundations allow them to offer a true alternative. This distinction would save us from tinkering at the margins of the current accounting system in the continued belief that it is capable of providing an adequate response to the fundamental problems facing the twenty-first century. One example of the pitfalls of this way of thinking may be found in the Stiglitz Commission's ambiguous proposal that monetised assessments of volunteer and domestic work be integrated into national accounting. While it would allow society to recognise previously marginalised activities, and for that reason might be welcomed as a social advance, it also denies the true nature of these activities – namely, that they are voluntary and unremunerated – by subjecting them to the laws of the market.

We therefore conclude by suggesting that indicators may be a point around which a legion of scattered forces for change can rally to resist society's reduction to profit-driven principles of governance, that they may be seized upon as the Trojan Horse that finally cracks the citadel of GDP and national accounting, bearing not arms, but the aspiration to greater humanity, altruism, and possibility.

Notes

1 Université catholique de Louvain and Belgian National Fund for Scientific Research
2 Collège d'études mondiales, Paris (France). For further information see authors' biographies at the front of this volume.
3 All translations are our own.
4 This section echoes and elaborates on previous publications; see Cassiers (1995, 2009). For more on the Fordist model (1945–1975), see numerous works by the Regulation School, in particular Robert Boyer (1999). For a concise overview of this school of thought, see Boyer (2008).
5 This political and ideological turning point is examined in greater detail in previous publications; see in particular Cassiers and Lebeau (2005), and Cassiers and Denayer (2010). The Regulation School has also dealt with these questions at length. See also Marglin and Schor (1989).
6 Updated data from Cassiers and Delain (2006).
7 See especially: Gadrey and Jany-Catrice (2006); Stiglitz *et al.* (2010); FAIR (2011); IWEPS (2011); Fleurbaey and Blanchet (2013); Hak *et al.* (2012) and Thiry *et al.* (2013).
8 We previously defended this thesis in Cassiers and Thiry (2009), and Thiry and Cassiers (2010).
9 The arguments contained in the following paragraphs are treated in more depth in Thiry and Cassiers (2010).

References

Boyer Robert (1999), Une lecture régulationniste de la croissance et de la crise. In: Pascal Combemale and Jean-Paul Piriou (eds), *Nouveau manuel. Sciences économiques et sociales*. Paris: La Découverte, 476–496.

Boyer Robert (2008), Regulation. In: *The New Palgrave Dictionary of Economics*, Second Edition, 126–128.

Bruno Isabelle (2010), La déroute du "benchmarking social". La coordination des luttes nationales contre la pauvreté et l'exclusion en Europe. *Revue Française de Socio-Economie* 1(5): 41–61.

Cassiers Isabelle (1995), Comptes et légendes. Les limites de la comptabilité nationale. *Reflets et perspectives de la vie économique* 34(6): 507–520. [Later published in *Problèmes économiques* (1996) 2467: 27–32].

Cassiers Isabelle (2009), Pour changer de cap, dégrippons la boussole. *Revue Nouvelle* 3: 53–61.

Cassiers Isabelle and Delain Catherine (2006), La croissance ne fait pas le bonheur: les économistes le savent-ils? *Regards économiques* 38: 1–14.

Cassiers Isabelle and Denayer Luc (2010), Concertation sociale et transformations socio-économiques depuis 1944. In: Etienne Arcq, Michel Capron, Évelyne Léonard, and Pierre Reman (eds), *Dynamiques de la concertation sociale*. Bruxelles: CRISP, 75–91.

Cassiers Isabelle and Lebeau Etienne (2005), De l'État Providence à l'État social actif: quels changements de régulation sous-jacents? In: Pascale Vielle, Philippe Pochet, and Isabelle Cassiers (eds), *L'État social actif: vers un changement de paradigme?* Bruxelles: PIE – Peter Lang, 93–120.

Cassiers Isabelle and Thiry Géraldine (2009), Au-delà du PIB: Réconcilier ce qui compte et ce que l'on compte, *Regards Economiques*, décembre 75: 1–15.

Clark Andrew E., Frijters Paul, and Shields Michael A. (2008), Relative income, happiness, and utility: an explanation for the Easterlin paradox and other puzzles, *Journal of Economic Literature* 46(1): 95–144.

Costanza Robert, Alperovitz Gar, Daly Herman, Farley Joshua, Franco Carol, Jackson Tim, Kubiszewski Ida, Schor Juliet, and Victor Peter (2012), *Building a Sustainable and Desirable Economy-in-Society-in-Nature*, Report to the United Nations as part of the Sustainable Development in the 21st century (SD21) project implemented by the Division for Sustainable Development of the United Nations Department of Economic and Social Affairs.

Dardot Pierre and Laval Christian (2010), *La nouvelle raison du monde. Essai sur la société néolibérale.* Paris: La Découverte.

Desrosières Alain (2008), *Gouverner par les nombres. L'argument statistique II.* Paris: Presse de l'École des Mines.

Easterlin Richard A. (1974), Does economic growth improve the human lot? Some empirical evidence. In: Paul A. David and Melvin Warren Reder (eds), *Nations and Households in Economic Growth: Essays in Honor of Moses Abramovitz.* New York: Academic Press, 89–124.

FAIR (2011), La richesse autrement, *Alternatives Economiques*, Hors-Série 48.

Fleurbaey Marc and Blanchet Didier (2013), *Beyond GDP: Measuring Welfare and Assessing Sustainability.* Oxford: Oxford University Press.

Foucault Michel (2004), *Naissance de la biopolitique. Cours au Collège de France (1978–1979).* Paris: Gallimard/Seuil.

Gadrey Jean and Jany-Catrice Florence (2006), *The New Indicators of Well-Being and Development.* London: Macmillan.

Georgescu-Roegen Nicholas (1971), *The Entropy Law and the Economic Process.* Cambridge: Harvard University Press.

Global Footprint Network (2012), *Living Planet Report 2012.* Gland: WWF International.

Hak Tomas, Janouskova Svatava, Abdallah Saamah, Seaford Charles, and Mahony Sorcha (2012), *Review Report on Beyond GDP Indicators: Categorisation, Intensions and Impacts*, Brainpool Project (FP7), Deliverable 1.1, October.

Illich Ivan (1973), *La convivialité.* Paris: Seuil.

IWEPS (2011), Développement d'indicateurs complémentaires au PIB. Parie 1: revue harmonisée d'indicateurs composites/synthétiques, *Working Paper de l'IWEPS* 4: 1–11.

Jackson Tim (2009), *Prosperity without growth: Economics for a Finite Planet.* London: Earthscan Publications Ltd.

Lachaize Pierre and Morel Julien (2013), *Les usages du PIB*, Shift Project, Tome 1.

Layard Richard ([2005] 2011), *Happiness, Lessons from a New Science.* New York/ London: Penguin.

Marglin Stephen A. and Schor Juliet B. (eds) (1989), *The Golden Age of Capitalism: Reinterpreting the Postwar Experience*. Oxford/New York: Oxford University Press.

Meadows Dennis, Meadows Donella, Randers Jørgen and Behrens William (1972), *The limits to growth: a report for the Club of Rome's project on the predicament of mankind.* New York: Universe Book.

Méda Dominique ([1999] 2008), *Au-delà du PIB. Pour une autre mesure de la richesse.* Paris: Flammarion.

OECD (2011a), *Divided we Stand: Why Inequalities Keeps Rising.* Paris: OECD Publishing.

OECD (2011b), *Toward Green Growth: Monitoring Progress.* Paris: OECD Publishing.

Ogien Albert (2010), La valeur sociale du chiffre. La quantification de l'action publique entre performance et démocratie. *Revue Française de Socioéonomie* 1(5): 19–40.

Rockström Johan, Steffen Will, Noone Kevin, Persson Åsa, Chapin F. Stuart III, Lambin Eric F., Lenton Timothy M., Scheffer Marten, Folke Carl, Schellnhuber Hans Joachim, Nykvist Björn, de Wit Cynthia A., Hughes Terry, van der Leeuw Sander, Rodhe Henning, Sörlin Sverker, Snyder Peter K., Costanza Robert, Svedin Uno, Falkenmark Malin, Karlberg Louise, Corell Robert W., Fabry Victoria J., Hansen James, Walker Brian, Liverman Diana, Richardson Katherine, Crutzen Paul, and Foley Jonathan A. (2009), Planetary boundaries: exploring the safe operating space for humanity, *Ecology and Society* 14(2): 32.

Stiglitz Joseph, Sen Amartya, and Fitoussi Jean-Paul (2009), *Report of the Commission on the Measurement of Economic performance and Social Progress.*

Stiglitz Joseph, Sen Amartya, and Fitoussi Jean-Paul (2010), *Mismeasuring our Lives. Why GDP doesn't add up. The Report by the Commission on the Measurement of Economic Performance and Social Progress*. New York/London: New Press.

Thiry Géraldine and Cassiers Isabelle (2010), Alternative Indicators to GDP: Values Behind Numbers. Adjusted Net Savings in Question, *IRES Discussion Paper* 18: 1–21.

Thiry Géraldine, Bauler Tom, Sébastien Léa, Lacroix Valérie, and Paris Sébastien (2013), *Indicators Beyond GDP. Characterising Demand: Institutional Analyses and Actors' Consultation by "Road Show"*, Brainpool Project (FP7), Deliverable 1.2, February.

UNDP (2013), *Human Development Report 2013. The Rise of the South: Human Progress in a Diverse World.* New York: UNDP.

Ura Karma, Sabina Alkire, Tshoki Zangmo, and Darma Wangdi (2012), *A Short Guide to Gross National Happiness Index*. Thimphu: The Centre for Bhutan Studies [www.grossnationalhappiness.com].

van den Bergh Jeroen C.J.M. (2009), GDP Paradox, *Journal of Economic Psychology* 30(2): 117–135.

van den Bergh Jeroen C.J.M. (2012), Growth, A-Growth or Degrowth to Stay within Planetary Boundaries? *Journal of Economic Issues* 46(2): 909–920.

3 Towards a transcultural definition of prosperity

Insights from the capability approach

Stéphane Leyens[1]

Redefining prosperity is an intrinsically normative undertaking. To agree on criteria for defining prosperity and on prosperity indicators means to agree on values and on conceptions of what society *should be*. In this sense, the concept of prosperity is an ethical concept. Thus, using the positive sciences – learning about what *is the case* – is necessary for an enlightened reflection on what prosperity is, but in itself it is not sufficient. To take a stand on the question implies to position oneself axiologically and morally.

This kind of reflection is of particular importance when considering prosperity in a globalised world. It is pointless to attempt to redefine prosperity only within the limited context of western liberal democracies, without consideration of the specific situations of developing and emerging nations. To give this necessary scope to our endeavour means to open up the field of values that underlie the conception of prosperity. Thus arises the thorny question of how to identify a single conception of prosperity that fits all value systems. This question is in fact that of the universality of values and of conceptions of quality of life, of human dignity, and of social justice. This central issue cannot be avoided and will be addressed in this chapter.

Scholars have long tried to frame a concept of "global prosperity". In the recent past their endeavour has mainly been undertaken within theories of development economics. For instance, the effort to build such a general and universal framework is characteristic of the work of the Indian economist and philosopher, Amartya Sen, who decisively shaped the thinking within the United Nations Development Program. Sen's theoretical framework will be widely referred to in this chapter. Sen's major influence on this issue is sufficient reason to consider his original thinking and to assess in which respects his theoretical contribution is of interest when redefining prosperity and, more specifically, when tackling the issue of the universality of values.

The approach of this chapter is fourfold. First, the logic of the concept of prosperity, and of related concepts, is analysed (section 1) in order to permit an understanding of the nature of the questions raised by the definition of these concepts (section 2). Second, on the basis of this conceptual clarification I will present Sen's position on prosperity (sections 3–5). Third, I will discuss some strengths and weaknesses of his theory to consider universal criteria of prosperity (sections 6–8).

Finally, I will conclude with a few practical considerations to redefine prosperity (section 9).

Before going further a preliminary remark is necessary. In Sen's work the concept of prosperity is not directly and explicitly discussed – prosperity refers to economic growth without further question as to the link between these notions. However, much of his work addresses technical issues that relate more or less directly to prosperity, such as issues of development, poverty, quality of life, or social justice. These issues are intertwined with the question of the conditions for social prosperity and refer to what is constitutive of a "happy" society. Isn't development aimed at a state of well-being? Isn't poverty a lack of social success? Doesn't social justice suppose realisation of a fulfilled life? Hence, the discussion on poverty, on development in emerging nations or on social justice arguments – inspired by Sen's writings – contributes to the debate on a redefinition of prosperity.

1 Prosperity as an ethical concept

The concept of prosperity, and related concepts such as poverty or development, has some characteristics that are worth analysing. First, the definition of prosperity is a human convention. It expresses the criteria used to distinguish the more prosperous from the less prosperous. For instance, if the definition is expressed in terms of quantity of material goods available, then the quantity of material goods available is the criterion one should take into consideration to determine the state of prosperity (of poverty, of development) of a given situation.

Criteria of prosperity are conventions in the sense that they result from human choices and that they could be different; prosperity could also be defined in terms of satisfaction of preferences or in terms of happiness. However, the type of convention at stake has to be specified. Indeed most definitions are conventions. For instance, the concept of horse is well-defined by convention. Designating a type of being by the word "horse" is not a necessity; it is a linguistic convention. But there is an important difference between the conventions used to define prosperity and the conventions used to define horse.

The truth, or the falsity, of the sentence "this is a horse" is determined by the state of the world it refers to (a being with such and such characteristics) and by the linguistic rules shared by all members of the English linguistic community. If I use the word "horse" to designate what all other members of the English linguistic community call "hammer", I use another linguistic convention, which is logically possible. By adopting different linguistic conventions concerning concepts such as horse or hammer, however, I exclude myself from the English language community in the sense that I can no longer communicate within it.

On the other hand, the truth, or the falsity, of the sentence "this society is prosperous" is determined by the state of the world it refers to (a society with such and such characteristics), by some linguistic rules shared by all members of the English language community *and* by value judgements not necessarily shared by all members of the English language community. Shared linguistic rules permit members of a given linguistic community to *communicate* with each other about the prosperity of a society, while value judgements are the reason why such members must *debate* to determine if that society is prosperous or not. Shared linguistic rules determine a *general* definition of prosperity (e.g. a state of well-being) whereas value judgements determine a *specific* definition (e.g. the possession of a given quantity of material goods). Defining prosperity is not only a matter of shared linguistic rules and conventions. It implies axiological choices, which can be divergent among members of a same linguistic community, i.e. sharing linguistic rules. Axiological choices underlying a definition of prosperity can always be debated, revised, and changed without affecting shared linguistic rules. I can have a different definition of prosperity than other members of the English linguistic community have, and still be able to communicate with them.

Second, the specific definition of prosperity expresses *positive* value judgements. This means that to say that a situation or a society is prosperous is to recommend such a situation or society. For instance, to define prosperity in terms of quantity of material goods (specific definition) is to recommend that a situation be characterised by a given quantity of material goods, that is, to recommend policies that will contribute to the acquisition of a given quantity of material goods. The concept of prosperity, and related concepts such as poverty or development, is a "thick concept" in the sense that it has both a *descriptive* and a *prescriptive* dimension (Williams, 1985: 140–142). To reflect about what is a prosperous society is to reflect about what a society *should be*. The concept of prosperity is an ethical concept.

2 Formal definition, conceptual definition, and indicators

I will discuss here the concept of poverty, which can be considered as the negative mirror image of prosperity, because it has been extensively scrutinised and has given rise to many important studies. Conceptual reflections and empirical data about poverty are very useful in consideration of the concept of prosperity.

Many indicators of poverty have been devised within development theories. Identifying what poverty is consists in answering the question: "who should be considered as poor?". This question has two components. One is concerned with the nature of poverty (poor in which respect?); the other is about the threshold of poverty (poor from which point?). Though the question of the threshold is important, the question of the nature of poverty is more essential because it is about the criteria that define poverty.

Determining the nature of poverty calls for reflection at different levels. At a formal level, poverty is defined, for example, as the condition in which people cannot live in a sufficiently decent manner. Such a definition is formal in the sense that it leaves open the meaning to give to "sufficiently decent living". What a "sufficiently decent living" means is made explicit at the conceptual level.

While a formal definition can easily be agreed upon, a conceptual definition provokes a debate because it expresses a particular conception of what it is to live decently. For instance, at the conceptual level, poverty can be considered from a biological approach and characterised by the insufficiency of earnings "to obtain the minimum necessities for the maintenance of merely physical efficiency" (Sen, 1981: 11). Without going into too much detail, it is worth noting that several elements of this definition need important clarifications. What counts as "earning"? Does it only refer to goods and money acquired as remuneration for recognised labour or does it also include goods acquired through activities other than legal labour, such as mendacity, stealing, or prostitution? And what is "physical efficiency"? Does it refer to the minimal conditions of physiological survival or rather to the physical conditions necessary to enjoy a fully accomplished family, cultural, sexual, and intellectual life? And what are "necessities"? Are they universally the same for all human beings or are they relative to the needs of each person, keeping in mind that the experience of indigence can condition what is necessary to mere physical functioning? Further, should the food "necessities" be specified in terms of "commodities" such as rice, bread, and meat, or in terms of "characteristics" such as calories, proteins, and vitamins, which typically ignore cultural diet customs? Each element of the definition deserves careful scrutiny, as each will determine which persons and situation should be classified as "poor" (Sen, 1981: 11–14).

Finally, a third level of definition, closely linked to the conceptual level, relates to the indicators of poverty. Once a conceptual definition is chosen, one needs tools to identify persons and situations that are "poor" according to that definition. There are at least two reasons why conceptual content and indicators are closely related. First, a sufficiently precise specification of the conceptual meaning of poverty by itself implies determinant indicators. As we have just seen, specifying the "necessities" for the maintenance of physical efficiency involves determining indicators (e.g. proteins or meat), and the specification of what is "physical efficiency" designates particular behaviours and activities (e.g. cultural activities), which are used as indicators of poverty. Second, the need for empirically useful indicators determines in some way possible conceptual definitions. Only concepts of poverty implying more or less directly empirical indicators are practically useful. Adopting a definition of poverty in terms of "unhappiness", with no more specification, is not of much use to develop a policy aiming at reducing poverty.

Once the nature, or the concept, of poverty is determined, one should fix a minimal "quantity" of the definitional criteria (for instance, available commodities) that a situation or a person must have to be considered as not "poor". To determine such a threshold requires one to determine the quantity of the definitional criteria necessary to be able to "live sufficiently decently" or to live in a state of "non-poverty". Because "poverty" and "living decently" are *thick concepts* as defined above, *assessing* a situation as being below the poverty threshold implies *recommending* improvement of that situation.

3 Amartya Sen and the informational basis

More than the formal definition and the determination of indicators, the conceptual level of definition is of particular importance to reflect about concepts such as prosperity, poverty, or development. It is precisely this level of definition that is central to Sen's work, in which the criteria of a conceptual definition are called "informational basis".

Three fields of research bring Sen to focus on the informational basis issue. The first is related to the social choice theory. In the mid-twentieth century, Kenneth Arrow demonstrated the impossibility to deduce democratically and rationally a coherent social choice from individual preferences. Sen showed that such impossibility is partly due to the narrowness of the informational basis, i.e. to the consideration given only to the utilities or preferences satisfaction. According to Sen, a coherent social choice theory must broaden its informational basis (1999a).

The second field concerns the theory of development and Sen's investigations on poverty (1981, 1999b). Classically, the level of development of a society is assessed on the basis of material goods that it produces and that it can enjoy. When the society under consideration is a national state, the statistics of national accounts are considered as practical and reliable indicators of the level of development experienced by the people. The Gross Domestic Product (GDP) per capita is the standard measure of development and the level of poverty is estimated on the same basis.

Two main reasons explain the importance given to the GDP per capita in assessing the level of development. The first seems obvious; income is an essential condition for well-being and quality of life. The second reason is pragmatic and no less important. Any development programme necessitates criteria (a) to describe the actual state of development, (b) to select a policy that will improve the actual state of development, and (c) to assess the impact of the policy in improving such state of development. Such criteria must be accessible for empirical observation and quantified measurement, and must allow comparisons among different places, different times, and different societies. To talk about development in terms of happiness is certainly meaningful as it meets our intuitions about what human flourishing consists of, but it is not very helpful in elaborating and evaluating concrete policies – how could one determine an improvement in happiness? On the contrary, incomes and material goods available to people are easily measured, quantified, and compared. Thus a major asset of the GDP indicator, and of the related criteria of available material goods, is its very high potential for evaluation necessary to any development policy.

Amartya Sen has been actively involved in the UNO reflection about the relevancy of the GDP as indicator of development and he has defended the idea that assessing prosperity solely on the basis of the criteria of income (at the personal level) or of the GDP per capita (at the State level) cannot be sufficient. Incomes, be they personal or collective, are certainly important means to implement development policies and to reduce poverty. But they cannot constitute the only assessment indicator of development or poverty. Sen's scepticism about material goods and incomes as relevant criteria of prosperity finds a foundation within a third field of research – political philosophy, and more specifically, theories of social justice to which I turn now.

4 Beyond utility and resources

One can understand Sen's originality in tackling the issue of social justice from the criticisms he made of two of the most influential contemporary theories: utilitarianism and Rawls' political liberalism (Sen, 1982, 2009).

According to utilitarianism, the criterion for assessing social justice is the sum of the utilities of all the members of a society; a society is fair and just as long as it tends to maximise the sum of the utilities. Different definitions of utility have been provided but each of them refers to a subjective state of well-being such as pleasure, happiness or, more generally, the satisfaction of individual preferences. Sen's criticism of this view on social justice is twofold.

First, the aggregate sum of preference satisfactions of all persons as a criterion of justice cannot be sufficient because an aggregate sum is blind to possible inequalities of distribution within a society. The criterion does not allow for differentiation in regard to social justice between two societies having the same sum of utilities, one being very unequal (a few have a lot and many have very little), and the other one being fairly equal (everybody has more or less the same). This runs counter to our intuitions of justice as a principle of equality (although various strategies, e.g. rule utilitarianism, have been devised to cope with the problem of unequal distribution, utilitarianism is an aggregative theory that neglects by its very nature the issue of distribution). The aggregation criticism is commonplace and Sen's originality lies rather in his second criticism of the informational basis of utilitarianism, to which I now turn.

Sen holds that well-being alone cannot be sufficient to evaluate the state of a society in regard to social justice. He writes:

> a person may value the promotion of certain causes and the occurrence of certain things, even though the importance that is attached to these developments is not reflected by the advancement of his or her well-being, if any, that they respectively cause.
>
> (1988: 41)

Promoting human rights, fulfilling commitments, and defending values are a person's "actings" not necessarily conducive to her well-being but that are nonetheless essential components of her quality of life. Such actings should be taken into account in a theory of social justice.

Furthermore, focusing on the satisfaction of the *expressed,* or *manifest preferences* of persons to assess the level of justice reached by a society is highly questionable. On the one hand, it is far from certain that everyone has an equal opportunity to express one's preferences in a given society. Indeed it is often the case that members of minority or marginalised groups do not have the same opportunity as members of the majority group have to express themselves in decision-making bodies. On the other hand, many expressed preferences are adapted to or conditioned by social and cultural context – such preferences are called "adaptive preferences". Thus a person living in very precarious conditions (e.g. a drought) will have basic preferences related to her survival in those conditions (e.g. drinking some liquid). According to a theory based on the satisfaction of expressed preferences, a society that satisfies those adaptive preferences (e.g. by providing a scant quantity of drinkable liquid) should be considered prosperous and developed, which obviously is not the case.

Central to those criticisms is the questionable relevancy of a subjective approach based on personal well-being in order to develop a theory of social justice, of the quality of life, and of prosperity. Does this mean that one should adopt a more objective approach not based on personal well-being to tackle the issue of social justice? Sen's response to this question can be found in the critical analysis he made of Rawls' theory of social justice.

According to Rawls, two fair principles of justice would emerge from deliberations done in a situation of impartiality in which one avoids being influenced by one's personal interests, priorities or prejudices. The principles are stated as follows:

1 Each person is to have an equal right to a fully adequate scheme of equal basic liberties, which is compatible with a similar scheme of liberties for all.
2 Social and economic inequalities are to satisfy two conditions. First, they must be attached to offices and positions open to all under conditions of fair equality of opportunity; and second, they must be to the greatest benefit of the least advantaged members of society.

(Rawls, 1993: 291)

To be fully meaningful, the second principle has to be specified so as to determine who are the least advantaged and in which respect they are least advantaged. To this end Rawls introduces the concept of "primary goods", which can be understood as an objective informational basis for interpersonal comparisons. The least advantaged are those who have the smallest amount of primary goods. Primary goods are the resources that everyone needs to achieve one's personal long-term plan of life and to live according to one's personal conception of the good. They include rights and liberties, powers and opportunities, income and wealth, and social basis for self-respect (Rawls, 2001: 58–59).

To illustrate the shortcomings of Rawls' theory, Sen asks us to consider the case of a severely handicapped person living in a society organised according to Rawls' principles of justice. In that society, this person enjoys fundamental rights and liberties (first principle), and gets an equitable amount of primary goods (second principle) – equitable in the sense that an unequal distribution among members of the society is allowed as long as the least advantaged persons benefit from that unequal distribution of primary goods (power, income, and wealth), which means that their power and income are increased through the unequal distribution.

Such disabled person has civic and political rights and an equitable socio-economic status. However, it can appear that unlike a person with no disability, she cannot make the most of her socio-economic resources in order to accomplish the rational plan of life she values. For instance, she cannot offer her children the schooling she wishes because she cannot fulfil certain conditions that such a project implies (e.g. attending parent teacher meetings) despite her formal right to her children's education and her equitable income. Taking into account objective primary goods, or resources, is not sufficient to assess how socially just a situation is.[2]

5 Freedom and participation as criteria of prosperity

Based on the criticisms of utilitarianism and of Rawls' theory of justice, Sen defends the idea that more important features one should concentrate on in assessing justice are the real opportunities a person has to achieve the "beings" (e.g. being educated) and the "actings" (e.g. going to school) she has reason to value – "beings" and "actings" are called "functionings" and the real opportunities to achieve them are called "capabilities". Given human diversity, it appears that different persons have different opportunities, that is, different capabilities, to use their material resources and their formal rights (Rawls' primary goods) to achieve the functionings they value.

Different persons having similar incomes, and the same formal liberties and rights might have very different experiences in terms of prosperity. While some have the real opportunity to translate their income and their rights into the plan of life they value (e.g. offering education to their children), others may not have similar opportunities. This might be because there are no universities in the vicinity where they live and no public transport to travel to a distant college, or because discrimination against the social group to which their children belong (gender, caste, race, etc.) is commonplace and is a serious obstacle to their children's integration into the university culture. The real opportunity that a person has in order to achieve the "functionings" she values – her capability – depends not only on the material goods and the formal rights she has, but as well on several factors (environmental, domestic, social, biological) that help, or prevent, her use of those goods and rights to achieve her plan of life.

Sen's approach to social justice – the capability approach – presents three important features worth noting. First, the focus is on the opportunity – the real *freedom* – that a person actually has to achieve some beings and actings and not on the achievement itself. The reason for this becomes clear when one considers the following example. Two persons who obtain a similar level of achievement of the functioning "being educated" – neither of them studies – may experience prosperity very differently: one chose not to study and to rely on her parents' wealth to make a living, while the other one had to work from early childhood with no chance to study. It is not what one achieves that matters the most, but the freedom to choose to achieve or not what one values. Second, Sen stresses the importance of the person's *participation* in decision-making relative to her life. Everyone should be fully agent of one's own life, i.e. being able to express her own values and her conception of the good, to act accordingly, and to be held responsible for it. Third, the capability approach focuses on the *individual*. Sen does not deny the importance of the community, from domestic to national level, in achieving prosperity. But he insists that the final consideration of any policy should concern individual persons.

6 Scope and limit of the capability approach

The capability approach offers an informational basis for describing and assessing the state of a society and of its members, be it in terms of prosperity, development, and social justice or, negatively, in terms of poverty. A society will be considered more or less prosperous, developed, just, or poor, on the basis of the capabilities it generates. One of the major assets of this informational basis is that it offers the qualities of both criteria of utilities and Rawlsian resources while avoiding their drawbacks.

On the one hand, the value of a utility-based approach to prosperity is that it meets our intuition that a society should satisfy the personal preferences of its members as much as it can. In this sense, the preference satisfaction criterion of utilitarianism is a subjective criterion. However, it has a major drawback. As seen above, the preferences expressed by a person might not reflect her real conception of quality of life. They might be adapted to the actual precarious situation the person experiences, hiding what she really expects from life. To assess prosperity using a subjective informational basis – through personal expressed preferences – might be conducive to conservatism and social status quo, which are hardly compatible with a prosperous society.

On the other hand, objective criteria such as Rawlsian resources avoid the subjective drawback by focusing on the objective means necessary to achieve a personal and subjective plan of life. But this approach neglects the fact that different persons have different capacities to translate the resources they have into an accomplished plan of life.

The capability approach offers an informational basis that has an objective dimension while paying attention to personal subjectivity. The real opportunity to achieve a valued functioning (e.g. being educated) is assessed on the basis of objective features such as available material resources, school accessibility, social discrimination, etc. But the objective opportunity concerns a being or acting (being educated, going to school), which is valued by a particular person. By focusing both on an objective assessment of a situation and on the subjective preferences of those concerned, the capability approach offers the assets of both utilitarianism and Rawls' resourcism while eliminating their respective drawbacks.

One may rightfully ask oneself whether the capability approach can be implemented in order to assess concrete situations. This point goes beyond the scope of this chapter; I will simply point out that the issue of capabilities measurements and indicators is extensively investigated in several research centres and is the topic of numerous publications. It is doubtless that there are practical assessment possibilities.

Furthermore, the individualist stance of the capability approach is questionable, especially in the context of a criticism of mainstream economics. On this point, I will note only that Sen's theory is a kind of ethical individualism, according to which well-being of individuals should be the aim of any policy or action. Nevertheless, it departs from an ontological or methodological individualism for which the only relevant explanation unit is the individual. The "individualism" of the capability approach allows, and requires, taking into account social and community dimensions of the quality of life.

Finally, the capability approach belongs to the political liberalism paradigm and one might wonder if an approach to the quality of life centred on individual freedoms is relevant to address issues in non-liberal societies. This point, which raises the difficulty to give a definition of prosperity that has a global scope, is of particular importance. In fact it would not be sensible to reduce the scope of a definition only to modern western societies with no consideration to other cultural and political contexts. This issue is that of value relativism, to which I now turn.

7 Capabilities and the issue of relativism

Criteria for defining prosperity are expressions of values, that is to say social conditions that are valued, about which an agreement should be reached. As in any ethical issue, value pluralism is a fact one has to deal with. In the case under consideration, the question raised by global pluralism is, which is the definition of prosperity that would be agreed upon by the different cultures and societies from all over the planet? Should we aim at a common definition based on universal values? Or on the contrary, should we acknowledge the irreducibility of particular value systems that are relative to various cultures? Or finally, could we make do with a very general definition accepted by all that would allow various interpretations adapted to specific cultural contexts?

My point here is not to answer those important and highly complex questions but rather to understand to what extent the capability approach can deal with them. My aim is twofold: first, to propose some beacons to reflect on the issue of value pluralism as part of our endeavour to redefine prosperity; and second, to better understand, through those questions, the originality of the capability approach.

From the outset, we can rule out two unreasonable extreme positions, between which we'll have to position ourselves. The first could be named "uncritical universalism". This position consists in raising particular values to the status of universal values without having critically compared them to other axiological systems. This is a form of ethnocentrism that is unacceptable within some intercultural context such as North–South relations.

The second position is the opposite of the former. It consists in condemning the fact of judging other value systems for the reason that any value system is meaningful only within the culture or society it is related to. But this normative ethical relativism, which amounts to a principle of non-interference, is self-defeating. Though it advocates the relativity of all values, it defends a universal value, that is, the moral obligation of non-interference.

This being clarified, how is the capability approach to be considered regarding the issue of the status of values? Does it allow avoidance of uncritical universalism and normative relativism? First, as I noted above, the central importance that Sen's theory gives to the individual freedom is highly questionable; isn't to raise individual freedom to the status of universal value to display outrageous western dogmatism? An articulate answer to this issue cannot be developed here; however I will argue, following Nussbaum (2000: 38), that claims and fights for fundamental personal rights and for individual freedom is not a specificity of Western culture, but can be found in many "traditional" cultures. Once we accept that line of argumentation, the issue is ready to be discussed within the framework of the capability approach.

In Sen's theory, a capability is the real opportunity one has to achieve beings and actings (functionings) that one has reason to value. In order to assess capabilities, social sciences provide tools to describe and evaluate the *real opportunity* people have and the *functionings they value* (Alkire *et al.*, 2008). But determining if one has *reason to value a functioning* remains an open question, directly related to the relativism–universalism issue.

Do the "reasons to value" refer to the rational coherence of a particular person, which means that *any* functioning that blends with her values and her way of life is considered rational and valuable? Or do they refer to a universal human rationality which is independent of particular preferences and values? The former meaning is a relativist type as the rationality of a functioning is assessed in relation to a particular way of life, which cannot be judged from the outside. As long as a functioning matches the way of life and the conception of the good of a person, it is considered rational, and it is therefore justified. For instance, the functioning "being submitted to female genital mutilation" is rational and valuable provided that it is consistent with the way of life in which it takes place, i.e. in a community where female genital mutilation is socially valued.

The later meaning is universalist in that the "reasons to value" are related to a common human reason which is the source of universal norms and values. According to this view, the rationality of a functioning does not rest upon the consistency with a particular way of life because some ways of life and value systems are universally valuable while others are not. For example, a universalist could judge unacceptable a way of life that values female genital mutilation because she holds that there are some universal norms and values on the basis of which one can distinguish valuable from non-valuable ways of life. The challenge is to avoid both relativism, according to which every way of life and value sets are equally valid, and dogmatic universalism imposing norms with no consideration to cultural diversity.

In relation to the issue of redefining prosperity, this challenge can be summarised as follows. Prosperity is a thick concept with a positive connotation, e.g. to judge a situation prosperous implies to recommend such a situation. Once we define prosperity using capabilities as informational basis – a society is prosperous provided that it strengthens its members' capabilities – social policies *should* strengthen the capabilities of all, i.e. the real opportunity one has to achieve the functionings that one values.

Let's imagine the case of people valuing capital accumulation (a functioning) with no regard for social justice and environmental considerations. In order to determine what the right policy should be, e.g. if a policy should strengthen the real opportunities to accumulate capital, the key issue is to know if those people have "reason" to value that functioning. To tackle this issue, one has to choose between the two meanings of rationality – relativist or universalist – and, accordingly, to answer one of the following two questions: (a) do they have reason because the functioning is consistent with their way of life (relativist stance), or (b) do they have reason because of universal values independent of their particular way of life (universalist stance)? In a way, those stances are compared to the subjectivist and objectivist approaches to prosperity discussed above. Within the capability approach, they correspond to two strategies, defended respectively by Amartya Sen and by the philosopher, Martha Nussbaum.

8 Contextual and universal capabilities

In regard to the epistemic status of capabilities, Sen's position is practically relativist. Indeed he rejects the idea of defining a priori fundamental and universal capabilities. The functionings that persons have reason to value are determined within a given context. In this sense, his theory is underdetermined, which explains that it presents a great flexibility of application to various contexts (1992: 48–49).

In Sen's view, reasons to value a functioning should be discussed, and then either accepted or rejected, through a participatory process. A major role of participation is in forming and clarifying values and their priority. Indeed, participation in focus groups and in decision-making procedures allows persons to exchange their points of view on a matter and leads to informed awareness of their interests, values, and commitments.

Participation not only allows one to defend and enforce one's point of view, but it also permits one to confront different points of view in order to assess their respective value as much as their weakness. It allows development of one's commitments and values; it has a constructive effect. In this sense, the participatory process is a major means of ethical rationality, e.g. of critical reflection on what should be valued, thereby enabling one to determine what are the functionings one has reason to value. According to this conception of value formation, the capabilities are contextually determined (Alkire, 2002: 129–143).

However, to implement a real participatory dynamic raises many difficulties. In a discussion group, one can wonder who organises the discussion, who expresses one's view, who is persuasive enough, and finally who decides. Behind the democratic ideals of participation, manipulation and the law of the strongest can loom large. Participation processes are hardly fully impartial and it is not sure at all that they are adequate to handle the adaptive preferences issue. The reason for this is that social pressure and unfair balance of power can strongly influence public discussions. For instance, gender-based discrimination can often condition the preferences expressed and prevent equal consideration to male and female points of view in decision-making. Therefore to pinpoint manifest preferences that are socially conditioned – adaptive preferences – requires devising specific strategies, which is a difficult task. Though participatory procedure can doubtless be an interesting tool to tackle this issue, it is certainly not a solution in itself.

Taking seriously into account shortcomings of such a purely procedural approach, philosopher Martha Nussbaum chooses a different path, which is best understood by considering how she approaches the adaptive preferences problem (2000: 137–139). Nussbaum notes that one can have unrealistic aspirations such as to fly like a bird or to be the best basketball player ever. Most people become easily aware that, given their own capacities, such aspirations are out of reach, and they adjust their preferences to what they can reasonably achieve; they adapt their preferences to their own condition. Such adaptations are often a good thing because they contribute to human flourishing by avoiding frustration.

In such cases, adaptation is not problematic because it concerns unrealistic aspirations that are not essential to our human condition. On the contrary, when social and cultural circumstances drive people not to aspire to physical integrity, or to political equality, and drive them to hold an adaptive preference for genital mutilation, for example, or for political submission, this is problematic. The reason is that such adaptive preferences run against human dignity and human flourishing. According to Nussbaum, there is no reason to value such functionings, and the freedom to achieve such adaptive preferences cannot be used to assess the well-being of a society.

The distinction between these two types of cases brings Nussbaum to defend a universal conception of human nature and a substantive theory of goods that are necessary to delineate valuable from non-valuable functionings. On the one hand, some functionings – beings and actings – are essential to, and constitutive of, human nature. In order to contribute to one's own flourishing, one should have the real opportunity to achieve those essential human functionings. On the other hand, some functionings jeopardise the flourishing of human nature. People shouldn't have reason to value these functionings, which are considered "irrational". Though they can be the objects of manifest valuation in specific contexts, some functionings shouldn't be taken into account to assess the prosperity of a society.

Nussbaum establishes a list of ten universal functionings that are part of our universal human nature (2000: 78–80): being able to live to the end of a human life of normal length; being able to have good health; being able to move freely, to be secure and to have opportunities for sexual satisfaction; being able to use the senses, to imagine, think, and reason; being able to have attachments to things and people outside ourselves; being able to form a conception of the good and to engage in critical reflection; being able to live with and towards others and to engage in various forms of social interaction; being able to live with concern for and in relation to the world of nature; being able to laugh, to play, to enjoy recreational activities; and being able to participate effectively in political choices, to hold property, and to work. A society will be judged prosperous provided that it secures real opportunities to achieve the functionings essential to human flourishing. Capabilities, according to Nussbaum, are universal goods.

Nussbaum is right to point out that any procedure, be it participative or not, implies some particular values which have to be made explicit and to be recognised as such. In this sense, her list of universal capabilities can be considered as an axiological background necessarily implied in a participatory process. But it is doubtful that the list of universal capabilities can play the role that Nussbaum intends to give them, that is, to be the universal criteria for determining the functionings that one has reason to value. Indeed it is one thing to acknowledge the relevance of the very *general* capabilities of the list and quite another to assess the rationality of a *specific* functioning such as "being submitted to female genital mutilation". A major difficulty to assess such specific functionings is due to the fact that they can refer to several general universal capabilities: should the rationality of female genital mutilation be assessed in relation to the universal capability "being able to have opportunities for sexual satisfaction" or rather to the universal capability "being able to live with and toward others and to engage in various forms of social interaction"? In the first case, it wouldn't be rational to value mutilation as it jeopardises sexual flourishing whereas in the second case, it would be rational to value it because it is a condition of social integration. Is the list practically useful?

One could argue that imposing a list of universal capabilities is a form of ethnocentric dogmatism. In response to this, one can follow Nussbaum when she notes that her list of universal capabilities corresponds to various "spheres of life" shared by all human beings, such as death, health, distribution of goods, attitude towards the ill fortune of others, living together, etc. Everyone develops an attitude towards those spheres: "no matter where one lives, one cannot escape these questions, so long as one is living as human being" (1993: 247). Of course, every culture has its appropriate ways to conceive what are correct attitudes. But those spheres of life, and the corresponding capabilities, are universal and make up the common background of values against which intercultural dialogue can take place.

However, those common values can be used as universal criteria by virtue of the fact that they are general enough and underdetermined; they necessarily call for a contextualised specification allowing understanding of what is precisely the right attitude in a given sphere of life in a specific context. Only then can one practically delineate essential human capabilities from nonessential ones and hope to assess how prosperous a specific society is.

At this point, it looks as if the tension between relativism and universalism remains intact. But at least one major ethical requirement is met, that is, the requirement to make explicit and to recognise the values that lie behind any assessment of a situation and which should be reflected and discussed in a participative way. Prosperity has to be defined against a background of universal values *and* on the basis of a participative process.

9 Redefining capabilities: capabilities, participation, and universal values

Which recommendations for redefining prosperity can be made from our discussion?

First, it was noted that prosperity is an ethical concept that has a descriptive component (definitional criteria) and a prescriptive component (what is defined as prosperous is recommendable). This means that a definition of prosperity must provide useful indicators to guide policies intended to improve prosperity. Furthermore, defining prosperity implies making ethical commitments, in terms of values. These commitments should be made explicit, recognised, and shared through the definitional criteria, which express what is valued and recommended.

Second, in a globalised world, the definition of prosperity must take into account cultural diversity, that is, value pluralism. A major challenge is to propose a definition with a scope broad enough to fulfil the pluralism requirement. Two shortcomings should be avoided: on the one hand, western ethnocentrism with an uncritical universalist claim; on the other hand, relativism that considers all value systems equally.

Third, definitional criteria should have an objective dimension and a subjective dimension. The objective dimension is necessary to meet a requirement of impartiality and to develop practical indicators. The subjective dimension makes room for concerns of individuals. The capability approach accommodates the two dimensions and is therefore an interesting template for a definition of prosperity.

Finally, the issue of value universalism raised by a "globalised" definition of prosperity must be addressed on a twofold basis: first, on the basis of a participative process giving voice to all parties involved and integrating value systems concerned, and second, on the basis of a universal conception of the good which is general enough to suit value systems concerned and which will be contextually specified through a participatory procedure.

Notes

1 Université de Namur. For further information see author's biography at the front of this volume.

2 Rawls recognises the existence of special needs for those who are clearly disabled. But according to Sen, the way he deals with this issue has a "limited reach" because special needs are taken into consideration only after the principles of justice have been established (Sen, 2009: 261).

References

Alkire Sabina (2002), *Valuing Freedoms: Sen's Capability Approach and Poverty Reduction*. Oxford: Oxford University Press.

Alkire Sabina, Qizilbash Mozaffar, and Comim Falvio (2008), *The Capability Approach: Concepts, Measures and Applications*. Cambridge: Cambridge University Press.

Nussbaum Martha (1993), Non-relative virtues: an Aristotelian approach. In: Martha Nussbaum and Amartya Sen (eds), *The Quality of Life*. Oxford: Oxford University Press, 242–269.

Nussbaum Martha (2000), *Women and Human Development: The Capabilities Approach*. Cambridge: Cambridge University Press.

Rawls John (1993), *Political Liberalism*. New York: Columbia University Press.

Rawls John (2001), *Justice as Fairness: A Restatement*. Cambridge: Belknap Press of Harvard University Press.

Sen Amartya (1981), *Poverty and Famines: An Essay on Entitlement and Deprivation*. Oxford: Oxford University Press.

Sen Amartya (1982), Equality of what. In: Amartya Sen (ed.), *Choice, Welfare and Measurement*. Cambridge: The MIT Press, 353–369.

Sen Amartya (1988), *On Ethics and Economics*. Oxford: Basil Blackwell.

Sen Amartya (1992), *Inequality Reexamined*. Cambridge: Harvard University Press.

Sen Amartya (1999a), The possibility of social choice, *American Economic Review* 89(3): 344–378.

Sen Amartya (1999b), *Development as Freedom*. New York: Knopf Press.

Sen Amartya (2009), *The Idea of Justice*. London: Allen Lane.

Williams Bernard (1985), *Ethics and the Limits of Philosophy*. Cambridge: Harvard University Press.

4 Consumerism and positive liberty

Jean De Munck[1]

The prominence of consumption is difficult to ignore in contemporary everyday usage of the notion of "prosperity". Historically, Western Europe and the United States were the first societies to found "real consumerism", but it is now so firmly established throughout the world that one may – for the first time in human history – speak of "global consumerism" (Bauman, 2008). The promise of more and more consumption is the most powerful force driving mass adherence to the "cult of growth"; it motivates the considerable efforts put forth by so many countries to convert to capitalism. Household consumption is one of the most common measures used to evaluate a country's level of economic development. In short, all over the world, economic prosperity is more often than not confused with consumerism. In a broad-reaching approach to the question of prosperity, this confusion justifies an examination of consumerism as a phenomenon unto itself. We must raise the question: *What, if anything, is wrong with consumerism?*

It should be noted from the beginning that providing a response to such a question would be inconceivable from within neoclassical economics, which recognises only private preferences, considered exogenous to the exchange system. From such a perspective, critiquing a mode of consumption reduced to the "tastes" of consumers making private and arbitrary choices is simply impossible. From the sociological point of view taken here, however, consumerism may be thought of as a way of life that is collectively produced and reproduced, and structured by norms as well as preferences. Approached from this angle, a critique of consumerism becomes possible.

My first goal here is to show that a critique of consumerism may be made from three discursive angles. First, the critique may be founded on an idea of justice: mass consumption reproduces inequalities. Taken on its own, this critical problematic is weak, since it confronts the distribution of consumption more than it does consumerism itself. The second critical approach is cultural. It looks at consumerism in terms of quality of life – and therefore presupposes an idea of what is good (and not merely what is fair, as in the first approach). The final angle is economical, using the lens of environmental impact to focus on the volume of goods consumed.

My second goal is to examine with particular care the second of these three critical angles, as, from a normative point of view, it is by far the most problematic.

The cultural critique presupposes a set definition of what philosophers would call "a good life". This, in principle, is something a liberal society does not permit itself to do. But at the same time, consumerism itself represents a certain definition – or at least a culture – of "the good life". Operating from behind a façade of total respect for individual choices, it imposes norms – norms that are unchosen, and, what is more, non-deliberated. Our central aim here will be to pinpoint, within this critical approach, where the normative standard for a critique of consumerism may come from. Without providing a definitive answer to this difficult question, I would like to suggest that it is possible to distinguish normative tensions that are *internal* to consumerism, and which attest to the fact that consumerism offers only an extremely impoverished version of positive liberty.

My third goal is to draw attention to the fact that a true and thorough critique of prosperity must include the three normative angles described above, rather than dissociating them. Politically and conceptually, combining these three angles is far from simple, and the temptation to avoid such a combination by seeking to "boil down" critiques of consumerism to a single or perhaps two dimensions is understandable. But any critique of prosperity that cannot work in at least three normative registers runs the risk of falling short of its own goals. Using the critique of consumerism as an example, I shall argue for a complex critique of prosperity based on a balanced articulation of these three registers.

1 What is consumerism?

First, a definition of consumerism is in order. Consumerism describes something other than consumption, which, biologically, is merely a function of living: an organism must consume environmental resources to survive. Economically, consumption describes the purchase of goods and services and their subsequent use. Clearly, any form of human activity, whether or not it is reified in lasting physical objects, requires some form of consumption. In this sense, therefore, consumption and consumerism cannot be the same thing.

The suffix "ism" refines the idea of consumption with two intertwined connotations. First, it draws attention to the fact that the bio-economical phenomenon of consumption is culturally overdetermined: the leap from consumption to consumerism cannot be made merely by adding a few symbolic dimensions to the bio-economical nature of consumption. The word "consumerism" designates a way of life; norms and standards for legitimate desire and for a successful life; and a means of transmitting messages, goods, and services. These cultural aspects of consumerism may vary through time and space. Broadly speaking, however, it is possible to point out several invariable characteristics which return, omnipresent and insistent, in most descriptions of the phenomenon: an individualist mode of consumption that is dependent on the market, quantitatively insatiable, invasive, hedonistic, focused on novelty, using signs rather than things, and prodigal in its use of natural and human resources. Baudrillard (1970) may be credited with drawing attention to this cultural dimension of developed capitalist societies.

Second, consumerism is a mode of consumption that is both *historically dated* and *geographically located*. It has no equivalent in past human societies. It has existed as a mode of consumption within developed capitalist societies since the 1920s. It became rampant following the Second World War and the emergence of the Keynesian state, which was entirely focused on what was then called the policy of demand. Consumerism survived the dismantling of Keynesian policies at the close of the 1970s, and continues to underpin policy in the post-Ford era. Though anchored in the West, it is spreading ever more rapidly to developing Southern-hemisphere countries, and in particular to so-called "emerging economies".

2 Three critical approaches to consumerism

The critique of consumerism has existed since the birth of consumer society. It is a complex critique, and is itself part of the much broader critique of capitalism. For a clearer vision of the vast terrain covered by the critique of capitalism, and to more precisely locate the critique of consumerism within it, we can identify three major normative themes around which the critique as a whole is organised.

1 The first critical approach to capitalism addresses the issue of inequality. As early as the nineteenth century, the serious promotion of the egalitarian principles espoused by the French Revolution threatened the most basic workings of a capitalist regime that had been built from the convergence of civil contract law, capitalist accumulation, and industrial production techniques. The two concepts at the core of this approach are the exploitation of the worker and the distribution of the wealth generated by work; it drove the Communist revolutions and motivated the emergence of the social welfare state. The key question it raises is whether or not policies to promote equality can be compatible with liberty. In an era when capitalism is gaining new vigour and running rampant across the globe, the egalitarian critique has retained all of its original pertinence.

In principle, the egalitarian critique touches on consumption as much as it does production. Historically, however, it has given far more attention to the latter that to the former. Socialism has largely preoccupied itself with *access* to consumption, rather than with consumption *practices*. Since participation in production is a precondition for access to consumption, the egalitarian critique has borne more strongly on work than on consumption (which is assimilated with "leisure").

And yet as Pierre Bourdieu showed in his celebrated work on the subject, the world of consumption is just as socially stratified as the world of production (Bourdieu, 1979). Following on his work, various *practices* of consumption and their potentially dangerous effects have often been observed. In the United States, for instance, the eating habits of the working class have been the subject of increasing attention, notably with regard to diet-related health problems such as obesity (see, for example, Sobal and Stunkard, 1989). The quality of food sold (meat, fast food, industrially processed or frozen foods, etc.) and the segregation of retail distribution channels are major markers of social inequality (be it class, gender, or race).

Though this first critical problematic can touch on concrete consumption practices, it is compatible with certain extreme forms of productivism and consumerism, and may even lead to recommendations for increasing consumption precisely where inequalities are the most dramatic. Thus, an egalitarian critique of capitalism may only become a critique of *consumerism* when it mobilises other critical approaches not based on the criterion of equality.

2 The second critique of capitalism is cultural. Here, the new lifestyle offered to the masses through increased growth is interrogated, not through the lens of equality, but rather by considering the idea of a "good and happy life". Such considerations may be expressed through the concept of "quality of life" (used, for example, by Nussbaum and Sen, 1993). The desirability of the way of life produced and reproduced by the growth of capitalism is thrown into question.

The idea of lifestyle did not originate in the twentieth century. Already in the nineteenth century, it had appeared under two main forms, both quite powerful: one, conservative and restorative, saw in the expansion of industrialised cities the disastrous destruction of fundamentally rural and religious lifestyles. The second was a progressive stance taken by artists and the modernist avant-garde seeking to break with the conservative and conformist values of the old aristocratic elite and at the same time to denigrate the "vulgar" and "philistine" bourgeois class which had taken society's helm. These critiques had little bearing on the broader populace. Nevertheless, socialist utopias that confronted the question of a better quality of life, from Fourierism to the founding of a variety of intentional communities, can be observed emerging during this era.

In the twentieth century, this critique changed courses. Starting in the 1920s, capitalism followed the course of the consumer society that spread across Europe after the Second World War. The cultural critique turned its attention to this new reality. It was developed in new forms of critical sociology, and propagated in the middle classes. It was a major force behind the discourse of May 1968 in the West. The classic expression of this critique was a refusal to participate in the "rat race", and it was levelled with equal vehemence at Ford-style capitalism and the real socialism of the Eastern-bloc countries. Consumerism became synonymous with alienation and conformity.

3 The third critical angle is ecological: its object is the extravagant, wasteful, and self-destructive nature of the growth of consumption. At root, normatively speaking, this critique is a classically economic one: its focus is on managing scarcity. Here, however, the definition of scarcity is broadened to encompass global ecological scarcity, which is barely accounted for in classical economics. The core argument of this critique is that development as it is currently practiced can be neither materially nor environmentally sustainable, since the type of consumption that gratifies the masses while offering equal access to wealth rapidly destroys the very natural resources that make production possible. This critical problematic took shape and gained political momentum starting in the 1970s. The oil crisis of 1974 was a moment of portent for advanced industrial societies,

and it brought with it pressures that would become more pressing and worrisome as time went on. An increasingly complex critical discourse grew from this historical moment, which included themes such as degrowth, alternative growth, sustainable development, and environmentalism.

Equality, quality of life, and ecological scarcity: a critique of consumerism draws more force from the values underlying the second and third critical angles described above than from the first. For all this, it would not be judicious to set aside the question of equality, for any radical critique of prosperity must draw upon all three of these themes. And yet, as we shall see, it does remain possible to build more selective critical discourses that employ only one or two of these angles.

3 The critique of consumerism, and the critique of the critique

Where do the social sciences stand with regard to consumerism? Starting in the 1950s and 1960s, challenging consumerism became something of a contact sport in the field of sociology (for an overview of this, see Schor, 2007). At the close of the Second World War, as the people strolled and surged through malls and department stores, sociologists viewed consumerism with a wary eye. The more conservative among them, such as Bell, believed it would threaten the moral cohesion of capitalist society, while those who tended towards the avant-garde, such as Adorno or Marcuse, feared it would destroy any possibility of a radical critique of capitalism. Tentatively, they traced out a second angle to the critique of consumerism. Bourdieu and his school followed in the footsteps of Veblen, renewing an approach to consumption that paid close attention to social inequalities. With Ivan Illich, Jean-Pierre Dupuy, and the "new left" of the 1970s, ecological themes made their appearance in the social sciences, mostly in the context of the third critical angle described above, opening the door to new utopian perspectives.

And yet, in the 1980s, a change in tone emerged in the social sciences, generally attributed to the advent of cultural studies as a discipline (or, in any case, to some aspects of that discipline). Essentially, two charges were levelled at post-war critiques of consumerism. The first was the insensitivity of these critiques to the *realities* of consumerism. Consumerism's persistence, expansion, and extreme creativity, so the argument went, were in the end much more impressive than the academy's critiques of it. Given its phenomenal scale, it would be difficult not to see consumerism as the concrete fulfilment of one of humanity's most basic desires. Whence the call in the 1980s for a "post-moral" sociology, beginning with the anthropological work of Marie Douglas and Baron Isherwood (1979) (Horowitz, 2004). Mass consumption, examined from up close using the tools of scientific ethnography, appeared far more polymorphic and dynamic than reluctant academics had previously believed. The emergence of new forms of individualisation and aestheticisation were observed (Jameson, 1991). Visions of the featureless masses grazing their way through a world of "passive consumption" evaporated, to be replaced by "active consumerism" that promised to respect consumers; to bring them action, adventure, travel; to mobilise them in all senses of the word (Urry, 1995). In short, so the argument went, before critiquing consumerism one ought to explain it, to understand it, and at the very least to admit that it satisfied a basic urge within the modern culture of liberty.

The second major charge levelled by this "critique of the critique" followed on the first, questioning the normative standards used to malign Fordist consumerism. The first assertion of this charge was of *elitism*: if consumerism was a vehicle for popular satisfaction, then weren't social critiques merely a last-ditch attempt to cling to an elitist version of aristocratic or bourgeois high culture? And had such a critique not been rendered obsolete by the democratisation of access to material and cultural goods? The second assertion contained in this charge was of *repressive asceticism,* expressed on all points of the critical spectrum, from Adorno to Bell to Galbraith. For these critics, unable to wrench themselves from the world of *anankè* and scarcity, no morality could be possible without suffering and privation. But why assign such moral privilege to asceticism? Was material prosperity truly incompatible with moral value?

4 For an immanent critique of consumerism

This "critique of the critique" of consumerism deserves to be taken seriously. Far from being an invitation to celebrate consumerism, it asks that more serious attention be given to its internal structure, rationale, and contradictions. Consumerism may in fact be examined as the fulfilment of entirely legitimate normative goals; it is true that the standards by which consumerism are evaluated should not be imposed from the outside in an elitist or ascetic manner. Indeed, I believe consumerism should be considered as an institution, so that its basic normative aims may be uncovered. In its very reality, we discern tensions and contradictions that belie the ways in which it falls short – and even fails – in keeping its promises.

Consumerism would certainly not have the force it does now if it did not present itself as a liberated lifestyle; that is, as a way for modern people to live out their freedom. This freedom manifests itself in two ways: first, for millions of individuals, it represents a formidable promise of emancipation from economic necessity. It is inclusive, *by principle* depriving no one of the right to access opulence. This promise of democratic opulence is what separates contemporary consumerism from the luxury consumption of the wealthy in the nineteenth century. Symbolically, it attains freedom for all. Second, consumerism achieves this collective liberation from economic necessity through individual choice, and its respect thereof. Placing the individual as sovereign at the nexus of the economic stage is central to consumerism. If it secures freedom for all, it is by mediating (rather than negating, as was the case with all outdated forms of collectivism) of each person's individual liberty.

Outwardly, then, we may say that consumerism presents itself as a culture of *positive* liberty. In effect, it includes and surpasses the principle of the market, since the latter is based on negative liberty. Negative liberty is formal, a set of rights which may be exercised without hindrance from others or from the government. In the sense of the market, consumerism presupposes negative liberty. But it also builds on that negative liberty, offering at the same time a *fulfilment* of liberty, channelling material and cultural means of gratification, proposing lifestyles, providing satisfaction. To freedom, it adds a culture of pleasure and happiness, transforming the negative liberty of the market into the positive liberty of the consumer.

And yet this culture remains unsatisfying: it generates its own normative contradictions. So while we remain justified in rejecting an "abstract" and "ascetic" critique that, from the outside, denounces a culture that surpasses it, we must instead attempt a kind of immanent critique of consumerism, one capable of revealing its inner axiological goals. Cultural criticism has everything to gain from observing consumerism's ambiguous motions from within, its oscillations and its contradictions, in order to attempt to understand what, in its very deployment, already designates something beyond its immanent normativity. To this end, accepted and tested critical approaches to consumerism may be reworked. At this juncture, it would be useful to recall four major normative tensions. They traverse *consumerism itself*.

5 Standardisation versus diversity and individuality

The first accusation levelled against consumerism is that its now global reach leads to the standardisation of objects, messages, and lifestyles. The price of this homogeneity is a decline in the quality of goods and services, due to several converging factors: deploying what is second best to stretch markets further; using economies of scale to reduce production costs; offering consumers peace of mind, etc. Every time another product or service is standardised, consumerism saps the overall quality of the cultural environment.

In early formulations of their *Critical Theory*, Horkheimer and Adorno made standardisation one of the defining traits of the mass culture industry. Little has changed since the 1940s; indeed, George Ritzer recently offered an updated version of this theme with the "McDonalidisation" of the world. His idea designates a form of consumption typified by fast food. Its characteristics are: the efficiency of consumption, taken and defined following a fully predetermined process; the calculability of the order (a Big Mac, large/medium fries, etc.) by the consumer; the predictability of the product and the service; the control of human activity by non-human technologies (uncomfortable chairs to encourage consumers to eat quickly and leave, limited menus, disposable objects thrown away in designated receptacles, etc.). Now, markets are systematically pursuing these four characteristics in other areas. The "McDonald's model" is overtaking a broad range of other goods and services – the commercial sex trade, food supply chains, hotel chains, credit cards, etc. (Ritzer, 2002). The idea of "Disneyfication" has been proposed by others in the same vein to define the trend for promoting theme parks designed along the Californian model and paired with the massive business of promoting related cultural goods.

Such standardisation violates two conditions necessary to cultural fulfilment: diversity and individuality. If individuals are to be truly free to choose their lifestyles and values, a sufficient range of possible ways of life (including products and of services) must exist and be truly available. Social and cultural diversity are resources for liberty. And liberty actualised can only lead to individuality. This is the primary ethical and aesthetic problem with consumerism: while it affirms positive liberty, it at the same time deprives that liberty of resources; personal and cultural individuality are drowned out in a process of universal serialisation.

Currently (and since the 1980s) consumerism seems conscious of its own contradictions. Studies of post-Fordist consumption have been correct to put the standardisation process in perspective (without denying it), as *flexible* capitalism has to some extent changed the contours of the landscape. The main feature of information and communication technologies is no longer their standardisation but the fact that they are interactive. There is an observable trend toward customisation, towards the individuation and personalisation of products and services. Furthermore, the modernist aspiration to constant novelty has taken over consumerism, fracturing temporally what is spatially constant. Now, new "generations" of products ceaselessly surge onto the scene, urging the consumer towards constant change.

As a result, and not without a certain amount of inconsistency, the critique of consumerism has begun to denounce this culture of constant change, rather than critiquing homogeneity. But at the same time, the preference for novelty is a core element of modern aesthetic freedom. With modernity, repetition is only desirable if it is the result of a choice in which interruption is considered to be a real possibility. Variation, renewal, unwonted combinations, modification – these are key elements of the culture of freedom that consumerism seeks, so to speak, to make consistently accessible.

In this way, consumerism offers us the image of a divided culture, torn between the implacable advance of standardisation, which destroys cultural diversity and individuality, and the cult of personalisation and continuous change, which constantly re-aestheticises merchandise and its use. It is this *contradiction* (rather than the two extremes considered separately) that we should see as the manifestation of consumerism's ethical inadequacy from the standpoint of fulfilled modern liberty.

Emancipated consumption supposes a culture that recognises uniqueness. The latter should not be confused with a mishmash of standardised options, however numerous they may be. Uniqueness relies on the expressive construction of a coherent individuality. Nor should the *recognition* of uniqueness be confused with a commercial offer of "customised" services and products. Such recognition relies on moral communication, rather than on commercial media, though the market may be used as a medium or supplemental tool.

6 The privatisation of value judgement

The second critical tension concerns freedom of choice. Consumerism presents itself as a cultural form that gives consumer choice a decisive role: he or she chooses whether or not to buy a product or service. In such a culture, the sovereignty of the consumer-who-chooses is supposed to represent freedom in its loftiest form. This is the liberal credo of consumerist culture: the greater this sovereignty, the greater the freedom.

But the freedom of the consumer, thus made private and boxed into his own individual calculations of preference, is illusory: after all, real deliberation requires public debate capable of providing individuals with the information and arguments they need to make informed choices. Even if we were to suppose (counter-factually) that the product market came with an adequate informational space, deliberation would remain a moot point so long as actual discussion – which is to say, free and open debate with others – had not occurred. But in the consumerist way of life, the act of purchasing is systematically cut off from the public space and manipulated by those doing the selling. It is true that choice comes into play, but with no true *deliberation.*

Even if we were to assume that no information had been manipulated, it is not certain that introducing commercial choice in all areas of material life is the best way to attain liberty (Gilbert, 2008: 557). Consumption is costly in terms of time and attention, and presupposes the availability and use of a battery of information. In reality, "letting the consumer choose" often means requiring him to choose among products whose qualities remain unknown to him. In this way, over the past two decades, policies aiming to privatise basic services have made much of the greater freedom potentially attained by broadening the available offer from competing telecommunications firms or power companies. But certain studies have revealed that consumers may prefer public monopolies (non-choice situations) whose standards are collectively monitored, since it is clear that rational *individual* choice among competing offers is impossible.

This difficulty inherent in commercial choice has not been overlooked by consumer culture. It has as a result sought to develop intermediary spaces for counselling, consulting, and expert advice to help customers exercise their sovereignty. Department stores offer information centres, appoint consultants for a variety of product ranges, provide specialists to help customers decide on kitchen appliances or apartment layouts, distribute eating and diet tips in supermarkets, etc. But since the deliberative space thus constructed is inscribed in the commercial space rather than in the framework of life as a whole, and since the offer, diverse as it may be, remains fixed, the possibility for deliberation remains structurally too primitive to count as authentic deliberation.

7 The primacy of well-being

A third tension inherent in consumerism is that, within the different criteria for prosperity, it creates an imbalance between well-being and other criteria for self-realisation.

Consumerism is founded on and reproduces an evaluation scale that is both monotonous and repetitive, and which may be qualified as *utilitarian.*

Contemporary capitalism disseminates a culture whose predominant focus is on individual well-being. Philosophically, this puts it in direct opposition to the Kantian and Aristotelian traditions, as well as to most religious traditions. It thus comes as no surprise that critiques of consumerism quite often turn to these thought traditions for justification. Measuring well-being, in the utilitarian tradition, may be done in a variety of ways: a positive measure of pleasure (and therefore a negative measure of suffering), or the satisfaction of preferences, for example. This moral approach is transmitted directly in advertising messages, which allude to the creation of this value: bodily well-being, culinary well-being, sexual well-being, mental well-being, less effort, no work, etc. Utilitarianism associates essentially consequentialist reasoning and a calculated cognitive approach with the value of well-being.

Thus, it would be appropriate to see consumerism as a kind of realisation of the postulates of utilitarian ethics at the scale of an entire culture. The result of this, as Horkheimer and Adorno have pointed out, is that consumerist culture seems incapable of holding altruism as a value. This feature of consumerism has serious moral and aesthetic consequences.

On the *moral* level, forms of altruistic commitment to others seem less and less culturally valued. As social values, community, citizenship, friendship, and love are fading compared with the value given to well-being. This weakens all social relations. Major developments of this disquieting phenomenon are well-documented in the social sciences. For example, anthropologists recently revealed the way in which this form of morality is invading privacy (Hochschild, 2003). On the *aesthetic* level, we may use what Adorno calls desublimation to describe the consumerist degeneration of the beautiful into the nice, and into hedonistic gratification. The problematic of desublimation is closely linked to that of the *de-autonomisation of art* diagnosed by many commentators of post-modernity (such as Jameson, 1991).

Nevertheless, utilitarian materialism is not fully sufficient to define consumerism. Colin Campbell (1987) emphasises this in his remarkable archaeology of consumerism. One of the defining traits of modern consumerism is to associate the sale and use of objects with messages evoking an imaginary "beyond", a life of adventure and escape, a romanticised dream existence, the sublime beauty of a landscape. In short, consumerism manages to inundate us with things by calling on the existence of Something Else. Consumerism can only sell hedonistic objects to the people by associating them with forms that transcend material satisfaction and the flat utility of the objects themselves. This taproot of romanticism feeds consumerist culture with a set of signs and symbols pointing to the non-utilitarian side of positive liberty. The pillage of Western culture's greatest works by the advertising industry, the attempt to include gestures, forms, and styles from modernist culture in consumer products, the constant aestheticisation of the store so typical of flexible capitalism – all of these amount to a sort of desperate attempt to forge a signifying link between utilitarian consumption and non-consumable significations. Kate Soper (2008: 577) gives a striking example of this:

> What has gone missing is the sense of the meal as prepared, shared, convivial event having its own intrinsic value in structuring time, fostering human exchange, and providing food for thought as well as bodily renewal. It will be pointed out, maybe, that more people are now visiting restaurants and spending "quality" time within them than before. But this only goes to prove the point that the primary momentum of consumerist culture is to reduce and drive out this time of expenditure from a more ordinary, immediate, trans-class and everyday experience. And if the need persists, as suggested by in the increase in restaurant eating, then that is no surprise. It is a manifestation of an "alternative hedonist" dialectic, through which the satisfaction denied or marginalized returns to claim attention in some other mode.

Rather than believe, as did the first Frankfurt School or postmodern sociology, that the result of this is that a monolithic complex of cultural consumerism is doing away with the divide between high and low culture, the avant-garde and mass industry, ideal and utility, it would be better to observe that the society of consumption leaves these contradictions alive in the very processes by which it disseminates its "utilities". Consumerism advances only by hiding behind the masks of authentic love, art for art's sake, faithful friendship, immortal works. In so doing, it exploits the very forms that contest it; at the same time, however, it provides the very yardstick that measures its inability to achieve its own aims.

8 The normalisation of the subject

The final tension: consumerism is perceived by its critics as a form of normalisation. As do the first three, this critique confronts consumerism's claims to achieve positive liberty for individuals.

Certainly, consumerism presents itself as a panegyric on the free realisation of the self. It is saturated with references to wants, desires, and personal promises. These references are presented under the idealised form of a society of individual desires in which constant change and insatiability are presupposed as ground rules. In this sense, few societies have so favoured individuality as a guiding principle for the good life. But at the same time, consumerist society is far from being a society "free from constraints". These constraints appear in two forms.

The first constraint is that consumerism generates a glut of standards, advice, and injunctions about individuals' well-being, their chances, their performance, their success. It uses the objects with which it bombards its customers as a vehicle for transmitting models in every normative register, from the gentle suggestion to the categorical imperative. Delivering myriad justifications with these norms, it offers templates – incoherent and contradictory ones – for hygiene, beauty, healthy living, physical self-realisation, fulfilled sexuality, ways to boost one's reputation, principles for excellence, etc. Oriented as it is towards choice and freedom, the consumer society balks at presenting these norms as actual imposed disciplines; however, it still employs a broad disciplinary framework of the sort described by Foucault to account for the normalisation of daily life, bodies, and desires with which modern society burdens its subjects. Of course, this normalisation has nothing to do with authentic normativity, which defines moral autonomy and true freedom. In a way, it is the counterfeit of authentic normativity, as it is characterised by incoherence, superficiality, and its constant coordination with the overall injunction to buy.

The second constraint is work. Work is the inevitable flip side of consumerist enjoyment. No purchase without labour; no consumerism without productivism; no blithe opulence without constant, engrossing, exhausting work. Daniel Bell (1976: 72) diagnosed the problem thusly "one is to be *straight* by day and a *singer* by night" – a contradiction which has yet to be resolved. It is for this reason that the society of opulence is in point of fact a disciplinarian society. The worker's submission is the truth behind the consumer's freedom.

To sum up our four themes, or tensions, consumerism proceeds as a form of positive liberty that is constantly contradicted in its own realisation. It is an institution of positive liberty, but offers only a stunted version of fulfilment. From this stance, a critique of consumerism is not a critique of cultural modernism. There is no question here of denouncing, as does Daniel Bell, the destructive and hedonistic stranglehold of an aesthetic that is supposedly linked to the avant-gardes. It is possible to see a force for emancipation in the modernist and post-modernist avant-gardes, and consumerism betrays that, rather than fulfilling it.

Consumerism's failure to fulfil its ethical and aesthetic aims is not conditional or transient; it is structural. The promise of liberty that consumerism extends will never be fulfilled by more consumerism – that liberty must come from something beyond consumerism. In other words, that freedom will come only when consumption and positive liberty are linked together in an entirely new cultural form, one that breaks with consumerism. This new phenomenon cannot obey some vague form of moral asceticism – its goal is not to limit freedom, but to demand more positive liberty, more freedom for personal fulfilment. Such a phenomenon would require that deliberation not be transgressed or limited by calculated choice; that pleasure retain its full force, undiminished by humdrum hedonism; that freedom not be confused with control conditioned by the market.

9 The third critical angle

We have just explored the four central tensions brought to light by a cultural critique of consumerism. The third and final critical approach to consumerism may be described as ecological. The ecological critique brings to light the unwanted effects of consumerism from the perspective of the management of scarcity. These effects may be divided into three thematic categories.

The first is the depletion of the planet's resources. Quantitatively, consumerism's demand for energetic, material, and cultural resources is constantly on the rise; at the same time, the technological tools used for the exploitation of natural resources continue to improve. Consumerism thus provokes the depletion of available resources. Dire forecasts for the future of fossil fuels, water, and uranium are familiar and extensively documented. Here, the damage done by productivism is directly linked to consumerism: the intensified use of natural resources is the direct result of the consumer's infinitely expanding desires. Without resorting to any intrinsic moral considerations, it is possible to argue for the harmful effects of widespread consumerism in purely consequentialist terms.

The second type of unwanted effect brought about by consumerism is waste production. Carbon dioxide, radioactive and chemical waste, the vast garbage dumps at the outskirts of overpopulated cities: the detritus produced by the technological and economic workings of our society has become the main threat to the survival of the human race. Consumerism is the form of consumption where the quantitative growth of waste remains out of control.

Third and last, consumerism is in a sense counterproductive, as it constantly creates new needs. This stimulates production that is structurally unsatisfactory on two interconnected levels. First, the quantitative production of goods and services and their built-in obsolescence is uneconomical, as it tends towards an overall decline in product quality, something that may be measured in objective terms. Poor quality meat is edging out high quality meat in fast food facilities; film productions target the middling tastes of culturally mediocre audiences, generating lacklustre products that are universally consumable. Urban planning opts for consumerist approaches when organising space, which leads to a drop in service quality (decline in the availability of local services or their weakening via the promotion of self-service, etc.). As the quality of products and services declines, it naturally creates new needs, and thus new dependencies on new consumable products and services. Jean Pierre Dupuy and Ivan Illich offer a particularly illuminating study of this aspect of consumerism's systematic counterproductivity.

10 Against a reductivist critique of prosperity

Having identified the different approaches to the critique of consumerism described above, it is easy to understand that falling back on just one or two of them is, politically speaking, nearly irresistible, unsatisfactory as it may be from a theoretical standpoint. Two such "critical fallbacks" may be identified in the contemporary political landscape.

The first has its roots in social democracy. Historically, the social-democratic left has shared with capitalism a blind faith in the progress promised by productivism and consumerism. It has for the most part shied away from the cultural critique of consumerism, even if certain aspects of the growth of consumer society have slowly but surely chipped away at the foundations of collective action upon which social democracy was built. Social democracy's goal is to encourage everyone's access to consumption. It has dealt with income as a set of rights for the realisation of individual autonomy, meaning that the levelling of income is crucial as a social and political model. In the face of the environmental crisis, however, the social-democratic left has been obliged to re-examine its faith in the automatically beneficial effects of growth. But since it must do so without engaging the cultural critique of consumerism, the social-democratic left has had to align itself with capitalism and take up the functionalist arguments of this third critical angle, with a minimally reformative approach.

As a result, the solutions proposed rely on intervening with key variables of *quantitative* over-consumption: consumer waste, demographic excess among consumers, technological solutions (the quest for clean, energy-efficient technologies). "Eco-management", "environmental law", and "eco-trade" all stem from this; they are the dominant forms used by contemporary societies to deal with environmental risk. Their hope is to continue consumerist emancipation as it is conceived now by "greening" the conditions under which it is managed. The best approach here would be to make ecological cost endogenous to markets, either externally (through taxation), or by organising more efficient markets of limited resources (bonuses for clean cars, etc.). Today, this is the approach behind most efforts made in industrially developed countries to ensure "sustainable" development. This ecological reformism – which is resolute and proactive to varying degrees – attempts to pursue the dream of emancipation by improving our societies' technico-economic apparatus. In no way does it question the *cultural* parameters of the socio-economic freedom driving consumerism. After all, if ecology is merely a *functional* issue, why seek *cultural* responses to it?

This "critical fallback" is therefore built on an avoidance of the cultural critique, and may be summed up in a slogan, which is currently the basis for a new political consensus: "Don't make the consumer feel guilty!" In contrast to this technico-economic reaction, a second "fallback" has been taken up by clusters of minority groups demanding that the cultural limits of consumerism be taken seriously. Taking up the four critical tensions I have outlined above, these alternative groups embody a moral and aesthetic conscience, squaring off against what is presented as a dense technico-economical-political system supported in equal parts by international capitalism and the social welfare state. Political scientists and analysts began noting the appearance of this "post-materialist" consciousness starting in the 1970s, and its expression continued through new social movements throughout the 1980s and into the beginning of the twenty-first century. The problem with this type of critique is that it remains, at base, very cultural. If a critical approach is to encompass the normative preoccupations of equality and collective management of scarcity, it is difficult to use quality of life as a starting point. As a result, this critique remains susceptible to accusations of elitism and asceticism. In comparison, the egalitarian emphasis at the core of the critical approach taken by socialism retains all its force, since it takes into account a shared demand for *mass* access to opulence. If the cultural "critical fallback" can find no way to meld its preoccupations and those of egalitarianism, it will remain highly vulnerable, closed off in a prophetic but ineffective role in the world of practical policy.

11 Rearticulating the critique of prosperity

A thorough and effective critique of consumerism, and therefore of prosperity, must push beyond these two unilateral "fallbacks" which threaten to attenuate it.

A critical theory and political practice must systematically identify ways to link the three critical angles discussed above, without devaluing any of them. This political challenge is also one for theorists of development.

Indeed, for the latter, linking these three critical approaches has been no easy task. A structure for collective development that takes these three normative requirements into account has yet to be created. Amartya Sen's recent attempt to elaborate a normative philosophy of development may be taken as an example. Sen offers an exciting way to reconnect the question of equality (the first critical line) to the issue of quality of life (the second critical line) by using the vocabulary of capability to reconceptualise positive freedom. In many ways, we may consider the Capability Approach as a response to certain cultural critiques of consumerism: a diversified set of evaluative frameworks that push beyond utilitarianism (in particular by considering agency in addition to well-being); the creation of viable spaces for public deliberation; a demanding idea of individual liberty – these are the basic ingredients of his project for the political economy. But even if Sen is aware of the pressing issues of our day and personally conscious of growth's ecological dead ends, one cannot say that his critical economic theory takes into account this new normative dimension of scarcity. In this regard, New Economics (Seyfang, 2009) or work on degrowth (both selective and broad-range) seem more promising.

A second example also deserves our attention: a Marxist approach, such as that of James O'Connor (1998). Here, an attempt is made to connect a classic Marxist critique of prosperity (our first critical angle) with the ecological critique (our third), in order to apprehend the ecological crisis from a solidly Marxist perspective. O'Connor thus offers a theory of the "second" immanent crisis in capitalism. The first is well known: according to Marx, a crisis in overproductivity will emerge naturally from the pursuit of the accumulation of capital, leading to the harsh impoverishment of the working masses, coupled with an expansion of the forces of production, thus generating a backlog of products that cannot be sold. But according to O'Connor, Marx did not see that capital would *at the same time* lead to a crisis in under-production. As capitalism seeks to reduce the cost of reproducing human labour (education, social welfare, etc.), as well as the cost of using the environment, it does not properly account for the degradation of its own environment, and therefore can no longer reproduce (or, as O'Connor puts it, it "under-produces") the conditions of its own existence. Because they seek to maximise profit over the short term, capitalist enterprises neglect "to maintain over time the material and social conditions of their own production, for example, by neglecting work conditions … degrading soils … or turning their backs on decaying urban infrastructures" (O'Connor, 1998: 242).

The current ecological crisis is therefore, from a Marxist perspective, inherent to the system of capitalist accumulation. There is no mention, in this explanation, of the *cultural* pathologies inherent in consumerism; no hypothesis regarding the logic that is internal and specific to modern(ist) culture, which becomes reflection, or superstructure. The essence is elsewhere, in the mechanisms of production. In this perspective, the normative foundations that allow us to confront the crises in capitalism are egalitarian and ecological, never moral and aesthetic.

On a theoretical level, it is difficult to be satisfied with this Marxist avoidance, just as it is difficult to accept political perspectives that ignore ecological scarcity or the demands of egalitarianism. A *weak critique* of prosperity therefore chooses one or two critical angles, while a *strong critique* includes all three. To choose the latter route, a critique of consumerism requires the creation of indicators of prosperity that are sensitive to equality, cultural values, and ecological scarcity. Clearly, the normative foundations of such a critique are necessarily complex. This supposes a new critical social theory fully capable of providing a normative and causal articulation of these three ways of qualifying reality.

Note

1 Université catholique de Louvain. For further information see author's biography at the front of this volume.

References

Baudrillard Jean (1970), *La société de consommation: ses mythes, ses structures*. Paris: Gallimard.

Bauman Zygmunt (2008), *S'acheter une vie*. Paris: J. Chambon.

Bell Daniel (1976 [1979]), *The Cultural Contradictions of Capitalism*. London: Heinemann.

Bourdieu Pierre (1979), *La Distinction: critique sociale du jugement.* Paris: Éditions de Minuit.

Campbell Colin (1987), *The Romantic Ethic and the Spirit of Modern Consumerism.* Oxford/New York: Blackwell.

Douglas Mary and Isherwood Baron (1979), *The World of Goods: Towards an Anthropology of Consumption.* London: Routledge.

Dupuy Jean-Pierre and Jean Robert (1976), *La trahison de l'opulence*. Paris: Presses universitaires de France.

Gilbert Jeremy (2008), Against the commodification of everything. *Cultural Studies* 22(5): 551–566.

Hochschild Arlie (2003), *The Commercialization of Intimate Life: Notes from Home and Work.* Berkeley: University of California Press.

Horowitz Daniel (2004), *The Anxieties of Affluence: Critiques of American Consumer Culture, 1939–1979*. Amherst: University of Massachusetts Press.

Jameson Fredric (1991), *Postmodernism, or, the Cultural Logic of Late Capitalism.* Durham: Duke University Press.

Nussbaum Martha C. and Sen Amartya (eds) (1993), *The Quality of Life*. Oxford: Clarendon.

O'Connor James (1998), *Natural Causes: Essays in Ecological Marxism*. New York: Guilford Press.

Ritzer George (2002), *McDonaldization: The Reader*. Thousand Oaks: Pine Forge Press.

Schor Juliet (2007), In defense of consumer critique: revisiting the consumption debates of the twentieth century, *The Annals of the American Academy of Political and Social Science* 611: 16–30.

Seyfang Gill (2009), *The New Economics of Sustainable Consumption: Seeds of Change*. Basingstoke/New York: Palgrave Macmillan.

Sobal Jeffrey and Stunkard Albert J. (1989), Socioeconomic status and obesity: a review of the literature, *Psychological Bulletin* 105(2): 260–275.

Soper Kate (2008), Alternative hedonism, cultural theory and the role of aesthetic revisionism, *Cultural Studies* 22(5): 567–587.

Urry John (1995), *Consuming Places*. London/New York: Routledge.

5 Prosperity in work

Thomas Périlleux[1] *and Julien Charles*[2]

The intention of this chapter is to contribute to a redefinition of prosperity in the realm of work. Identifying with what Jean De Munck has, in this volume, called the "cultural critique of capitalism", we seek to challenge a system of production that is inherent to capitalism which defines prosperity with no regard for the worker's "quality of life". We believe that, as part of a broader conception of prosperity, one must consider the multiple dimensions that constitute quality of life at work (which we also call the experience of living work).

Etymologically, the term prosperity, borrowed from the Latin word *prosperitas,* refers to a "happy situation". At times, it has the secondary meanings of "well-being" and "physical health". *Prosperus* signifies "that which lives up to one's hopes, propitious, favourable". To be prosperous is "to be fortunate, happy, favoured with success, often with the secondary notion of beautiful appearance, when speaking of a plant, an animal, and, ironically, a human being" (Rey, 2006: 2982).

These indications demonstrate the concept's semantic complexity, which belongs to a configuration in which it echoes "well-being", "fortune", "happiness", "abundance", and "success", without being reducible exclusively to economic wealth. True, the metonymic senses of "fortunate event" and "healthy appearance" have not been preserved in modern usage. The economic sense of "state of abundance, increased wealth (of a community, of a business)" (Rey, 2006: 2982), has, however, become predominant.

Now that it has entered the vocabulary of political economy, the concept of prosperity has at least two characteristics that we believe are worth mentioning in introducing our argument. On the one hand, it refers to a particular social condition, and, as such, must be considered in macroeconomic and macrosociological terms. Yet it must also call our attention to local and singular work experiences. We thus propose to examine how one might "grasp" the work experience in all its complexity, without crushing it under the weight of an overly general and reductive conception of prosperity.

On the other hand, while classical and neoclassical economics have borrowed the term as a criterion for evaluating a "population's well-being", it has also been taken up by the critical tradition. It still contains a critical potential, which could challenge the connection between economic wealth, happiness, and human self-realisation. Thus for the young Marx, "the most prosperous state of society ... means stationary misery for workers" (1972: 12)[3]; the key problem (and communism's deep meaning) is that of replacing false opulence with true wealth – humanity's creative potential, based on the "human manifestation of life" through human needs. Hence the second question that will inform this chapter, to which we will offer a succinct answer in the conclusion: how can we go beyond an approach to prosperity – at work and through work – that has been traditionally formulated in the utilitarian terms of well-being and life satisfaction? How might we rethink the conditions needed for work that is "prosperous" in that it allows its practitioners to experience the vital energies of exploration and creation?

This chapter consists of three parts. First, we discuss the conception of prosperity that prevailed in Europe during the post-Second World War period. Within the framework of a compromise between collective solidarity and productive capacities, collective well-being was assumed to depend on social prosperity, understood as increasing and shared economic wealth. Statistical indicators were created during this time to evaluate economic growth, social justice, and well-being at work. Because they were associated with a particular way of conceiving politics (and, implicitly, the subjective experience of work), these indicators entered into a state of crisis beginning in the mid-70s. We demonstrate that other ways of grasping work in all of its different facets had a difficult time establishing themselves, despite the introduction of the category of "psycho-social factors" into surveys of working conditions.

In part two, we will attempt to describe contemporary malaise in the workplace. This volume's editors encouraged us to consider the discrepancy between the continuous economic growth in all European countries during the post-war period and the decline in subjective indicators of personal satisfaction. How can this incongruity be explained? Were promises of growth not kept? Individual job-related malaise was obviously not lacking during the Fordist era, but it could be "justified" by a conception of work in which toil was seen as legitimate to the extent that it contributed to improving the lot of future generations and advancing social justice. These connections have become unravelled, even as new manifestations of work-related malaise have begun to appear. Adopting a clinical approach, we will consider social malaise and particularly social pathologies, the origins of which can be traced back to new ways of organising the production of goods and services. We propose to address what we call "pathologies of engagement", which are characteristic of contemporary capitalism. In this way, our analysis interrogates ways of accounting for the dark side of economic prosperity through the elaboration of statistical indicators and clinical symptoms.

In the final part, we will attempt to define, not prosperity and well-being at work as such, but the ways to account for the experience of work in all its complexity, such that it would renovate our approach to defining living work for a different kind of prosperity. In our view, sustained reflection on the characteristics of the work experience and ways to grasp it collectively should be central to any redefinition of prosperity. These efforts must be the foundation of an alternative approach to prosperity, one that could undo the bond that is too often preserved between opulence, economic growth, and well-being. The approach we have chosen could lead one to refuse to sacrifice "quality of life" at work to the imperatives of economic growth – unless a new compromise, following the post-war Fordist compromise, proved capable of challenging the most widespread of contemporary assumptions concerning life satisfaction and consumerism.

1 The crisis of Fordist conceptions of prosperity

Statistical indicators in general, and those of prosperity and well-being in particular, are not simply mathematical representations of society, which are limited only by the development of techniques of calculations. They are closely tied to particular ways of representing the social world.[4] Representation, whether statistical, political, or cognitive, can be thought of as an act of positing equivalencies, making it possible to treat people and things "in general". In order to treat things in general (or "conventionally", in the sense of the French "economy of conventions" tradition), a form of equivalence must be established between the entities in question by characterising them in a particular way – in other words, by "investing in form" (Thévenot, 1986). This operation transforms particular entities (such as groups of workers), integrating them into more general wholes (for example, social classes) and situating them along a common horizon (such as the advent of communism).

In this way, the indicators of prosperity and "well-being", which flourished after the Second World War, drew on a particular way of thinking about politics.[5] After briefly describing it, we can then consider the way in which these kinds of representation – which are both statistical and political – have been criticised, and in the name of which other forms.

"Prosperity" under the Fordist compromise

From 1945 to the mid-1970s, political and statistical representations of society generally drew on a compromise between two principles of justice: the civic and the industrial (Boltanski and Thévenot, 1991). The result was to consolidate the compromise between collective solidarity and productive capacities. The first of these two principles valued solidarity, social justice, and seeking the general interest, and drew on a movement to formalise collective rules. The second, industrial principle promoted utility. It was aided by the standardisation of production and long-term investment. The establishment of a compromise between these two principles was stabilised through the introduction of workers' rights, the social state,[6] and labour organisations, as well as the development of collective bargaining agreements, demands for security, the negotiation of salary scales, and so on. This "civic-industrial" compromise implied a state that was able to plan and respond to the needs of the productive system.

> It is expected that the state acts "on average," covers risks, and ensures that individuals are equalised for statistical and insurance purposes. It strives to reduce the social inequalities described in statistics generated through poll-based surveys. The Keynesian government minister seeks to adjust aggregate supply to aggregate demand, using macroeconomic models based on national accounting tables.
>
> (Desrosières, 1997: 275)

> During the period between roughly 1950 and 1975, an effort existed, at least as a trend, to unite economic and social debates through a common language, that of planning and Keynesian macroeconomics, growth and national accounting, the sociology of social inequalities and statistical indicators, state-sponsored collective negotiations between employers and unions, and a redistributive system of social protection based co-managed by labour and business.
>
> (Desrosières, 1992: 143)

In short, productivity and the general interest were, in this context, linked to the elaboration of a common good that would guide the actions of management and labour. Collective well-being was based on social prosperity, understood as increasing and sharing society's wealth. At a practical level, industry's efficiency and performance made solidarity possible through social security. Statistical measures supported the ideal of equalising opportunity (through education) and improving the conditions of the underprivileged. Regulations were based on future projections. Institutional decisions were justified on the basis of expertise and implemented by a centralising state.

This compromise was, moreover, founded on a future-oriented sense of time and "delayed gratification": one worked without expecting immediate satisfaction, in order to further "social progress" and help society down the right path. At the same time, the strong presence of unions and, in particular, the pillarisation of Belgian society encouraged workers to grasp their professional activities in the categories of the civic-industrial compromise. This can be see with such concepts as "social class" or "profession", which generalised the conditions under which people participated in work. Socio-professional categories, once they had left the offices of statisticians and began to influence public debates, also contributed to this generalised representation of the work experience and to the integration of personal experience into collective categories and shared horizons.

The forms of public action that were rooted in the civic-industrial compromise drew on statistical indicators that generalised professional activity, understood as the execution of a plan (Thévenot, 1995) or the realisation of a task. In companies, this meant that the coordination of various individual activities was conceived as the execution of formal rules, based on an intentional conception of action and the objectification of such action in a plan (the classic example being a Taylorist industrial plan). The worker fulfils his role insofar as he accomplishes what is formally expected of him. In this context, his environment is seen as a series of means that have been made available in order to achieve a goal: the realisation of the task. This form of planning, with its particular conception of the person, the environment, and action, was generalised under the civic-industrial compromise we have just described: the plan's temporality and the construction of efficient action were put to good use in the industrial conception of the common good, as were the definition of tasks and the development of collective bargaining agreements in the civic order.

Within this framework, the worker's well-being was evaluated in terms of standards of hygiene and workplace security, which grasped the physical and physiological constraints that weighed down upon the worker.[7] The latter was frequently considered from a more collective perspective, one that was attentive to wage conditions, which were themselves integrated into socio-political categories. "Working conditions" were considered from the standpoint of workload, pay, and the relationship between socio-professional categories. At a different level, these elements were incorporated into indicators of growth and productivity (Gadrey, 2001): in short, workers' activity consisted in achieving expected tasks which contributed to the valorisation of production. Statistics, in this way, played a role in distributing the fruits of collective efforts.

The Fordist compromise thus rested on a compromise between the ideals of economic progress and those of social progress. The problem of difficult work, to which we will shortly return, was not lacking, but it tended to be tolerated, as it could be integrated into a more general model of delayed satisfaction: work, experienced as duty or sacrifice, had to contribute to improving the lot of later generations before gratifying the worker himself. Obstacles to well-being were seen as lying almost exclusively within the realm of workplace security and hygiene and were checked against wages. In this way, work had powerful political effects. Indeed, wage conditions and participation in institutions of social dialogue (such as unions), when tied to such representations, became spaces in which the contradictions of social life could be experienced from the standpoint of the worker's sense of what was just and unjust (Ferreras, 2007). But these ways of grasping work, which are characteristic of the Fordist compromise, entered a state of crisis at the same time as the civic and industrial justifications.

The crisis of the Fordist compromise

The conception of work as the execution of plan, as well as the entire Taylorist model of work to which it belongs, have been widely criticised (among others, by sociologists of labour) as unrealistic and far removed from work's reality and for being in any case practically undermined by workers' self-regulation. Moreover, others have denounced the dwindling regularity of professional tests under the Fordist compromise, which depended on a relatively stable and closed statutory system (witness the rigidity of professional careers). The Taylorist model was accused of leaving no room for innovation and individual competence, which were crushed by its authoritarianism. A flexible approach to organising work, one that was supposedly more open to communication and initiative, came to be valued. These charges were rooted in principles of representation that differed from those of the Fordist compromise.

Much criticism was also rooted in commercial criteria. Competition came to be integrated into every organisational stage, burdening all employees with its constraints (of which the presence of clients at production sites was a powerful illustration). The timeframe required for judgement was tightened in the short term and accompanied by demands for diversification and production renewal. According to Boltanski and Chiapello (1999), capitalism rebuilt itself around the idea of the network. In this context, it was deemed important to engage in projects and extend one's networks. This demands a great capacity of adaptation and flexibility of the individual. Mobility was valued to the extent that it allows for mediation between several networks.

With each of these critiques, work seen through the categories of the civic-industrial compromise came to be seen as oppressive and even alienating. Rooted in a long-term outlook, these categories were viewed as excessively rigid and as threatening individual interests, mobility, and freedom. Bureaucracy and technocracy allegedly impaired the speed of commercial exchange and reticular dynamics. The Fordist model, it was argued, disdained the most personal ways of engaging in work, as well as each individual's unique traits.

A new vocabulary emerged for understanding the social world and justifying new organisational structures, granting greater importance to individual action and personal responsibility. In a way, this was a response to the critiques of May 1968 (Boltanski and Chiapello, 1999). The greater consideration now given to the personal aspirations of workers was supposedly a response to the need for creativity and autonomy. Flexible production appeared as a solution to the unresponsiveness of ponderous hierarchical structures. This new organisation of labour sought to be open to creativity and to allow self-development. At the same time, thanks to theories of human capital, management began to understand the work experience in terms of competencies that had to be made to bear fruit in order to increase individual employability. But this required significant self-mobilisation, which "intensifies subjective engagement and puts to work the employee's affects, values, and relational dispositions", which previously had been firmly confined to the private sphere (Périlleux, 2003: 243). Engagement in a company depends on appeals to personal experience, initiative, individual responsibility, and openness to opportunities and challenges. The competencies expected are no longer those associated with Fordist discipline, but rather those of the "performing subject", who is pulled between self-mobilisation and the imperatives of generalised competition. This subject must be active and competitive, calculating and prudent, and nomadic and buoyant (Sennett, 1998; Périlleux, 2004, 2009).

In keeping with this perspective, new characteristics, requiring the elaboration of new indicators, began to appear in surveys of working conditions: the use of new technology, cognitive development at work, access to training, and so on. The will to take into account and evaluate these new traits necessitated the development of innovative measurement tools that could recognise how individual performances contributed to completing a project. This led in particular to the elaboration of indicators and rankings that incentivised collective and individual actors, while also forcing them to compete.

While these new indicators imply a new conception of work, it seems to us that the older criteria of judgement have not yet been "replaced" by equivalent forms of judgement. Rather, they have been supplanted by evaluations that are no longer directed at justice in a general sense, but limit themselves, in keeping with the principles of liberalism (i.e. the political philosophy), to focusing on divergent "private" interests, which can, at best, be aggregated. Indeed, the experience of work is no longer grasped in the generalised forms of the Fordist compromise. The private is integrated into the public realm on a contractual basis, which is particularly suited to the market. The collective is constituted through the aggregation of individual entities and the good pursued is thus limited to the realisation of a project constructed on the basis on contractual relations (Thévenot, 1995). The lack of any reference to a principle of justice has given way to a conception of what is shared that no longer concerns itself with such generalities, but that focuses on situation-specific arrangements achieved through bargaining.

We should acknowledge that the positive effect of these developments is that they allow us to better grasp the individual at work, occupied with his daily tasks. The worker becomes a little less interchangeable and is recognised as having a kind of specificity, without being immediately absorbed into the public categories of the Fordist compromise. Yet that which is most personal in his professional engagement is grasped in terms of interests and efficiency, at the expense of such familiar forms as "tricks of the trade" and other local habits. At the same time, though the Fordist perspective has been criticised from the standpoint of commercial and "connectionist" justifications, the horizon of a common good in work has gradually dwindled. The "common" in work no longer means anything more than the sum of interests, leading to a rejection of questions of social justice as they relate to work.

2 The search for new representations of work

It is important to note the profound ambivalence of the way in which working conditions have developed. A number of (technological, organisational, and cultural) advances have freed some workers from thankless, stigmatising tasks, offering them new opportunities for choice in their "varied" and "flexible" lives. But at the same time, there are numerous symptoms of a decline in working conditions that has reintroduced, though in new forms, the oppression, alienation, and exploitation that the capitalist system of production has never ceased to generate.

In this way, we see a deepening chasm between managerial promises focused on the self-realisation of the autonomous and responsible individual (freedom from servitude, self-entrepreneurship, living intensely at the crossroads of opportunities, satisfaction and motivation at work, and so on) and the silent malaise that often expresses itself indirectly, through symptoms that are reinterpreted as "problems that must be managed" – when they are not quite simply exploited for productive ends.

In this way, the crisis of the Fordist compromise raises two questions: how can we, at present, grasp the dark side of prosperity in the working world? Is it possible to rebuild a conception of the common good, to define prosperity differently, without neglecting the distinct malaise that many feel in their professional experiences?

This twofold challenge enjoins us to return to the problem of indicators of well-being at work and to consider their limitations. To advance further in our diagnosis of current problems, we will examine the contributions of work clinics. The latter allows two displacements to occur: from the question of indicators of well-being to that of symptoms of workplace *malaise*; and from overall life satisfaction to the distinctive experiences of *living work*. These displacements will allow us to reconstruct a broad political perspective on the conditions required for "prosperous" work, to which we shall return in the Conclusion.

Work indicators: two challenges

We have seen how the indicators constituted around the Fordist compromise participated in a social compromise of which they were the conventional markers. Yet because they lacked a sensitive grasp of "lived" work (Breviglieri, 2004), they were also powerful tools for crushing the personal experience of work.

In the contemporary period, the extension of indicators of well-being to "psycho-social factors" represents an attempt to further integrate the subjective appreciation of working conditions.[8] Though exposure to "health and security risks" and the physical burdens of work are still significant indicators, current surveys, particularly at the European level, now attach considerable importance to issues relating to the organisation of work and the way in which workers experience it.[9] This represents a significant advance in redefining the conditions for prosperous work. Yet even so, we wonder if, in its very construction, this way of grasping "well-being" makes it possible to articulate all the levels of the work experience, from the most personal of ordeals to work's political and moral implications, by way of its technical and instrumental characteristics. In this way, indicators of "quality of life" at work pose two challenges:

1 "Upward", in their relationship to the common good, they risk becoming detached from any reference to justice, thus obstructing or short-circuiting political deliberation. This is true of rankings relating to the "social performance" of corporations, which are used only to make comparisons and which refuse to reconsider the underlying productive models and the principles of justice upon which they could be based. This is usually known as the technocratic use of indicators.

2 "Downward", in their relationship to the situations they grasp, they risk tearing experiences away from the life context to which they owe their own singular truth. This is what we see in the example of surveys that ask respondents to state their "life satisfaction" in absolute terms, independently of any referential context (the same is very often true for indices of work satisfaction[10]). Entire swathes of experience are generalised and rendered equivalent through statistical charts. But while it may be possible to measure rates of absenteeism (for example), or even rates of depression, can one quantify the experience of suffering in order to generalise it without doing violence to its individual character?

Liberal critiques of the Fordist model showed us that conceptions of work that are exclusively focused on justice transform the worker into a disembodied being, a single component of a larger entity. But the liberal anthropology that promotes the idea of a performing and responsible individual scorns, in turn, certain aspects of our daily engagement in work, by reducing the personal to the private (Foessel, 2008) and disdaining the (potential) relationship between work and the common good. Such characterisations and judgements *distort* certain forms of activity, other ways of engaging in work that depend on different ways of treating people. It is in this context that the lessons of the work clinic prove illuminating.

From indicators to symptoms: clinical displacements

The work clinic concerns the way that individuals engage in their tasks by confronting the organisation's failures and the obstacles that rein in their creative powers. The activity of working engages the worker's subjectivity; it affects him "for better and for worse". In this sense, work, as a source of pleasure and of suffering or malaise, is always experienced in an individual way and this is what must be explained clinically.[11]

But the work clinic also has political significance: it makes silent, work-related suffering apparent, using it as a standpoint from which social critique can re-emerge (Renault, 2008; Périlleux and Cultiaux, 2009). One of its contributions is to identify what it calls the "new pathologies of work", thus displacing the question of indicators towards in favour of that of symptoms and their existential and political meaning.

Two traits distinguish a clinical symptom from a statistical indicator. First, unlike indicators, which immediately place all information on the same level of impersonal equivalence, the existence of symptoms and their meaning is formulated by individuals through a process whereby they are listened to and "risk" speaking. In other words, a symptom is always addressed to someone who is capable of hearing and, in this way, some of the individual's distinctive truth is made apparent (Dejours, 1993). To speak of symptoms is to grasp in a particular way the individual's troubles in relation to his milieu. Decoding them requires a theory of the subject and a theory of activity, which are often lacking in contemporary indicators of well-being at work.[12] This means, however, that the shift from the particularity of the symptom to the generality of the analysis will be a difficult one.

Second, unlike indicators, which tend to freeze particular conditions (satisfaction, well-being, stress, burn-out, depression, absenteeism, and so on) in time, symptoms imply an ambivalent dynamic. They consist of the individual's most personal contradictions, in addition to those of his milieu. They create stability in the way one lives and acts, but at the same time result in crisis. They can, paradoxically, be regarded as original – albeit thwarted – expressions of an individual's creative forces, even if they can simultaneously diminish it.

For the social sciences in general and discussions about prosperity in particular, these developments pose the question of the legitimacy of an approach based on symptoms and pathologies: do they medicalise social problems? Do collective pathologies exist? Can one speak of social pathologies?

Let us dismiss any concepts that are simple analogies and excessively functionalistic, which see society as an organism that could be considered sick or healthy.[13] We can then see social pathology as a concept of considerable critical scope, to the extent that it refers to processes that threaten or destroy the practical conditions for human fulfilment – or, more precisely, in relation to the question that concerns us, the conditions for the development of living work, which would allow human beings to experience, in their practical lives, their own vital forces.

Social pathologies undermine "the relationships to oneself and to the world without which life loses its value and quality", writes Emmanuel Renault (2008).

> They are above all a critique of a social condition that is felt to be alienating, lacking meaning, reified, and even sick.... This negativity must be evaluated not narrowly, as a failure in relation to principles of social justice, but much more broadly as a violation of the conditions of a good or successful life.
>
> (Renault, 2008: 86, 105)

In particular, social pathologies make it difficult to practice living work, understood as real work, the subjective praxis of the individual, his activity as dictated by the prescriptions of the life inside of him – the realisation, in other words, of his vital forces, of his capacities for being and acting.[14]

As we understand it, the idea of social pathology is far from medicalising social problems and the way in which they are expressed or treated. To the contrary, it opens up an original path, leading to the search for the origins of clinical symptoms in the social conditions of life and work. Furthermore, the concept of social pathology cannot be separated from the (historically relative) norms that define the negative processes of "perverse" social development, "normal" situations, and the horizons of emancipation; it thus requires that critique make explicit its own criteria for political and moral evaluation. It is in this sense that the clinic seems justified in renewing our representations of work and prosperity.

3 Elements of a clinical approach to prosperity in work

Let us turn to the symptoms that the clinic encourages us to consider as manifestations of "new pathologies of work", which traditional indicators of prosperity are incapable of grasping due to the concept of work upon which they are based. We will then present our own contribution, relating to the idea of "pathologies of engagement".

The "new pathologies of work"

According to Christophe Dejours' description (2006), there are, in the first place, *pathologies of overwork*, to which we often refer using such poorly defined terms as "stress" or "burnout", to which we must add the musculoskeletal disorders that are typical of Taylorised production. The clinic puts these problems in perspective by identifying any number of trends in the organisation of production: work intensification (i.e. doing more in less time), combined with distressing interruptions in the completion of tasks; the accumulation of industrial and commercial constraints at every hierarchical level and increased time pressures resulting from direct contact with clients (Gollac and Volkoff, 2000; Askenazy *et al.*, 2006); burdens of responsibility without the necessary resources (Clot, 1998); and the feeling of having to choose, in isolation, between the contradictory demands of production quality and quantity (Dejours, 2006).

Next are the *pathologies of harassment*, which testify to a dramatic degradation of the conditions of collective living. In this case, the symptoms assume several forms: on the one hand, a sense of solitude and the experience of being isolated in confronting the actual difficulties of a work-related task; on the other, different forms of direct or indirect violence, aimed at others or oneself. This description, which cannot be discussed at length in this chapter, raises several questions that are essential to our way of thinking. First, it illustrates increased sensitivity to the most subjective aspects of the work experience. In this way, it parallels trends that exist in the organisation of production individual. In the representations of capitalism's spokespersons, work, which is no longer reducible to the realisation of a plan, now appeals to each worker's most personal qualities – his initiative, his psychological availability, his relational abilities, and so on. The trend is towards what might call the "subjectification of work" (Périlleux, 2003). It is not surprising that it is accompanied by the forceful emergence of subjective problems at the workplace.

Second, there is clearly a need to revamp our understanding workplace malaise, in ways that go beyond the indicators inherited from the Fordist era. The ravages of Taylorism and Fordist production have not gone away; in some sectors, they have multiplied and worsened. But they can no longer be detached from the way in which work is experienced through new "troubles". Work experience must now be elaborated by exploring with the subjects themselves the inner dynamic of their relationship with work.

Third, there is the question of the pervasiveness of these pathologies per sector, hierarchical level, or category of workers.

For the work clinic, the source of these work pathologies lies in the applications of new management methods to the organisation of production – most important of which consist of individualised performance evaluation and "total quality" procedures – which are themselves tied to the transformation of capitalism after it found itself economically exhausted and culturally contested after 1968.[15] It is worth noting that we are indeed talking about sources rather than causes: what is being sought is the symptom's origins, their active core in the mutually shaping relationship between individuals and their work environments.

These "pathogenic" management methods, however, transcend the boundaries separating different kinds of work and different categories of personnel. According to surveys on working conditions, some symptoms affect specific personnel categories preferentially – in other words, unequally. For example, assembly-line workers are more likely to suffer from musculoskeletal disorders, and women are more exposed than men; symptoms of professional exhaustion first hit those in healthcare professions; and so on.

For its part, the work clinic maintains that most pathologies transcend the boundaries of the newly segmented labour force, while accentuating the inequalities arising from wage labour's increasing precariousness. Thus while new pathologies have everything to do with hierarchical relationships at work and what Isabelle Ferreras (2007) calls the "domestic regime" that prevails in companies, the clinicians believe that they affect professionals in positions of power in hyper-flexible companies more than precarious employees, as for the former are themselves enmeshed in the mechanisms of "domination" they wield over the latter (Dejours, 2006).

But this question revives the delicate methodological and epistemological issue of grasping work experience in all its richness. The elaboration of clinical symptoms makes it possible to hew as close as possible to experience, but their integration into pathology charts, the question of their social pervasiveness, and the denunciation of their social origins makes it necessary to rise to a higher level of generality through other information formats (epidemiological surveys, statistical charts, large scale chronological perspectives, and broad references to justice). We thus need a new way of articulating these plans for elaborating experience to identify malaise at work and redefine a new path to prosperity. Before returning to this problem, we will conclude this section by proposing a transversal interpretation of what the clinic encouraged us to regard as pathologies of work.

Pathologies of engagement

The work experience consists of engaging oneself in various regimes of activity in which one experiences reality's resistance to the one's task.[16] If one accepts this proposition, it is possible to understand the symptoms described by the work clinic as social pathologies of engagement. We do not intend, with this term, to propose a single way of reading social pathologies. Rather, we seek to redeploy clinical analysis through a transversal framework that can account for lived experience in all its richness.

The term "engagement" calls attention to the "mutual fashioning" of the individual and his environment (Thévenot, 2006: 14). It emphasises the engagements that give the individual a certain existential consistency through his various multiple relationships with himself, others, and the world. Indeed, engagements respond to highly variable demands, ranging from familiar situations, in which engagement flows through routine forms, to spaces of political deliberation, where there is a heavy demand for political justification. Finally, the term engagement emphasises the idea of a *guarantee* that is implicit in the word *"gage"* – in French, a promise as well as proof – and which supports the power to speak and to act.

In work, guarantees are at once conventional (contracts, statutes, protections guaranteed by law), functional (assurance of the effectiveness of certain gestures), and routine and familiar, ensuring basic confidence in the way an activity transpires, making it possible to inhabit the workplace (Breviglieri, 2004). In this way, the worker accesses a number of goods, including common goods, the realisation of the project, and a sense of ease (Thévenot, 2006).

In our view, it is on the basis of these goods and their articulation that an alternative vision of prosperity must be reconstructed. It strikes us as particularly important not to limit ourselves to a conception that would be disconnected from these goods. We favour an approach that is also interested in articulating engagement's problems and successes, thus rendering meaningful the sense of "subjective consistency" experienced in tests that are not simply moments in an evaluative process, but which can also be demanding on the individual (Périlleux, 2001; Stavo-Debauge, 2009).

But successful engagement can be hard to find. This leads to a different set of problems. From an existential standpoint, guarantees are always precarious and engagement always risky. To engage in a work-related activity is to risk encountering the unexpected[17]: disturbed routines, failures of planned coordination with colleagues, and often brutal clashes between different sets of values over what is considered just. The work experience is a confrontation with reality, and to engage with it is to wager [*gager*] one's competencies, sensibility, moral principles, imaginative powers, and even one's health, without knowing what will come of it.

Many of the symptoms mentioned by the work clinic can be reconsidered from this standpoint. Numerous observers have called attention to the problem of *excessive engagement*: as if the identification with the ideal of performance (Aubert and de Gaulejac, 1991; Aubert, 2004; Dujarier, 2006) and the imaginary passion of risk (Ewald and Kessler, 2000; Hamraoui, 2007), in the form of a *subject of performance*, led one to devote one's body and soul to it, without restraint and to the point of exhaustion. Other analyses now highlight a *lack of engagement* in work relations: as if the desire to withdraw from the pathological effects of "overwork" and "abuses of power" led to the avoidance of encounters with other people, with all the encroachments they necessarily entail on one's private life (Lebrun, 2007).

It is possible, however, that the distance between excessive and insufficient engagement is not quite as great as it seems, since both participate in the *logic of avoiding* the existential risk implicit in engaging oneself in work.

In this sense, one might speak of a social pathology of engagement in the sense that new methods for organising production, associated with capitalism's redeployment over the past forty years, threaten the practical conditions that make possible the challenge of living work. Justifying the implementation of these management methods, which value the autonomous and performing individual, managerial ideology has dangled the promise of exciting work – at least for qualified professionals – to be found in the wide variety of projects and intensity of tasks. In reality, there is reason to fear that it has presented work as intense living, the obligation to enjoy as the freedom to choose, "the burden of production as the buoyancy of work, sickness as health, the individual pushing forward as physical extravagance"; in short, it has presented "death as the face of life" (Barkat, 2008: 18).

4 Towards a redefined prosperity?

On this basis, how should we reconsider prosperity in work? In the first section, we reflected on the nature of the statistical indicators that purported to grasp and guide prosperity during the Fordist period and the crisis they went through beginning in the mid-70s. In the second part, our attention turned to the different ways in which work is represented at present. The final stage addressed ways of explaining the pain experienced by living work through the clinical elaboration of work-related malaise. If the guiding thread of our argument has been the experience of work in all its complexity, it is because we believe the latter must be the foundation of an alternative approach to prosperity, one that is capable can unfasten the bond that is too often maintained between opulence, economic growth, and well-being (which surveys call "life satisfaction").

We can now affirm that contemporary "measure" of work should satisfy the demands for justice contained in the engagement in work and in its subjective basis, as both are inherent to the work experience. The question is thus whether it is possible to grasp work's pluralistic nature, which is rarely grasped as such. As a result, work is often problematised in what Isabelle Ferreras calls a "dismembered" way (2007). The challenge of redefining prosperity is thus twofold: on the one hand, it seeks to address the epistemological critiques regarding the indicators' limits; on the other hand, it seeks to go beyond the approach based on "well-being" and "life satisfaction", which is steeped in contestable utilitarian assumptions.[18]

The Fordist compromise was rooted in the goal of connecting economic and social progress. This model has undergone a profound crisis, which has had an impact on the indicators that can gauge the quality of life at work. The statistical apparatus created at the end of the Second World War understood the activity of the work as the realisation of a plan, while integrating it into the realisation of a much broader common good, formulated in terms of social justice, so that engagement in work contributed to social progress. Obstacles to "well-being" were seen as lying almost exclusively in such realms as workplace security and hygiene and were often checked against wages.

While these aspects are included in "measures" of the work experience, they have ceased to be dominant. The perspective to which they belong has been widely challenged since the second half of the 1970s, from a perspective privileging commercial and connectionist justifications. The quest for the common good that is unique to these two approaches has been stretched increasingly thin, thanks to a liberal perspective in which the common consists only of the diversity of interests, thus dismissing the question of justice. At the same time, management put forth the notion of a "performing subject" that is expected to be autonomous and responsible.

We presented two of the challenges with which this development saddles work indicators: "upwards", in their relation to the common good, and "downward", in their relationship to the situations they grasp.

One possible answer to this twofold challenge could be gleaned from an approach in terms of symptoms and pathologies, which highlighted the pathologies of engagement resulting from new methods of organising production. In considering the description of these symptoms, there is a powerful temptation to see work as the locus *par excellence* of oppression, and even alienation, and thus to advocate an alternative form of prosperity based on abandoning the "work society".

It seems to us that a redefinition of prosperity cannot avoid the task of reflecting deeply on the experience and organisation of work, lest it reimpose a burdensome denial onto the vital experience of work, its pathologies, and its accomplishments. Our proposal is rather to consider that prosperity at a societal level necessarily requires a less pathogenic way of organising work, in that it would respect the practical conditions for deploying the multiplicity of work experiences. This requires us to consider that prosperity cannot be reduced to increasing economic wealth, and that it can even be opposed to the latter: what does prosperity mean in a society where "one wastes living by earning one's living"? Where work does not challenge the worker's vital forces, but crushes them? Where the quality of life is sacrificed to the imperatives of economic growth, understood in its most restricted sense?

Some might consider that the indicators of "decent work" meet the criteria that we have proposed in this chapter, in that it cares about the "quality of employment" (see Méda, 2009). True – and this is not negligible – they are concerned with what we called the "upward" challenge, by placing their work clearly within the horizon of quest for justice in and through work. Yet it seems to us that too little attention has been give to the "downward" challenges, which are less preoccupied with the quality of employment than with subjective engagement in work. It is true that indicators of decent work do not confine themselves to unemployment rates and are also interested in evaluating other dimensions of work, such as "quality of life" and "possibilities for individual achievement" (Anker *et al.*, 2003); but the aspects of work that they consider in practice, and the parameters according to which they propose to measure them, do not manage to grasp subjective engagement in professional activity in its own terms, nor do they connect it to the other goods that we have identified as constitutive of genuine prosperity in work: common goods relating to workplace justice and functional goods relating to work efficiency.[19]

What we would like to encourage is not only an improvement of statistical indicators, so that they can better account for a fuller reality, but also and especially new connections between personal experiences arising from work's familiar terrain, functional decisions at the level of the organisation, and socio-economic system's overall regulations. As we see it, an alternative conception of prosperity must take the need to articulate very different kinds of goods head on. It must promote social justice and the functional realisation of sustainable productive projects, as well as the subjective experience of living work; it must also take into account the articulations of these goods and of their potential tensions.

It is thus appropriate to situate the place of these indicators of prosperity and well-being (whether they be alternative or not). This should not be done from a systemic perspective, which would amount to defining the indicators' sphere of relevance and rendering them impermeable to other accounts of work experience, but rather through an approach emphasising procedure and the evaluation of quality of life at work, based on indicators of well-being and prosperity that are attentive to the intrinsic plurality of the experience of engagement at work. Promoting a process that is exclusively focused on work's political and general aspects is not, in this way, sufficient. The point is rather to conceptualise forms of evaluation that rest on political constructions of the "common" and recognise subjectivity.

These paths make it possible to go back and forth between local experiences and broader deliberations, thus allowing work to be grasped politically in a pluralistic and composite way. The goal is to conceptualise a way of connecting the identification of symptoms to the public's qualification, without ignoring the need for these measure to be efficient. More than anything, redefining prosperity thus requires that we attentively consider the spaces where these new indicators – which must be receptive to the plurality of work experiences – can be formed.

Notes

1 Université catholique de Louvain.
2 Belgian National Fund for Scientific Research. For further information see authors' biographies at the front of this volume.
3 Translator's note: this is a translation of the French translation of Marx's remark, as in available English translations, Marx does not use the word "prosperous".
4 On this topic, see the work of Desrosières and Thévenot listed in the bibliography.
5 This perspective is particularly adapted to the French situation, where statistical tools are more developed than in Belgium, thanks to the INSEE and the INED, two institutions which are also research centres.
6 We include the social state as a component of this compromise. Indeed, it must be grasped as the consequence of a particular form of representation, given that various forms of generality can be folded into a compromise. Because it is of the same nature as statistical indicators, it cannot explain them.

7 This is obviously not unconnected to the fact that the heavy manufacturing and, to a lesser extent, agriculture comprised a significant majority of all workers, who were thus more exposed to dangers than those in the tertiary sector, which employs most of the workers at present. Even if these questions have not been erased from contemporary surveys of working conditions, they are now integrated into a range of different cognitive and normative factors, which emphasise, for example, the quality of information about work-related risks. We will return to this point at the end of the section.

8 In France, it was in 1987 that a first national study of the "psychological conditions" of work was conducted. At the European level, it is noteworthy that "moral harassment" is the number one reason for health-related absenteeism. "Work intensity" is also the object of statistical analysis, which indicates that it has accentuated in recent years, even as the exposure to "physical" risks (vibrations, noise, temperatures, repetitive movements, painful positions, and so on) is very stable over time. In light of these results, it is surprising to note that general satisfaction regarding working conditions also remains very stable over time.

9 For example, through reflections on the possibility of choosing or modifying work rhythms and methods, the feeling of being competent in executing one's work, perceptions of health threats, and so on. We should recall that the introduction of these indicators did mean that more traditional ones were abandoned. For example, evaluations of "work's impact on health" can exist alongside evaluations of "perceptions of work's impact on health". Similarly, indicators of "satisfaction with working conditions" can be found side-by-side with charts of "income and remuneration systems" (fourth European survey working conditions survey, 2007).

10 In surveys on satisfaction, the question often takes this form: "Generally speaking, are you satisfied with your working conditions?" Researchers at the European Foundation for the Improvement of Living and Working Conditions (Dublin) make the point themselves: their survey presents a "complex and multifaceted portrait" of European working conditions, but it also calls for "new research in order to better understand, interpret and contextualise the data". It remains to be seen how to make this interpretation operational, while avoiding a simple juxtaposition of statistical surveys and qualitative data out of respect for different facets of the work experience, including its most unusual aspects.

11 Christophe Dejours has based his analysis on the concept of *suffering* at work. We will continue to use the term *malaise*, as it refers to the ambivalence of the work experience. In contrast to utilitarian assumptions, it makes manifest the fact that the human capacity for freedom is limited (Freud, 1995). According to Freudian anthropology, malaise is unavoidable. This does not, however, rule out struggles against the sources of unjust suffering, nor a reconsideration of prosperity on this basis.

12 One could plausibly think that things have not always been this way. As we demonstrated in part one, it is indeed possible to see statistical indicators as *conventional* and to integrate them into a general theory of action and personhood.

13 For an overview of models of social pathologies in the social sciences, see Renault (2008).

14 See, on this point, Michel Henry's reading of Marx. In the capitalist system of production, living work is placed under the domination of an external and coercive reality: exchange value and its equivalent, money. Living work and its production value *are incommensurable*. To grasp the reality of work, one must come back to its "*subjective determinations*" (Henry, 1976, 2004; Dufour-Kowalska, 1980).

15 Without going into the details relating to the new forms of production organisation, the following traits can nonetheless be mentioned: the shift from work productivity to systemic efficiency; production flexibility and the individualisation of wage relations; the shift to "stockholder governance" concurrently with the financialisation of the economy.

16 In this instance, the term "real" has a precise definition. It refers to that which escapes the worker's mastery through knowledge and know-how (cf. Dejours, 1993, 1998).

17 We find here one of the possible meanings of the concept of "test" (*épreuve*), which is widely used in the field of sociology.

18 Without presenting the critique of these assumptions in detail, let us say that if one questions the concept of growth, one must be prepared to abandon that of well-being, which rests on anthropological bases that are in our view untenable. Well-being is a word with multiple meanings, with roots in utilitarianism that are so deep that utility, satisfaction of desires, and well-being are often considered synonyms (Kymlicka, 1999). Yet it is important to distinguish desires from needs. Unlike needs, which can be counted, desire is characterised by a lack. Recognising this means embracing a more tragic view of the human condition – and more critical of capitalism and its exacerbation of artificial needs (Arnsperger, 2005).

19 Thus the proposals devoted to "decent work" (Anker *et al.*, 2003) consist of six constitutive elements: the possibility of working, the conditions of freedom, productive work, work equity, security at work, and dignity of work. Eleven parameters are considered: the possibilities of working, the acceptability of work, remuneration and productivity, length of work, stability and work security, work/family life balance, fair treatment at work, work-related security and health, social protection, social dialogue and relations of production, and socio-economic contexts. This ultimately results in a list of thirty indicators from which what we called subjective engagement in work, brought down to the principles of social justice, finally disappears from the study.

References

Anker Richard, Chernyshev Igor, Effer Philippe, Mehran Farhad, and Ritter Joseph A. (2003), La mesure du travail décent: un système d'indicateurs statistiques de l'OIT, *Revue internationale du travail* 142(2): 159–193.

Arnsperger Christian (2005), *Critique de l'existence capitaliste: pour une éthique existentielle de l'économie.* Paris: Cerf.

Askenazy Philippe, Cartron Damien, de Coninck Frédéric, and Gollac Michel (eds) (2006), *Organisation et Intensité du travail.* Toulouse: Octarès.

Aubert Nicole (ed.) (2004), *L'Individu hypermoderne*. Paris: Érès.

Aubert Nicole and de Gaulejac Vincent (1991), *Le Coût de l'excellence.* Paris: Seuil.

Barkat Sidi Mohammed (2008), L'évaluation, le travail et la vie. In: François Hubault (ed.), *Évaluation du travail, travail d'évaluation.* Toulouse: Octarès, 3–12.

Boltanski Luc and Chiapello Ève (1999), *Le Nouvel Esprit du capitalisme.* Paris: Gallimard.

Boltanski Luc and Thévenot Laurent (1991), *De la justification. Les économies de la grandeur*. Paris: Gallimard.

Breviglieri Marc (2004), Habiter l'espace de travail: Perspectives sur la routine, *Histoire et Sociétés* 9: 18–29.

Clot Yves (1998), *Le Travail sans l'homme? Pour une psychologie des milieux de travail et de vie*. Paris: La Découverte.

Dejours Christophe (1993), *Travail, usure mentale. Essai de psychopathologie du travail.* Paris: Bayard.

Dejours Christophe (1998), *Souffrance en France. La banalisation de l'injustice sociale.* Paris: Seuil.

Dejours Christophe (2006), Aliénation et clinique du travail, *Actuel Marx* 1(39): 123–144.

Desrosières Alain (1992), Discuter l'indiscutable. In: Alain Cottereau and Pierre Ladrière (eds), *Pouvoir et Légitimité. Figures de l'espace public*. Paris: Editions de l'EHESS, 131–154.

Desrosières Alain (1997), Du singulier au général, l'argument statistique entre la science et l'État. In: Bernard Conein and Laurent Thévenot (eds), *Cognition et Information en société*. Paris: Editions de l'EHESS, 267–282.

Dufour-Kowalska Gabrielle (1980), *Michel Henry. Un philosophe de la vie et de la praxis*. Paris: Vrin.

Dujarier Marie-Anne (2006), *L'Idéal au travail*. Paris: Presses universitaires de France.

Ewald François and Kessler Denis (2000), Les noces du risque et de la politique, *Le Débat* 109: 54–72.

Ferreras Isabelle (2007), *Critique politique du travail. Travailler à l'heure de la société des services*. Paris: Presses de la Fondation nationale des sciences politiques.

Foessel Michaël (2008), *La Privation de l'intime*. Paris: Seuil.

Freud Sigmund ([1929] 1995), *Le Malaise dans la culture*. Paris: Presses universitaires de France/Quadrige.

Gadrey Jean (2001), Nouvel esprit du capitalisme et idéologie néolibérale, *Sociologie du travail* 43(3): 389–402.

Gollac Michel and Volkoff Serge (2000), *Les Conditions de travail*. Paris: La Découverte.

Hamraoui Éric (2007), *L'image de l'homme véhiculée par le nouveau rapport de travail*. Strasbourg: Communication, Association "Alsace-Santé-Travail" (AST).

Henry Michel (1976), *Marx. I. Une philosophie de la réalité, II. Une philosophie de l'économie*. Paris: Gallimard.

Henry Michel (2004), *Auto-donation. Entretiens et conférences*. Paris: Beauchesne.

Kymlicka Will (1999), *Les Théories de la justice: une introduction*. Paris: La Découverte.

Lebrun Jean-Pierre (2007), *La Perversion ordinaire. Vivre ensemble sans autrui*. Paris: Denoël.

Marx Karl ([1844] 1972), *Économie politique et Philosophie. Manuscrits de 1844*. Paris: Éditions sociales.

Méda Dominique (2009), *Travail: la révolution nécessaire*. La Tour d'Aigues: Éditions de l'Aube.

Périlleux Thomas (2001), *Les Tensions de la flexibilité. L'épreuve du travail contemporain*. Paris: Desclée de Brouwer.

Périlleux Thomas (2003), La subjectivation du travail, *Déviance et société* 27(3): 243–255.

Périlleux Thomas (2004), Être éprouvé par le travail. Sujet entrepreneur et résistance à l'aliénation. In: Jean Giot and Jean Kinable (eds), *Résistances au sujet – Résistances du sujet*. Namur: Presses universitaires, 143–157.

Périlleux Thomas (2009), Travail sur soi et affairement. Les voies de la subjectivation du travail. *Working papers du CID* 8, Louvain-la-Neuve.

Périlleux Thomas and Cultiaux John (eds) (2009), *Destins politiques de la souffrance. Intervention sociale, justice, travail*. Toulouse: Érès.

Renault Emmanuel (2008), *Souffrances sociales. Philosophie, psychologie et politique*. Paris: La Découverte.

Rey Alain (ed.) (2006), *Dictionnaire historique de la langue française*. Paris: Le Robert.

Sennett Richard (1998), *The Corrosion of Character: The Personal Consequences of Work in the New Capitalism*. London: W.W. Norton.

Stavo-Debauge Joan (2009), Venir à la communauté. Une sociologie de l'hospitalité et de l'appartenance. PhD dissertation in sociology, École des Hautes Etudes en Sciences Sociales, Paris.

Thévenot Laurent (1986), Les investissements de forme. In: Laurent Thévenot (ed.), *Conventions économiques.* Paris: PUF (Cahiers du Centre d'étude de l'emploi), 21–71.

Thévenot Laurent (1995), L'action en plan, *Sociologie du travail* 37(3): 411–434.

Thévenot Laurent (2006), *L'action au pluriel – sociologie des régimes d'engagement.* Paris: La Découverte.

6 Out of the laboratory into the field

The stakes riding on a paradigm change

Gaëtan Vanloqueren[1] *and Philippe Baret*[2]

> We want to give our research facilities a pre-eminent place in the economic war that is raging in the world and will determine our status as a great scientific country and a great industrial country.
>
> François Mitterrand, inauguration of the French National Agricultural Research Institute's Biotechnologies Laboratory, quoted by *Le Monde*, 8 October 1988

Agriculture and food are without a doubt emblematic sectors of the paradigm change that is necessary to redefine a new form of prosperity. In addition to being an important economic sector, food is essential for survival; our daily physiological survival and long-term public health depend on it. But in addition, food is a component of our cultures. Rethinking our food systems calls for re-orienting our agricultural systems. Whilst the economic weight of this primary productive activity has declined steadily since the beginning of the last century, it still occupies a considerable part of our space, both physical space – half of the European continent's territory – and public space, e.g. mad cow disease, dioxin, the milk crisis, the "junk food" problem, and reform of the common agricultural policy.

This re-orientation will have to allow for the many aspects of our modern food systems that are challenged by people and the stakes linked to climate change and the depletion of certain natural resources. Rather than claiming falsely to give an exhaustive definition of this re-orientation, we shall explore one specific aspect of it, namely, the link with innovation. Scientific progress and innovation are at the heart of agricultural matters; they are constants in the middle of the upheavals that have accompanied the development of agricultural activity over the past fifty years.

Research and innovation in the service of agricultural modernisation have made it possible to feed a growing population but also to reduce the weight of food in the household budget, to improve farmers' working conditions, and to release agricultural labourers for the development of first industry and then services. Whereas the majority of the human population worked the land from the Neolithic Age until the twentieth century, the industrialised countries have moved beyond this situation. In these countries, the modernisation of agriculture has thus led to an almost complete disconnection between the majority of the population and the agricultural sector. Paradoxically, this modernisation has now entered a dead-end street.

1 Impasses

Innovation in agriculture is at the core of our societies' development. However, its place is now being challenged. Whereas agriculture no longer concerns more than a small percentage of the working population in the "developed" countries that set their sights on an economy based on services and knowledge, it is the sector in which one of the most important socio-technical controversies has been developing since the mid-1990s: the status of genetically modified organisms (GMOs).

In parallel with this polarisation of the debate about a very specific innovation, the entire process of generating knowledge to serve agricultural development has recently come under fire. The report of an "IPCC on agriculture" that was approved by sixty-four governments in Johannesburg in April 2008, in the middle of a global food crisis linked to the spectacular price increases on the agricultural commodity markets, demands a change of paradigm. The process mobilised 400 international experts who worked on this International Assessment of Agricultural Knowledge, Science and Technology for Development (IAASTD) for four years. Its aim was to assess the impacts of agricultural knowledge, science, and technology on the reduction of hunger and poverty, improvement of rural livelihoods and human health, and "equitable, socially, environmentally and economically sustainable development".

For these experts, agriculture and food systems are a "crossroads" (indeed, the report is titled "Agriculture at a Crossroads") and must be radically turned around. Their conclusion cuts straight to the chase: "The way the world grows its food will have to change radically to serve the poor and hungry better if the world is to cope with a growing population and climate change while avoiding social breakdown and environmental collapse" is how GRID-Arendal[3] sum up McIntyre *et al.*'s hefty report (McIntyre *et al.*, 2009).

Forced into the media spotlight by "hunger riots", this report was gradually abandoned by the very institutions that commissioned it. It was not even used to prepare the Global Food Security Summit that the FAO organised subsequently in Rome. The need to recast the agricultural model met too much opposition from both the decision-makers of the South, who were rushing to modernise their countries by copying the model of the North, and by the proponents of a simple marginal adaptation of the current models, i.e. agrochemical multinationals and their relays in the States and international institutions.

More generally, opposition to the dominant system no longer has the visibility of the 1999 demonstrations in Seattle, where the devastating impacts of inequitable international trade were denounced by the new alliance of proponents of global change and trade unions. Some people, such as the Canadian sociologist Harriet Friedmann, feel that this movement's failure to change the course of world affairs on the global level pushed a large swatch of its players to change their strategies and become involved on the "micro" level. Opposing the World Trade Organization has given way to building local alternatives such as the new schemes of direct relations between producers and consumers around direct delivery of local produce.

In this context, agriculture, which has been fed by innovations and feeds our societies, is the epitome of a democratic issue, for it connects the local and the global. Its re-orientation will be supported by scientific research understood as a public good with its own transparent scheme of governance. That, at least, is what this chapter shall try to prove.

Our analysis of transgenic plants – taken as a critical case of the dynamics of innovation – will show that the current governance of innovation, steeped in the philosophy of economic liberalism, is incompatible with the paradigm change that the international experts deem crucial. The priority given to purely biotechnological solutions effectively culminates in technological lock-ins that restrict the horizon of possibilities, that rein in the diversity of innovative pathways that are produced by science, especially those that could contribute significantly to a transition to more sustainable systems. After that, we shall ponder the changes necessary to break away from this system. Both the agricultural and socio-economic aspects of today's dominant agri-food model must first be considered in the light of the emerging alternative model or models in order to identify the levers of change that transition policies will have to use. Finally, the very policies of innovation and the role of expertise as places for the democratic definition of our technological choices must be thought through anew.

2 Innovation that is stimulated, supervised, but "locked in"

Agricultural systems and agri-food chains are constantly changing. The ways that they function are constantly influenced not only by technological progress but also by national and regional agricultural policies, international agricultural agreements, consumers' wishes, and the rationales of private sector players, from the major supermarket chains down to seed growers. Innovation is thus but one of the places where the horizon of our food is redefined. Its weight in this redefinition, alongside that of the WTO agreements or CAP reforms, is difficult to measure. It does, however, have a special characteristic: although it is often a product of chance, innovation is planned and put into effect by choices made in very specific innovation policies and systems such as the budgets and guidelines of the European Union's Framework Programmes for Research and Development (R&D). The horizon for what is deemed possible is thus set ten, twenty, or thirty years in advance.

The example of transgenic plants is very telling when it comes to this time issue: whilst the controversy about genetically engineered plants was triggered in Europe in 1996 with the arrival of the first boatloads of genetically-modified soybeans from the United States, the first transgenic plant was produced by a Belgian research team in Ghent with public research funds in 1983. Ten years earlier the production of the first transgenic bacterium had already triggered a wave of investment in biotechnology in the wake of decisions in Brussels and Washington alike. These are the discoveries that led to the commercial development of the first transgenic plants in the mid-1990s. They thus opened the door to a very singular type of prosperity, that of a few agricultural biotechnology multinationals, a few start-ups in the same sector, and, to a lesser extent, American farmers, whose competitiveness was enhanced. Other technological choices in the 1980s and 1990s could have reinforced the situations of other types of economic operator. The roles of scientific progress and innovation must be analysed with care, for the redefinition of the dominant economic models – dominant because they give "good performance" and are "competitive" – is rooted in a long time scale.

The critical case of transgenic plants

The development of transgenic plants affords a better understanding of the rationales by which agricultural innovation is currently managed collectively. Transgenic plants are a critical case, given the speed of their advance (170 million hectares in fifteen years) and the acute, persistent controversy that surrounds them.

The ways that our innovation systems and policies operate can be analysed at each of the five great stages that marked the development of the "transgenic plant innovation", i.e. R&D policies, the protection of intellectual property rights over living organisms, the regulatory assessment of transgenic plants to allow their release on the market, the organisation of their inclusion in agricultural systems, and the sale of the products of these modified organisms. This analysis shows that each stage is guided by principles that must be questioned today, given the IAASTD's findings.

R&D policies have become major political issues, as attested by the speed with which they have been ramped up in the European Union's construction. However, to sum up the role that our societies assign to R&D, no treaty equals the words of François Mitterrand that were quoted at the start of this chapter. We have to accept that, far from the very pure idea that the aim of science is to understand the world better, science and technology policies have long been understood and managed by all the major powers not only as tools for controlling the natural world according to the positivist tradition, but also and above all as tools to serve a nation's competitiveness. In our societies, where the economy progresses – or regresses – through creative destruction, as Joseph Schumpeter (1942)[4] showed, innovation is the place of competition between enterprises and thus between States. Innovation policies must enable the State to be competitive via universities of excellence, spin-offs with top performances, and national industrial champions. Now Europe – like the United States – decided as of the early 1980s that biotechnology, along with information and communication technologies, would be one of the two motorways of innovation for its future. So, a political choice – the identification of one (from amongst several) pathways of innovation as a choice for future prosperity – dictated the subsequent priorities of Europe's R&D budgets and supported a major technological development.

Supporting the development of transgenic plants through public R&D efforts was not enough. The second step on the road to innovation was to get the private sector involved. In the case of transgenic plants, a unique ruling of the United States Supreme Court made it possible to attract more investors than the strict scientific potential of the technology alone would have done. In 1980, whilst the U.S. Patents Office had been refusing to grant a patent on a genetically modified bacterium since 1971, the U.S. Supreme Court issued a ruling in *Diamond vs. Chakrabarty* that allowed the patenting of micro-organisms modified by man. This decision, which was subsequently broadened to include plants, was the milestone that triggered major private sector investments in biotechnology. Biotech start-ups raised funds on the money markets, agrochemical multinationals decided to launch major R&D projects in this field, and a "race for genes" began. The possibility of patenting genes and modified organisms guaranteed the security of investments in genetic engineering and gave the de facto green light to the development of technological innovations based on such engineering. The development of transgenic plants is thus closely intertwined with the current intellectual property rights system, the flaws and limits of which have been denounced repeatedly.

The commercial development of transgenic plants would have been impossible, however, without the third stage: permission to leave the laboratory. The controversy about transgenic plants has moreover focused abundantly on risk analysis before the release of a new object such as a transgenic plant for cultivation is allowed. Alexis Roy (2001) has shown that everything in the transgenic plant regulation schemes of OECD countries helped to "guide without hobbling" their development. The idea was to set up a system allowing these new objects to move gradually from the confined environment of the laboratory to the open environment of the field through a series of stages, tests, and learning phases. This was done not to be certain of their agricultural merits, but to guarantee their harmlessness, which in the case of transgenic plants means their compliance with the principles of biosafety (protection of public health and then the environment).

This logic of assessment that concentrates on the risks of innovations more than on their merits must be placed in the context of the economic liberalism that has been the dominant philosophy in our thinking since the Enlightenment. Indeed, economic liberalism provides for not only free trade, but also the freedom of enterprise, and thus the freedom to innovate, whilst controlling the potential risks of a new object such as a technological innovation remains a State prerogative, justifying the minimum rules that guarantee the people's safety but also the smooth working of the economy. Since the freedom of enterprise, and thus of innovation, is a right, it is therefore necessary to "supervise without hobbling" it. In the case of transgenic plants, such oversight to avoid risk is presented as a perfect application of the precautionary principle. It should nevertheless be underlined that just one narrow interpretation of the principle has been adopted. The interpretation of the precautionary principle that is enshrined in the European regulations in this field revolves around hazards only. A second interpretation, for its part, demands a target-oriented approach in which the precautionary principle is linked to a public ethic of sustainable development. If such a vision had been applied to transgenic plants, public institutions would have been encouraged to develop assessment schemes making it possible to determine whether the genetically modified plants proposed by companies or research institutions contributed to achieving democratically determined public objectives such as reducing pesticide use, increasing yields, improve nutritional quality, and so on. The public authorities, which remained focused on verifying biosafety risks in the case of transgenic plants, never truly assessed the *merits* or *usefulness* of innovations such as transgenic plants. Such an assessment is left up to the market, which would in a way allow assessment of an innovation's merits by aggregating the individual choices of all the parties concerned (farmers, processors, consumers, investors, and so on). According to this vision, an innovation that meets a demand and becomes a commercial success is useful and interesting whilst, *a contrario*, commercial failure is proof of an innovation's uselessness.

The fourth stage in the development of the "transgenic plants innovation" is that of the marketing of their seeds, that is to say, their cultivation in open fields. Here, the preponderant issue was the need to guarantee the co-existence of transgenic crops, conventional crops, and organic crops – a principle that is broadly accepted and recognised by all the players. Although it is rarely stated in this way, the idea was to guarantee the freedom of producers throughout the European Union to produce what they wanted to.

The fifth stage – that of marketing the products of transgenic plants – brings the consumer into the picture. The purpose of labelling foods that come from transgenic plants is to maintain the consumer's freedom of choice – a must in the eyes of the proponents of the approach described here.

Aside from the R&D stage, managing transgenic plants as innovations thus relies on the principles of liberalism: the freedom to innovate, to produce, and to consume are the founding principles of the regulations in this area. These freedoms may be curtailed only in the case of scientific risks (toxicity, etc.) proven by "sound science", even though the latter has shown some weaknesses when it comes to assessing transgenic plants.

In leaving a preponderant part of assessing the *merits* of technological innovations for society, i.e. society's technological choices, to the market, the current management scheme implements a liberal conception of innovation policy. In so doing, it delegates a large part of the work of determining each innovation's relevance and contribution to the agricultural model to the market and effectively abandons all political intervention in the gradual, collective definition of prosperity. This model can no longer stand up to the challenges of climate change and resource depletion, for it reinforces the current situation, whereas changing tack is necessary (De Schutter and Vanloqueren, 2011). A long-term vision of food systems requires opening up to alternative paradigms.

Diversity of progress versus technological lock-in

The intensity of the debate surrounding GMOs, in which the "pro-GMOs" are pitted against the "anti-GMOs", and the way the former caricature the latter's position as that of philosophical opposition to scientific progress, has hidden a major stake of innovation, namely, the many directions that progress takes. Indeed, it is possible to take several innovative pathways to deal with such problems as plant diseases, insect infestations, and low yields.

Just one of the many examples of the multiple possibilities of scientific progress concerns the management of insect infestations in cotton fields. Whereas man-made pesticides were the practically inevitable option for some fifty years, two new ways of protecting cotton plants emerged at the end of the twentieth century. The first option was to plant genetically modified cotton resistant to the insects' attacks (through the inclusion in its genome of a gene coding for the production of insect-repellent toxins in the plant's tissues). The second option was to use pheromones and biopesticides, i.e. natural substances that either repel or kill the insects. The scientific community tends to consider the first option to be an innovation, with the pheromone option being seen as going back to old practices. Yet in both cases an innovative product was developed through trials, mistakes and failures, seed selection trials, and the selection of substances from a pool of hundreds of possibilities. "Research and development" efforts were decisive in both cases, and there are probably as many differences between the first genetically modified cotton plant and the ones used today as between the first utilisation of a home-made plant extract and the current use of neem solutions to repel insect pests in Mali. The two options differ in terms of their environmental, agricultural, social, economic, and political implications. In the long run, and if we consider the host of choices to make for each crop, these logics of innovation give rise to profoundly different development pathways in both the North and the South.

The concept of technological pathways has been proposed to illustrate this phenomenon. Genetic engineering (genetically modified cotton) and biological pest control (biopesticides) are the outcomes of different technological pathways that follow different scientific paradigms. The main strategy pursued in genetic engineering is to modify the plants to optimise their ability to produce maximum yields under various environmental constraints (e.g. massive presence of pests in the field) or to modify their qualitative characteristics, such as changing their nutritional profiles. Biological pest control, for its part, belongs to the family of agroecological practices, in which the principles of scientific ecology are applied to agriculture to result in sustainable agro-ecosystems that use resources efficiently and respect nature's balances.

Some of these technological pathways are currently over-represented in agricultural research, whereas others are neglected, despite their major potential as ways to solve today's major problems. Genetic engineering has been the focus of an especially impressive research effort for close to thirty years, whereas until recently agroecology received only marginal attention (see below).

This state of affairs is not just the result of the different factors presented in the management of the "genetic plants innovation". It is clear today that, besides the strategic decisions made in R&D policies, a host of factors determines the directions of innovation. Until now, these factors prompted the development of genetically modified plants and curbed that of agroecology. Moreover, the current situation of agricultural research is best described as a "technological lock-in". This notion was coined by the economists of innovation who studied changes in industry in the 1980s. It characterises situations in which a dominant technology prevents the development of competing and potentially superior technologies (David and Arthur, 1985). The concept was popularised by the study of the QWERTY keyboard, a technology that became a success despite the existence of ergonomically superior alternatives. The QWERTY keyboard dominated at the dawn of typing. It remained in place thereafter because the transaction costs of switching to an "optimal" keyboard (for example, retraining all the users) were too great.

Agricultural research systems are partly locked today by a combination of public choices (R&D policies), standards (the current intellectual property rights regime), but also academic and cultural practices. All in all, about a dozen factors, ranging from researchers' training to market constraints, influence the development of the various technological pathways (Vanloqueren and Baret, 2004, 2009). The researcher is effectively urged, encouraged, or forced by a series of mechanisms to commit to certain research choices rather than others. For example, a molecular biologist can publish the results of the gradual decoding of an organism's genome every six months, whereas a scientist who is studying a wheat-poplar agroforestry system will have to wait until the plot is some fifteen years old to have publishable results. In an environment in which publications have a decisive influence on careers, the stakes riding on certain choices are clear.

It will not be possible to make the change of model that is required to be in line with the IAASTD experts' conclusions if work is not done on such obstacles. What must be done to change this system caught in an ultimately unsustainable rut? Two major fields must be explored. The first one is redesigning our agricultural and economic models in line with the IAASTD's conclusions (Section 3). The second one is to redefine innovation policies and scientific expertise (Section 4).

3 Redefinition of agricultural models, 1940–2010

The current debate about our food systems ties in with a past marked by a series of technical, but also social, revolutions. The history of agriculture, which is often seen from the Malthusian angle that links food production and population, was effectively marked by a strong connection with agro-ecosystems' fertility. Our countries' agrarian systems – the legacy of the twentieth century's "Green Revolution" – are based on an intensification paradigm that is currently reaching its limits.

The Green Revolution: a dominant model running out of steam?

Agriculture has always been dependent on the ecological capital that is made up of soil fertility, the availability of land, and agro-climatic conditions. In the long run, the prosperity of our societies is a function of the state of this ecological capital. The rift between agriculture and the natural system began forming in the United States in the late nineteenth century. This was based on principles developed in European scientific circles in the eighteenth and nineteenth centuries and a new understanding of organic chemistry and plant physiology. The combination of new techniques, such as the tractor and nitrogen fertilisers, with new cereal varieties led to a doubling of yields per unit area in just a few decades (Tilman *et al.*, 2002).

The exportation of this model shaped global agriculture of the twentieth century. In 1940, U.S. Vice President-elect Henry Wallace turned to the Rockefeller Foundation to improve the Mexicans' means of subsistence. The strategy that took shape gave priority to disseminating new wheat varieties but also training Mexican researchers and teachers. This programme entailed a threefold transfer: financial inputs, technical assistance, and the dissemination of a specific view of progress. Research choices were aimed at increasing output and a single avenue for reaching this objective, namely, the production of hybrid seeds, from amongst all the other possible research choices. Technically, the choice was successful: by 1956, Mexico was self-sufficient in wheat.

During the same era it became obvious that the global demographic boom due mainly to population growth in Asia would lead to famine if global agricultural production was not increased. Some countries embarked on agrarian reforms to redistribute the land to the poorest in order to stimulate agricultural production and reduce poverty and inequality, but also to prevent the possible spread of communism by instating the privatisation of the land in the countryside. However, the avenue of technological innovation prevailed in terms of magnitude. As of the late 1950s the Rockefeller Foundation, working in conjunction with the Ford Foundation and under the aegis of the United Nations, spread the Mexican approach to India and Asia by participating in the creation of the International Rice Research Institute (IRRI) in Los Banos, the Philippines. This research centre would disseminate the "Mexican model" throughout its regional sphere of influence. The American agricultural model thus spread to Latin America and Asia. The success of this transformation, which was christened "the Green Revolution", was recalled at regular intervals in 2008/2009 when the global food crisis sparked renewed interest in agriculture, for in thirty-five years (from 1961 to 1996) global wheat production doubled and global rice production increased ninefold!

Technological innovation was at the core of the Green Revolution. The dissemination of new varieties of wheat, maize, and rice is what led to the intensification of agriculture and amazing productivity gains. The technical model was that of agriculture that relied on intensive inputs (chemical fertilisers, mechanisation, irrigation, and so on). This model's effectiveness can be measured in tonnes per hectare. The result in financial terms for the farmer is much less favourable: he sells more, but at lower prices and thus, overall, only those with large holdings increase their incomes and the well-being that may come in the money's wake. The bulk of the profits go to the middlemen (vendors of inputs, seed growers, and grain merchants) and, at the end of the chain, the (basically urban) consumers, for whom staple foods become cheaper.

Whilst today's knowledge, scientific research, and technology systems, which were inspired by the Green Revolution, can boast of having improved global food security, this model has also generated far-reaching social and environmental imbalances. In India, for example, the Green Revolution reinforced inequalities and the two-tracked nature of agriculture: the poor peasants did not benefit from and even suffered because of the new technologies. For example, many went into debt to adopt the technologies, which forced the most vulnerable to sell their land when their harvests were poor. Agriculture such as it is practised today in most of the systems in Europe, America, and South-East Asia has negative environmental consequences: degradation of water resources, increased soil salinity and erosion, chemical pollution, and loss of biodiversity. The industrial agricultural model uses more energy than it generates and helps to push the climate further off-kilter through emissions of greenhouse gases such as methane, whilst the increased use of pesticides has disastrous public health effects, especially when they are used by people oblivious to their toxicity.

Is this model still appropriate today? From the social perspective, a worsening of agriculture's dualisation is contrary to a progressive understanding of prosperity, for the latter is very much a collective rather than individual concept. Yet the application of the Green Revolution model to large swathes of territory in Africa that have been "cornered" by wealthy investors is on the verge of becoming a major trend. From the ecological standpoint, the awareness of the impact of human activities on the environment that began with Rachel Carson's 1962 book *Silent Spring* has taken on a planetary dimension with the problem of climate change. Today, all human activities must be seen within this context. The problem is not just deciding how to cope with this change, but above all how to limit agricultural activities' contributions to climate change. Now, the IPCC estimates that agriculture accounts for some 10–12 per cent of anthropogenic greenhouse gas emissions, or almost as much as the transport sector. Beyond these quantitative dimensions, a new vision of agriculture must incorporate the necessary uncoupling of prosperity and growth (Jackson, 2010). In this context, agriculture must no longer set its objectives according to the logic of increasing production alone; it must factor in the issues of consumption, waste, the nutritional quality of foods, and so on.

Rather than analysing each of these issues in detail, we feel it is important to examine the matter of alternatives to the intensive, industrial model of the twentieth century.

Agroecology, an emerging alternative model

When faced with crises and criticism, the temptation to correct the problems caused by overly industrial agriculture by means of injunctions often prevailed, i.e. reduce fertiliser use, ban the most harmful pesticides, regulate the use of antibiotics on stock farms, etc. Whilst this approach is definitely necessary and effective, its induced effect has been to hide the debate on the scientific fundamentals and socio-economic dimensions of the agricultural system. Paradoxically, in creating a feeling of urgency, the crises have in part masked the debate on the reference agricultural model, a debate that could give rise to a new way of looking at agriculture involving both a new scientific foundation and social, economic, and environmental coherence.

The dominant agricultural model, one should remember, is solidly rooted in history. The scientific bases of agriculture were laid down in the late nineteenth and early twentieth centuries around agricultural chemistry, mechanisation, the first man-made insecticides and fungicides, and improved plants (especially hybrid varieties). The arrival of biotechnologies in the last quarter of the twentieth century back up this disjointed approach, in which each of the components of the agrarian system is analysed by a different scientific field. This reductionism still lies at the heart of the current practice of intensification, the expectations of which are met by transgenic plants, precision agriculture, and sophisticated agrochemical solutions.

However, a new scientific field at the intersection of ecology and agriculture developed in the early 1970s. Agroecology was built around the notion of the agro-ecosystem as a system connecting living things, environmental conditions, and economic conditions as an alternative to a reductionist vision centred on agricultural yields. The first examples of agro-ecological models showed the value of biological pest control (combating a pest by means of natural organisms that are its antagonists) and associated or companion cropping (a cropping scheme consisting in growing several plant species or varieties on the same plot at the same time), with strong involvement of the farm communities in implementing these systems. The aim was to maximise the ecosystem's systemic properties, such as the ability to limit disruptions, the natural renewal of soil fertility, photosynthesis as an energy source, and the maintenance of recycling abilities. This is the model that got the support of the IAASTD report, which underlines the necessary contribution of agroecology to the development of alternatives to the current productivist agricultural model (De Schutter and Vanloqueren, 2011).

From the social standpoint, agroecology initially focused on the peasants of Latin America, Asia, and Africa, usually in the framework of cooperation projects between NGOs and a few scientists. The communities living in areas of low fertility and "forgotten" by the Green Revolution's experts were very receptive to this model. So it is that a new model was thought up in these marginal environments. Although it is still quantitatively marginal today, agroecology has since been put to the test in a complete range of agricultural systems, including the mechanised systems of the North. More recently, the field of study and application of agroecology has broadened to consider the comprehensive food system, from the field to the final consumer. Indeed, it is clear that re-orienting our agrarian systems today will involve all the players in each commodity chain.

In livestock farming, for example, the attention paid to the sustainability of production must be accompanied by a reduction in meat consumption. Similarly, it is often impossible to change agricultural practices without modifying those of consumers, as many "local" organic schemes have found out.

This broadening has important potential for a paradigm change. The construction of alternative food systems effectively corresponds to the emergence of new political fora, in the sense that the citizens who are involved – sometimes individually, sometimes organised in social movements – are finding ways to re-invent not only food systems, but also democratic practices and forms of civic commitment. The emergence and spread of *Groupements d'achat solidaires* (GAS) (solidarity purchasing groups) and associations for the maintenance of small-scale farming (AMAPs in France, etc.) in which consumers become partners of farms in industrialised countries and the decentralised, consultative forms of certification of the Slow Food International movement in the countries of the South are encouraging initiatives (Friedmann and McNair, 2008; Whatmore *et al.*, 2003; Lamine, 2005). New food, social, and economic models are thus being tested and their influence goes from "field to table" up until the European Parliament.

Transitions

Whilst agroecology is an alternative to the dominant agricultural model that relies on biotechnology and agrochemistry, the matter of the transitions between the various models is strongly marked by the issue of the technological lock-in described earlier. To date, the main technological pathway linked to biotechnology has hogged the bulk of the human, technical, and financial means available to agriculture. The initiatives described above have not yet truly weakened its sway.

The socio-technical regime in agriculture can nevertheless be reconfigured by combined actions on the macro level (the institutional landscape, macro-economic elements of the system, and actions of social movements) and micro level (especially the concerted action of multiple niches of innovation[5]) (Geels and Schott, 2007). Change can come about when certain micro level modifications, including in niches of innovation, act in synergy with macro level changes, to the point of challenging the dominant socio-technical regime and forcing it to be reconfigured, even to the point of causing an alternative regime to arise. This is what may gradually come about with agroecology today. The agroecological innovations being made in the field and which emerge in niches of innovation may combine with macro level political and institutional changes (McIntyre *et al.*, 2009) or those effected by the actions of social movements (Via Campesina, Slow Food International, etc.) (Claeys, 2012). These macro level changes can effectively protect, push for, legitimate, and facilitate the convergence of niche innovations that correspond to desirable or necessary changes. Organic farming, which was born in a niche protected by a label and government funding, has already had an impact on the dominant regime, especially on consumers' expectations, although the sector's certification and standardisation have drastically limited its strength to effect social changes.

"Agroecology in action" could thus be considered not only a horizon of sustainability and prosperity but also a transition model based on partnerships of networks of ordinary citizens, farmers, researchers, and various groups that would also generate new knowledge (Warner, 2007; Stassart *et al.*, 2012).

4 Redefining innovation policies and expertise

Such a transition will require new agricultural, economic, and social policies as well as major institutional arrangements. To delve into the issues of innovation policy, we propose five tasks or "worksites" on which we feel ground must be broken.

Today it is vital to go beyond the simplistic slogan that consists in wanting to reach a symbolic figure (devoting 3 per cent of the gross domestic product to research) and to redefine the role of innovation in the pursuit of a redefined prosperity in opposition to the current governance of innovation and to the technological lock-in that prevails in our research systems, one that also takes account of the current food, climate, energy, and economic crises. Innovation must be doubly re-embedded: embedded in civic aspirations (to extend the sphere of democracy to science) and in natural constraints (climate and energy crises, resource depletion, and so on).

A first crucial task will be to give new meaning to the concept of innovation. The word "innovation" is effectively far too often followed by such adjectives as *technological* and *scientific*, which restrict its scope drastically. Innovation ("novelty" or what is new) actually has many forms: it can be institutional, social, or political. In taking up the challenges that concern us here, these possibilities often co-exist. The aim will thus be to promote first and foremost those innovations that contribute to a redefined prosperity.

Several examples can illustrate the range of possibilities. When it comes to food, the nutritional value of the meals served to children in Western countries' school cafeterias is becoming – happily – a public issue. The political debate about limiting the availability of soft drinks in school that was sparked a few years ago has (finally) put its finger on the growing problems of malnutrition and child obesity. What are the best innovations to deal with such problems? It's a good bet that the impact of omega 3-enriched foods, for example, will be negligible compared with those of certain social innovations. A few nutritionists and teachers have effectively launched projects in their schools *cum* laboratories to reform the cafeterias and get pupils interested in their diets so as to lead to lasting changes in everyone's eating behaviour. These social innovations have positive impacts on child health – and the agricultural commodity chains involved – even though, once again, there are too few studies of such subjects. These subjects, which are "too" applied, "too" interdisciplinary, and non-patentable, are hard put to compete with research into functional foods, which is currently raking in huge subsidies. Another example, this time limited strictly to the field of agriculture, is the creation of farmer field schools in developing countries. In these schools, integrated pest management (IPM) practices to control insects are promoted and discussed by the farmers and have sometimes led to more significant production improvements than those obtained by the search for new chemical compounds, which are constantly needed to replace insecticides that have become obsolete because of the extreme adaptability of the plants' predators, which become resistant to the insecticides used (Uphoff, 2002). Yet, research into the best forms of participatory knowledge generation with small farmers remains marginal, whereas companies receive tax rebates when they develop new chemical compounds.

These are not the only examples of what can be done. A diverse range of social innovations has been emerging on every continent for the past fifteen years, whether these innovations are steered by the largest distribution groups (e.g. the GlobalGAP certification standards and the new models that they promote) or by new or emerging movements and social networks (e.g. the alternative food systems promoted by Slow Food International). Whilst in this article we have given priority to analysing developments on the level of the farmer's field rather than in the whole food system, rebalancing support, in terms of both vision and means, for technological and social innovations throughout the food system will be necessary not just to maintain the level of food security reached by a few privileged countries in the face of new energy and climate challenges, but also to enable a larger proportion of humankind to enjoy this same level of security. Indeed, these social innovations need more than subsidies to be implemented. They need and deserve to be accompanied and improved by research efforts (especially action research, which enables the players themselves to improve their reflexivity).

The second task would be to devise innovation policies that could materialise this new vision of innovation in the current context of globalisation. We know that the States, put under pressure by international finance and multinational corporations, must have competitive economic, tax, labour, and environmental laws to attract foreign investment, i.e. the key to stability or growth in a deregulated, globalised economy (Cerny, 1997). The example of GMOs reminds us that this prompts States to adopt innovation policies that contribute to their competitiveness, even though having States compete in this way reduces possibilities for democratic choices and ultimately leads to the erosion of democracy itself (Cerny, 1999; Hertz, 2002; Coutrot, 2005). Whereas the State is thus itself working to reinforce the multinational private sector that reduces its room for manoeuvre, it will be tricky, but vitally important, to devise innovation policies that will support the emergence of innovations "serving a redefined prosperity" without probably being able to stop the support for innovations "serving competitiveness" in one go.

A third task is to encourage recognition of progress's multiplicity at the very heart of technological innovations and thus the need for technological choices. This means going beyond the debate "for" or "against" transgenic plants to decide more generally what means we must give ourselves to orient research and to promote one innovation track over another. Participatory forecasting efforts that include possibilities of technological choice must be included in this work to look ahead to and assess the choices to make today.

The aim of the fourth task is to unlock the innovation systems by reducing the influence of the obstacles that thwart the development of innovations that are essential for a transition to more sustainable food systems. If science is understood to be a public good and the diversity of progress and innovative tracks a necessity, the situations of technological lock-ins effectively warrant public intervention (Callon and Bowker, 1994). So, we shall no longer be able to content ourselves with "supervising without hobbling". Government research will have to turn more towards the technological pathways, such as agro-ecological ones, that the private sector either neglects or does not investigate sufficiently. This will be a substantial change, for today government research agents and agencies are encouraged to work on precisely the same technological pathways as the ones that the private sector favours. Finally, provided that they are promoted by pro-active policies, the niches of innovation that stimulate agro-ecological approaches will be necessary levers and vital "worksites" for democratic experiments.

The fifth task will have to deal with expertise. The transition to new forms of innovation cannot avoid this issue, which is omnipresent in agricultural decision-making chains. The controversies such as those triggered by GMOs, cloning, and mad cow disease have reinforced experts' weight as referees. Now, experts are by definition called upon to give their opinions on matters that are at the fringes of knowledge, given that the information at hand must be interpreted or is incomplete. The expert must thus take a very precise stand on a fuzzy line between the known and unknown. This singular role, which is indispensable for making policy decisions, must be recognised but guided (guaranteed by the transparency of the procedures, possibility of feedback on the decisions taken). Increasing the number of fields represented is an essential element of this reframing of expertise. As described for the special situation of GMOs, a division of roles has taken root for assessing most agricultural innovation projects: the market assesses the innovation's relevancy, whereas risk management is left for the most part to regional, national, and European administrations. This has led to a certain number of misunderstandings, as the citizens discovered little by little that these two dimensions could not be separated completely and thus it was impossible to content themselves with a scientific appraisal *sensu stricto* without including at some point an assessment of the innovation's economic and social dimensions and, in so doing, to look at both sides of the balance sheet – impacts and relevancy – so as to strike the right balance between risks and benefits.

This broadening of expertise is having trouble taking root: the possibility of connecting new dimensions, such as the existence of technological choices or the socio-economic impacts of transgenic plants, has been limited so far. Yet some progress has been made in certain countries. In April 2009 France initiated a new process by instituting a Higher Biotechnology Council composed of a multidisciplinary scientific board but also of an economic, ethics, and social affairs committee that includes local elected officials, MPs, associations, and professionals. The aim is to construct an opinion between these two poles that can inform political decisions about GMOs as fully as possible. The other originality of this system is to analyse GMOs in the context of the alternative practices and innovations that pursue the same objective. This mechanism contributes to a better assessment of the relevancy of innovations in this field, which is vital for the transition to new food systems of a society that would take up technological possibilities instead of being subjected to them. Such institutional innovations would effectively help to democratise expertise, which has too often been phagocytised by expert civil servants, to place expertise in the democratic sphere once again. Given the complexity of innovation projects, highly qualified civil servants, whether national or European, have effectively taken on a growing role in carrying out assessments. Whereas their roles were initially limited to the administrative organisation of such projects, they gradually took on the work of pulling together the conclusions of the assessments submitted by the various experts in their specific fields and also of interpreting the legal framework. So, at the end of the day they have decisive impacts on the decisions taken, all the more so as a large proportion of them have a positivist view of science.

Broadening and democratising expertise will have to concern all the levers of innovation: not just those that act at the moment of approving a new technology's market release, but also those that kick in when research priorities are being set.

5 The paradox of urgency

Agriculture was at the heart of our socio-economic development well before industry and the service sector appeared. The agri-food sector continues to have an important place in the prosperity of our nations, which today argue bitterly in international agricultural agreement negotiations and use market dispute settlement mechanisms to decide on agricultural biotechnology issues with the aim of improving or maintaining their positions. In challenging agriculture and food, we are thus raising questions about one of the vital elements of our prosperity.

The issues of climate change, fossil fuel dependency, and the biodiversity crisis, combined with those of the social bankruptcy of agriculture's modernisation, the persistence of food insecurity for one-sixth of humankind, and overweight or obesity for a comparable proportion of the population, make it necessary today to redefine the paradigms that influence our food systems, i.e. agri-food models and pathways of innovation, in order to accelerate the transition to more sustainable production and consumption patterns. Natural constraints are converging with civic-minded aspirations to make our food systems more democratic, sustainable, and socially equitable.

In today's context of deep crisis, the right elements have come together to give rise to a transition towards the pursuit of another form of prosperity in our food systems. These elements are awareness of the limits of the industrial model and its biotechnological avatar, the emergence of agricultural and agri-food models that are compatible with climate change, and better understanding of the mechanisms of a transition. Agroecology – this new approach to agricultural practices and food systems – is helping to redefine prosperity as prosperity built upon principles of sustainability and social justice, in counterpoint to a model of intensive production in which the only indicators are the maximisation of yields and profits. Although the players that profit from the current productivist system continue to control most of the levers of influence, such a transition is technically possible and socially desirable.

Paradoxically, one of the factors blocking this transition is the rhetoric of urgency: the urgency of doubling global food production to feed the planet; the urgency of innovating to increase competitiveness and win market share; and the urgency of combating climate change. Such urgent needs have pushed the States caught in the logic of competition into the impasses of intensive monocropping of transgenic plants and the expansion of biofuel production at a rapid rate. Yet giving way once again to the productivist models that are incompatible with both the natural constraints on humankind and social aspirations will merely worsen and delay the magnitude and difficulty of this transition.

Notes

1 Université catholique de Louvain
2 Université catholique de Louvain and ICHEC-Brussels Management School. Further information see authors' biographies at the front of this volume.
3 www.grida.no/news/press/1462.aspx
4 Schumpeter popularised the concept of creative destruction in his book *Capitalism, Socialism and Democracy* (1942). In evolutionist economists' dynamic view of the economy, the destruction of sectors of activity parallels the creation of new economic activities, which themselves are linked in particular to innovations and entrepreneurial activity.
5 Niches of innovation are protected spaces in which it is possible to stray from the rules of the dominant technological scheme (Geels, 2004). They are places where radical innovations can burst forth, whereas incremental innovations usually develop within the dominant scheme. Several currently well-known technological innovations (wind turbines and hybrid cars) developed in such niches, protected from the dominant scheme by government subsidies, massive government research efforts, or a steady stream of public procurement contracts.

References

Callon Michel and Bowker Geoffroy (1994), Is science a public good? *Science. Technology and Human Values* 19(4): 395–424.

Carson Rachel (1962), *Silent Spring*. Boston/New York: Houghton Mifflin Harcourt.

Cerny Philip G. (1997), Paradoxes of the competition state: the dynamics of political globalization, *Government and Opposition* 32(2): 251–274.

Cerny Philip G. (1999), Globalization and the erosion of democracy, *European Journal of Political Research* 36(1): 1–26.

Claeys Priscilla (2012), The creation of new rights by the food sovereignty movement: the challenge of institutionalizing subversion, *Sociology* 46(5): 844–860.

Coutrot Thomas (2005), *Démocratie contre capitalisme*. Paris: La Dispute.

David Paul A. and Arthur Brian (1985), Clio and the economics of QWERTY, *American Economic Review* 75(2): 332–337.

De Schutter Olivier and Vanloqueren Gaëtan (2011), The new green revolution: how twenty-first-century science can feed the world, *Solutions Journal* 2(4): 33–44.

Friedmann Harriet and McNair Amber (2008), Whose rules rule? Contested projects to certify "local production for distant consumers", *Journal of Agrarian Change* 8(2–3): 408–434.

Geels Frank W. (2004), From sectoral systems of innovation to socio-technical systems: Insights about dynamics and change from sociology and institutional theory, *Research Policy* 33: 897–920.

Geels Frank W. and Schot Johan W. (2007), Typology of sociotechnical transition pathways, *Research Policy* 36(3): 399–417.

Hertz Noreena (2002), *The Silent Takeover: Global Capitalism and the Death of Democracy*. London: Arrow Books.

Jackson Tim (2010), *Prospérité sans croissance. La transition vers une économie durable*. Brussels: Etopia/De Boeck.

Lamine Claire (2005), Settling shared uncertainties: local partnerships between producers and consumers, *Sociologia Ruralis* 45(4): 324–345.

McIntyre Beverly D., Herren Hans R., Wakhungu Judi, and Watson Robert T. (eds) (2009), *International Assessment of Agricultural Science and Technology for Development: The Global Report vol. 1: Agriculture at a Crossroads*. Washington, DC: Island Press.

Roy Alexis (2001), *Les experts face au risque: Le cas des plantes transgéniques*. Paris: PUF.

Schumpeter Joseph (1942), *Capitalism, Socialism and Democracy*. New York: Harper and Brothers.

Stassart Pierre M., Baret Philippe, Grégoire Jean-Claude, Hance Thierry, Mormont Marc, Reheul Dirk, Stilmant Didier, Vanloqueren Gaëtan, and Visser Marjolein (2012), L'agroécologie: trajectoire et potentiel. Pour une transition vers des systèmes alimentaires durables. In: Denise Van Dam, Michel Streith, Jean Nizet, and Pierre M. Stassart (eds), *Agroéocologie entre pratiques et sciences sociales*. Dijon: Educagri, 25–51.

Tilman David, Cassman Kenneth G., Matson Pamela A., Naylor Rosamond, and Polasky Stephen (2002), Agricultural sustainability and intensive production practices, *Nature* 418: 671–677.

Uphoff Norman (2002), *Agroecological Innovations: Increasing Food Production with Participatory Development*. London: Earthscan Publications.

Vanloqueren Gaëtan and Baret Philippe V. (2004), Les pommiers transgéniques résistants à la tavelure – Analyse systémique d'une plante transgénique de "seconde génération", *Le Courrier de l'Environnement de l'INRA* 52: 5–20.

Vanloqueren Gaëtan and Baret Philippe V. (2009), How agricultural research systems shape a technological regime that develops genetic engineering but locks out agroecological innovations, *Research Policy* 38(6): 971–983.

Warner Keith Douglass (2007), *Agroecology in Action. Extending Alternative Agriculture through Social Networks*. Cambridge: MIT Press.

Whatmore Sarah, Stassart Pierre, and Renting Henk (2003), What's alternative about alternative food networks? *Environment and Planning A* 35(3): 389–391.

7 Environment, growth, and prosperity

Possible models of integration

Tom Bauler[1] *and Edwin Zaccai*[2]

We live in a time when the classic models of economic development are being increasingly challenged by environmental questions. This tendency is evident among radical critics of economics, as well as students of economic history. In France, a typical example of this trend is Serge Latouche (2006). Until around 2000, his work consisted of a critique of Western-centric development models, at which point he turned to the concept of "degrowth". Subsequently, his call to "abandon economism" was based as much on the environmentally unsustainable character of our way of life as on his earlier arguments. Similarly, Geneva-based Gilbert Rist's work on the history of development criticised the incompatibility between development, on the one hand, and human needs and social justice, on the other (Rist, 2003). By 2010, Rist was arguing that ecological impacts must be a central factor in rethinking the approach to development. Daniel Cohen (2009), for his part, has undertaken a dense and instructive reflection on the world's economic history,[3] which brings us once again to a problem that in our age has become a truism: the unsustainability, from an ecological perspective, of replicating the West's resource-intensive model in countries like China and India. He concludes by emphasising the need to find alternative models for wealth creation and global prosperity. In Great Britain, the Sustainable Development Commission coordinated by Tim Jackson, has also called attention to the impossibility of "decoupling" the pursuit of a growth-based model of prosperity from its energy impact. While some economic reformers, such as Joseph Stiglitz, place less emphasis on the constraints implicit in environmental concerns, these preoccupations have now become commonplace in forward-looking thinking about economic development.

Beginning with this observation, this chapter will address the adjustment of the theory and politics of environmental protection with respect to Western models of development. A central concern of our analysis is the proper interpretation of the relationship between economic growth and environmental protection. Indeed, like other contributors in the present book, we believe that, in order to enrich our understanding of prosperity, we must rely on the multiplicity of existing analyses of the role and consequences of economic growth for existing models of development.

This chapter also proposes to put the topic into perspective by focusing on innovations in the governance of environmental policy. Based on environmental concerns, we seek, in this way, to consider the ways in which we might transition to a new socio-political dynamic. Particular attention will be given to innovations at the level of policy instruments, such as fore/backcasting and long-term planning. Beyond the concepts – slogans ("sustainable development", "degrowth") and political programmes ("Green Growth") – it has been argued that environmental policy, because it is "naturally" progressive, could become the experimental nexus for a broader reform of society, including our understanding of prosperity. Beginning with these hypotheses, we develop a partial assessment of these efforts to implement innovative environmental governance.

However prosperity is defined, the question of economic growth and its relationship to resource exploitation and its environmental impact must necessarily be posed. We need specific and sensitive indicators, but particularly processes that permit greater respect for the environment (compared to our current situation). Indeed, the redefinition of prosperity as a political and social project will inevitably require us to reshape how it is measured. These measures must improve the way we account for the connections between human activity and its resulting environmental impacts.

1 A diversity of environmental impacts

The term "environmental impact" comprises a range of phenomena of varying natures and degrees of importance. We must distinguish the *use* of renewable resources (for example, water, forests) and non-renewable resources (such as oil) from the *impact* (emissions, effluents, waste) of human activity on various aspects of the environment. This impact can be local (soil pollution), regional (air pollution), or global (climate change). Moreover, some impacts are partially reversible, as demonstrated by improvements in surface water and air quality in some areas, while others are not, at least for the foreseeable future, as with species extinction, climate change, or soil erosion. Concern with the impact of human activity on the environment generally leads to the consideration of four variables: the type of resources consumed; how critical they are (whether they are irreplaceable, indispensable); and both the nature and seriousness of the impact. Knowledge of these four factors, including how they inter- and retroact, is, however, limited. Because of this limited knowledge, when the relationship between humans and their environment changes, precautions must be taken.

In confronting these wide-ranging challenges, increased human activity is merely an indirect and incomplete indicator of threats to the environment. For example, in industrialised countries, the direct cost of energy consumption represents only a few percentage points of total GDP, whereas the expected impact of this usage on climate change constitutes a potentially catastrophic long-term threat and a factor that can weaken growth itself. By contrast, services in the same countries represent over half of GDP and generate proportionally less impact than industry or agriculture, even if they produce their own environmental consequences, notably in the realms of transportation and housing management.

Even so, it is reasonable to expect that increased human activity, roughly reflected in rising GDP, results in increased pressures on the environment, if these increases are sufficiently great and continue over the long term. Yet this trend, which has been characteristic of industrialised countries, is accelerating, as noted in the introduction, across the globe.

Today, one cleavage prevails (Zaccai, 2012). On the one hand, the environment is being harmed in a number of ways that are locally perceived and that involve relatively small amounts of pollutants, e.g. waste management, water pollution, air pollution. Solutions to these problems exist, even if they are neither automatic nor comprehensive, which are not fundamentally incompatible with economic growth. It is even possible to incentivise the economy to make investments that can offset or redress these problems through industrial and environmental policies imposing increasingly ambitious emission or production standards.

Massive consumption of *material flows*, however, leads to significant environmental damage, as evidenced in water consumption, the effect of territories on biodiversity, energy consumption, and the production of greenhouse gases. The amount of this second category of threats is estimated to reach millions or billions of tons annually on a global scale. If some of the impact of rising production can be mitigated at the local level (particularly in northern countries) by more ecological approaches to management, these measures are far from sufficient at the global level. In addition to the question of economic growth, it is our modes of production and consumption that are, in this way, being challenged. Each European is said to "consume" an average total of fifty tons of materials annually (either directly or indirectly); chemical compounds cause imbalances in ecosystems (through acidification and nitrification); and industrialised countries emit a significant portion of greenhouse gases. Among these problems, the rise in greenhouse gases is particularly troubling. According to international reports (such as IPCC, 2013 and World Bank, 2012), the possibility of limiting global temperatures to 2°C no longer seems likely. This kind of environmental damage can clearly harm economic development in its current form, particularly as it is pursued in other regions of the world. Nevertheless, on the broader issue of the compatibility between growth and the environment, three positions have emerged in recent research. Each of these will be considered in the following section.

2 Three positions on the compatibility between growth and the environment

The main positions on the relationship between economic growth and the environment can be broadly summarised as follows: growth as opposed to the environment; growth as compatible with the environment; and growth as favourable to the environment.[4] In this section, each position will be illustrated by one or two trends or representative works. Without claiming to be comprehensive, we will also attempt to connect each one to its typical "political programs".

Table 7.1 Classifying environmental policy approaches and movements against their understanding of economic growth

Environment vs growth	*Environment and growth*	*Environment with growth*
The Limits to Growth (1972)	*Brundtland Report* (1987)	Environmental Kuznets curves (1990s)
Decommodification and sufficiency movements (1970s)	Decoupling strategies (1990s)	Industrial ecology (1990s)
Steady-state economics (1970s and 1980s)	Sustainable development strategies (1995 onwards)	Ecological modernisation (1985 onwards)
Degrowth movement (2000s)	Transition management (2004 onwards)	Green new deals (2008 onwards)
Prosperity without Growth (2009)		Green Growth (2010 onwards)

This typology is summarised in Table 7.1. Each item is followed by a date indicating this position's initial emergence.

Economic growth as opposed to environmental protection

In the first place, the *Limits to Growth* report (Meadows *et al.*, 1972) and later studies exploring the idea of "degrowth" are illustrative of the position that economic growth and protecting the environment are irreconcilable. *Limits to Growth* was a landmark in the debate relating to the relationship between the environment and economic growth. In the scenarios it presents, production's growth dynamic results in systemic economic and social collapse by the mid-twenty-first century. Two factors would cause these upheavals: insufficient food resources to feed a rapidly growing population and the health consequences of production-generated pollution. *Limits to Growth* presents economic growth as inherently problematic and advocates "steady-state economics", which was theorised at the time by Herman Daly (1991). Daly, a leading figure in ecological economics, was influenced by John Stuart Mill (in the nineteenth century) and Kenneth Boulding (1981), who laid the foundations for evolutionary economics. Rather than increasing production, *stationary economics* seeks to use improved productivity to reduce the amount of time devoted to work in order to stabilise consumption and/or investment. It also supports to population control through strict demographic policies. Unlike some of the classical economists of the nineteenth century, who considered a stationary economy as the almost inevitable consequence of wealth accumulation and the consumption of scarce resources, contemporary and environmental versions of these theories see a stationary economy as a desirable goal that can be achieved through significant regulation. State interventionism and the need for "economic-environmental" governance have, moreover, proved to be constant features of research that favours limiting economic growth for environmental reasons.

Within this field, the term "degrowth" appeared in France in the 2000s. There are conceptual links between degrowth and other trends, such as steady-state economics, voluntary simplicity, decommodification, and even deep ecology (Martinez-Alier *et al.*, 2010). Latouche (2006) sees degrowth not as an ideal but as a reflection of the necessity of abandoning the principle of growth (which does not necessarily imply economic degrowth, as the less striking term of "a-growth" suggests), which is itself supported by the West's oppressive economic ideology. Theories of degrowth have been criticised, in substantive terms, for their practical shortcomings. Above all, the concept refers to an intellectual movement and a mobilising force, yet which, at least in the short term, lacks a well-defined programme of political action.

Work on degrowth has flourished in recent years. This fashion has been notably encouraged by the discouraging results of traditional environmental policies, which have failed to contain the effects of increasing environmental flows at a global level. In addition to these environmental constraints, the trend is probably also supported by the recognition that Europe seems to have entered a stage of economic degrowth, as well as by the relative decline of historically developed countries in an increasingly multi-polar world.

Economic growth as compatible with environmental protection

A second trend proposes a different interpretation of the connection between growth and the environment. It is exemplified by the Brundtland Report of the World Commission on Environment and Development (WCED, 1987) and the concept of "decoupling", which has been promoted notably by the OECD and the European Union and has played a significant role in shaping contemporary environmental policies.

A landmark in the emergence of the theory of sustainable development, on which it had a decisive impact, the Brundtland Report argued that developing countries should pursue the growth they need, provided that its fruits were better distributed among the population and that sustainable environmental conditions were respected. It favoured, in other words, a form of growth that was adapted to specific contexts, without being absolutely imperative, and that would, moreover, be socially equitable and ecologically sustainable. As we suggested earlier, this approach was able to produce results in a number of realms related to various problems, including air pollution (but not the greenhouse effect), water pollution, waste and toxic product management, and so on. However, while these concepts have become widespread, the sustainable development policies they inspired have encountered only limited success on a global scale.

Having gradually distinguished itself from the concept of sustainable development, *decoupling* – between economic growth, on one hand, and the emission of pollutants, on the other – has become a policy priority in OECD countries. The EU has invoked it on multiple occasions. Thus the European Environmental Agency notes that labour productivity in Europe (i.e. EU 15) increased by 270 per cent between 1960 and 2000, whereas productivity in material usage increased by 100 per cent and in energy usage by only 20 per cent over the same period.[5] At present, environmental and employment concerns are creating incentives to significantly increase "ecological" productivity and, perhaps, to decrease the pressure on human labour. This trend is known as the "double dividend". From this perspective, *eco-efficiency* is regarded as the best solution for softening the impact on the environment. It makes it possible to reduce resource consumption and the environmental impact of such economic developments as advances in technology and other types of consumer services.

The goal of decoupling is all the more convenient for rich countries in that it tends to occur in countries with large GDPs and increasingly service-based economies that are able to make productivity gains in natural resource and energy usage through procedures and technological innovation that are subject to environmental norms. In a context of economic growth, the effects of decoupling remain in practice quite limited: the consumption of a number of environmental goods and services continues to rise. Yet even on a limited scale, decoupling is far less advanced in other countries, particularly in developing industrial economies, which, like Europe during the industrial revolution, are experiencing a transitional rise in energy intensity (i.e. energy consumed per unit of wealth), notably for the setting of their infrastructures.

In terms of political governance, the quest for compatibility between economic growth and environmental efficacy has produced models of procedural and technocratic management inspired by the forms of central planning used during the 1980s and 1990s in other sectors (such as the aerospace and computer industries). Yet the goal in such instances is not simply to react to industrial and commercial change (such as computerisation), but to encourage innovation and to channel it in directions that lessen environmental impacts. "*Transition management*" (Shove and Walker, 2007; Boulanger, 2008), extended to socio-technical systems and systemic innovations, seeks to promote the integration of environmental innovations into the way production systems are organised. Some believe that the development and support for "alternative" niches and "innovation (and production) beehives" can improve the current system's environmental performance, without requiring a break with the current economic and commercial modus operandi. The kind of governance proposed rests on a form of procedural and communal self-management that no longer depends solely on the intermediary of the market in determining which goals are to be pursued.

Economic growth as favourable to environmental protection

Beyond the approaches emphasising the possible compatibility between growth and the environment, some authors – economists, for the most part – see these concepts as complementary: economic growth could improve environmental performance. In the mid-1990s, environmental economics began to speak of a bell curve, known as the *environmental Kuznets curve* (EKC),[6] representing the correlation between pollution levels and GDP growth in specific scenarios. Pollution levels as a function of production volume rises with industrialisation, but is said to fall as the revenue generated by economic growth leads to the acquisition of less pollutant infrastructure and as people become more "green". Empirically, this trend is evidenced in pollutants that are troubling or harmful only at short distances, at least when relatively cheap technological solutions can be found. Good examples include air pollution by NO_x and SO_2, the contamination of waterways, and deforestation.

Yet there are many phenomena to which it is difficult to apply this curve, such as mass material flows, resource and water consumption, but also waste generation. As for CO_2, even if an ambitious climate policy in wealthy countries (particularly in Europe) could provide retroactive justification for the environmental Kuznets curve, since emissions have recently demonstrated a (limited) tendency to decline, it would be difficult to extend this projection to the global level, at least within the timeframe required to protect the climate. It is worth recalling that, according to the IPCC, emissions would need peak globally by around 2020.

Furthermore, even when they do occur, correlations between GDP growth and declining pollution levels are hardly automatic. Empirical work on environmental Kuznets curves demonstrates that they are contingent on environmental policies. Moreover, the fact that they occur in the older industrialised economies of the northern hemisphere can be explained in part by the fact that their pollutants and emissions have been exported. Indeed, competition for comparative advantage on a global scale also affects the environment, leading certain world regions to overvalue their carrying capacity of pollutants and various kinds of waste.

While the EKC is, in a sense, the common economic software of those who believe that growth can benefit the environment, there are several other trends and schools which promote social and industrial change along these lines. Among the most important is *ecological modernisation*, a current that emerged in the late 1980s in Germany, the Netherlands, and the United States (Hajer, 1995). In this category one can also include the proponents of industrial ecology, even if, in its more utopian forms (which embrace a "circular economy"), its implementation does not depend on growth.

Despite its theoretical and practical limitations, the idea that economic growth could reverse the trend towards environmental degradation is very widespread. The great advantage of this view is that, like other economic factors, it creates incentives to seek growth, since many actors assume either out of conviction or ignorance that environmental benefits will result over the long term. Following the 2009 crisis, this position found its way into public policy debates in the form of Green New Deals. These national economic stimulus plans count, on the one hand, on innovations in green technology to revive countries still reeling from the banking and economic crisis and experiencing low or non-existent growth rates, and, on the other, to propel high-performing industrial or tertiary economies into a direction that is reputed for its high added value with low environmental impact and is seen as having a promising future (notably in terms of job creation), which has become known as "green growth". Were these economic support programmes to bear fruit, growth would no longer simply promote environmental performance; rather, the demand for improved environmental quality would favour economic growth. In practice, the effects of "green growth" have, for now, proved limited. They must be evaluated from the standpoint of a spectrum of environmental and social priorities.

A parallel question: how much could environmental governance be reformed?

Several points emerge from the previous discussion. It seems clear that environmental problems have, despite the discourse, been enlisted into efforts to achieve greater economic prosperity and, in many regions of the world, prosperity as such. Depending on the regions and the issue, economic growth is not necessarily antithetical to solving environmental problems, provided that certain priorities are satisfied, certain limits are respected, and investments and practices favouring the environment are promoted. These goals, however, require the implementation of diversified and ambitious regulations.

Furthermore, the global growth of natural resource flows and greenhouse gas emissions and, more generally, the inauspicious development of the quantity and quality of eco-systemic services are major causes for concern. This evolution seems to be inversely related to the rise in global GDP. A reconsideration of the concept of prosperity may contribute to modifying these trends and – by extension – the regulations to which they give rise. However, from an environmental standpoint, this reconsideration must take into account a diverse range of problems and crises.

A major question that is implicit in the three theoretical positions outlined above is the degree to which the economic system must be reformed if it is to respect environmental constraints. As one moves from the first to the third position, fewer reforms of the way in which our society operates are required. In short, these three currents offer different answers to the question "should we emphasise respect for existing institutions (and economic growth in particular) or respect for the environment?" In any case, government regulations play a preponderant role in shaping local and global environmental performance, including its relationship with economic growth. At the global level, some believe that, due to environmental governance's weakness in the realm of international relations, it has been supplanted by the only form of international governance that is effective on a global scale, namely, global trade. The superstructure that governs global relations – i.e. commercial relations which themselves are determined by the paradigm of economic growth – would seem to inhibit the emergence of environmental governance at various levels of state competence. In other words, the diffusion of the World Trade Organization's spirit and regulations has succeeded in limiting the scope of efforts to reshape global environmental governance.

In what follows, we will further consider the role that environmental governance could play in redefining prosperity, in order to explore whether some forms of governance innovations favour a broader structural reform of our social model. Put differently, does environmental governance have a proactive – and even exemplary – role to play in the process of redefining prosperity?

3 Environmental governance: a tool for reshaping prosperity

Our analysis will consist of two parts. First, we will present a number of methods and approaches that have been used in Europe to better *integrate* environmental concerns into "mainstream" politics. The "mainstream" European policy framework is mainly characterised by "Europe 2020" and the seven "flagship initiatives" with which it is associated. It consists, in short, of an effort to achieve economic growth throughout Europe by promoting a knowledge-based society, while keeping significant environmental and social impacts under control. In other words: smart, green, and inclusive growth. This programme thus offers the perfect institutional example of the quest for selective economic growth that is favourable to environmental protection (and thus compatible with the second and third positions discussed above). As an example, we will consider the current status of one the main issues that environmental governance faces at the European level, namely *the integration of environmental concerns into sector-specific policies* termed *Environmental Policy Integration (EPI).*

Second, we will explore the limitations of the EPI programme in order to draw a series of lessons that could more broadly be applicable also to the process of redefining prosperity. We will take our inspiration from state-of-the-art environmental governance in a realm that has proved particularly innovative in recent years, namely *fore/backcasting and long-term planning*. Our goal will be to understand whether innovation in environmental governance has lived up to the expectations that it could reshape environmental governance. Shortcomings in this particular area could indeed raise doubts as to the potential of the environmental polity and related governance procedures to contribute significantly to a broader reshaping of society's goals (such as the redefinition of prosperity).

But first let us consider the concept of "environmental governance". Often seen as an extension and expansion of the more coercive and traditional concept of "government" (Spaargaren *et al.*, 2006), governance can be understood as "the structured ways and means in which the divergent preferences of interdependent actors are translated into policy choices to allocate values, so that the plurality of interests is transformed into co-ordinated action and the compliance of actors is achieved" (Eising and Kohler-Koch, 1999: 5). The shift from "government" to "governance" offers a broader and more open interpretation of institutional mechanisms, notably insofar as they consist of more participatory (or at least deliberative) arrangements that aspire to incorporate multiple levels, actors, and dimensions. Governance also entails a broader definition of "institution": "politics" ceases to be limited to the realm of the state, while "institution" is no longer confined to the socio-political and "institutionalised" organisations that are responsible for managing acknowledged social problems. From this perspective, environmental governance concerns itself with coordinating and guiding actors towards the collaborative and integrated resolution of environmental problems.

Furthermore, some environmental problems possess characteristics – such as incommensurable uncertainty (in the case of climate change), irreversible risk (for nuclear waste), the emergence of controversial impact realms (as with electromagnetic fields), and long-term impact (i.e. the erosion of biodiversity) – which, according to some authors, requires the creation of new forms of consultation and negotiation through innovatively organised networks of public actors. In this way, environmentalism creates a demand for public management based on the principles of "governance".

On this twofold basis – the widespread emergence of governance and the ways in which modes of governance are shaped by the very nature of environmental conflicts and actors – is environmental governance really capable of innovating and trailblazing? In addition to generating models of interaction between economic growth and environmental policy (such as those addressed in this article's second sections), environmental concerns also require us, for this very reason, to reform *how* we see society and the future. They lead us to the question: to what extent can reforming environmental governance contribute to a redefinition of prosperity?

Integrating the environment into policy

Environmental governance seeks to construct itself through three kinds of integration: (1) the horizontal integration of environmental concerns and constraints into sector-specific policies; (2) the vertical integration of global environmental threats into local levels of governance (and vice versa); (3) temporal integration, by considering the "long term" when formulating and operationalising public action.

In (partial) reply to the question of whether environmental governance has a notable effect on the reform of governance as such, we use "horizontal integration" as an indication of whether innovation in the realm of environmental governance has occurred (or not). We do so because, in the first place, it is through horizontal integration that environmental issues directly confront the elaboration and reshaping of sector-specific policies. In the second place, horizontal integration has been formalised – unlike the other two forms of integration – as a basic principle in elaborating public action, particularly at the European level.[7]

The results of the process of integrating environmental concerns into sector-specific policies (Environmental Policy Integration, or EPI) are mixed, at the EU level[8] as much as at the national level (for federal Belgium, see the Cour des Comptes, 2005). Empirical comparative evaluations ultimately suggest that horizontal integration has been more easily achieved – until now, at least – in traditional and hierarchical institutional and political contexts than in more open and collaborative settings (Wilkinson, 2007). This may seem counter-intuitive, as one might assume that "governance"-based environmental policies, which tend to be more open and collaborative, have in principle a greater potential for governmental innovation and are thus more likely to operationalise novel environmental policy tools. Yet it strikes us that this kind of environmental policy has had a more difficult time operationalising the tools required to achieve institutional reform.

Further strengthening this claim, studies have shown that environmental governance has had difficulties in conceiving the new instruments of public action needed to take on complex environmental problems. Often, these instruments are simply translations (accompanied, admittedly, by significant procedural improvements) of instruments tested in other domains of public action (Halpern, 2007). To cite one example, the emergence of local environmental policies based on mechanisms for contractualising relationships between state entities and user networks, notably (in Belgium and France) in the case of managing the environmental quality of watersheds, can be understood as an instance of the broader shift towards contractualisation (which has been tested in peri-urban settings in France and in Belgian health care policy). The same is true of the economic instruments used in environmental policies, particularly in the case of trading schemes for carbon emissions or environmental services. In short, the latter represent no real innovation in terms of environmental governance, other than introducing monetary values and financial speculation into environmental management.

Even if the picture painted here is selective, the very innovativeness of the public management of environmental problems, which was initially presented as a catalyst for a broader reform of the concept of prosperity, must be qualified, at least if we are to judge it on the basis of concrete results. In particular, it would be naive to believe that environmental governance has managed to escape the broader trend in public policy towards emphasising efficiency goals, which, for logical reasons, relies increasingly on economic mechanisms and instruments. In this respect, environmental governance can be understood as the economic governance of environmental problems. The favourable reception given to efforts to assess environmental problems in monetary terms, the most recent examples of which are the Stern report (2006) for climate policy and the TEEB reports[9] for conservation policy, further illustrates this trend.

Governance innovation in the realm of environmental planning and fore/backcasting

The leverage that environmental governance could bring to redefining prosperity can be approached from another angle. If there are privileged moments at which society's purpose can be reconsidered and, by the same token, prosperity can be rethought, it is reasonable to assume that *fore/backcasting and planning processes* can inspire us to imagine what our lives will be like in the future. In recent years, deliberative and participatory exercises in planning and fore/backcasting, after having first emerged in the realm of environmental policy, have met with renewed interest.

If the central questions of fore/backcasting efforts in the environmental realm are aimed at softening the impact of our production and consumption patterns – by insisting on the need to give greater consideration to the environmental limits that our way of life is rapidly exceeding – we must return to a point made earlier: certain "sustainable" lifestyles challenge with more or less virulence the fact that prosperity's primary instrument should be economic growth. A majority of fore/backcasting processes acknowledge that the economic growth of the industrial era is a major source of environmental problems and advocate controlled economic growth (i.e. growth that is sustainable, green, and post-industrial) as an indisputable precondition of our society's future development. Yet in addition to this effect, which is related to the often-repeated need to give greater consideration to environmental limits, some see fore/backcasting as offering even more fruitful possibilities.

From a procedural standpoint, environmental governance could, more fundamentally, create incentives for new ways of conceiving our society's ends, goals, and expectations along more collaborative, open, and "reflexive" lines (Beck *et al.*, 1996; Newig *et al.*, 2008). Reflexivity as a requirement for fore/backcasting becomes essential to ensuring that the redefinition of society's goals is put into practice, notably by introducing learning functions into public institutions, which might also be directed at producers and consumers. This would consist of multiple forms of learning, which need to be generated and supported: "social or collaborative learning", "organisational learning", "policy learning", "governmental policy learning", "social policy-learning", "political policy-learning", and so on. These leaning processes must become necessary (but not sufficient) conditions for achieving "quality" fore/backcasting, making it possible to turn fore/backcasting into a broader cycle of strategy and action-plan building. Learning processes would thus ensure (at least in part) that lessons and new insights into the relationship between economic growth and environmental constraints would shape public action.

Yet in the context of environmental policy, which in principle lends itself to fore/backcasting and planning of a kind that is both ambitious and receptive to challenges to contemporary representations of prosperity, it would appear that, here, too, the expectations arising from the virtuous circle of shared and non-partisan knowledge and cumulative learning have yet to be fulfilled. Indeed, if one considers some of the integrated and reflexive exercises in fore/backcasting and planning (which are deliberative and participatory) that have taken place in Europe – particularly the "Transition Management" experiments in the Netherlands, which are probably the most advanced of these projects – one notes that they do not seem to be directing discussion (or resulting action plans) towards a redefinition of prosperity. To the contrary, it would appear, upon analysis, that the reflexive character of these ambitious exercises in new planning does not entirely diverge from the more conventional practices that can be encountered in sector-specific industrial innovation. Reflexivity seems to induce an exaggerated concern for honouring criteria of political feasibility and ensuring that recommendations are acceptable to "decision-makers". Consequently, radical reassessment and revolutionising contemporary intellectual frameworks (including notions of prosperity) are largely abandoned in favour of mild and incremental evolutions.

4 Conclusion

Our analysis has allowed us to illustrate and confirm the concerns expressed in our initial references to the current importance of environmental questions as they relate to the pursuit of classic models of development. While there are many environmental reasons for seeking new forms of prosperity, they cannot afford to neglect these questions. It is primarily at the global level, with the ever-increasing flows of resources and pollution, that environmental constraints, confronted with this kind of economic growth, encounter the most problems. Of these flows, the stakes of reducing greenhouse gas effects are particularly high.

But the tree of climate change must not prevent us from seeing the forest of additional problems relating to unsustainable development. If our analysis has identified progress in the management of environmental problems in some countries, other major threats continue to destabilise the earth's ecosystems and will, sooner or later, destabilise the societies that exploit them. Yet these problems are not new. Theories and policies have been suggested and implemented. We have tried to identify some of their most crucial aspects.

We have also mentioned innovations in governance that seeks to redirect society towards a more sustainable path, taking note of some of these results achieved in Europe. At the end of the day, the results of these experiments are rather thin and innovations have certainly not risen to the level hoped for. This does not mean that these directions offer no lessons regarding the development of means for revising the concept of prosperity, particularly in the realm of fore/back-casting. Over and above the various theories we have discussed, it remains to be asserted that policies promoting real and sustainable prosperity do in fact change, practically as well as theoretically, their relationship to environmental issues.

Notes

1 Université libre de Bruxelles
2 Université libre de Bruxelles. For further information see authors' biographies at the front of this volume.
3 For global analyses, see for example the OCDE's studies (2008).
4 A more complete analysis of these positions can be found in Zaccai (2010). For a typology of the key actors in sustainable development as they relate to social justice, on the one hand, and technological solutions, on the other, see Hopwood *et al.* (2005).
5 "Experience with the use of economic instruments in Europe", speech by Professor J. McGlade director of the EEA, March 2007, available at www.eea.europa.eu/media/speeches/19–03–2007 (accessed 5 October 2013).
6 This curve is named after the Noble-prize winning economist Simon Kuznets (1901–1985), who proposed a similar curve demonstrating the relationship between GDP and social inequality.
7 This has notably been shown at the European level through the Cardiff process.
8 See, notably, the conclusions of the EPIGOV project (www.ecologic.de/projekte/epigov/).
9 See, among others, the TEEB report, *The Economics of Ecosystems and Biodiversity for National and International Policy Makers – Summary: Responding to the Value of Nature 2009*. www.teebweb.org.

Bibliography

Bayon Denis, Flipo Fabrice, and Schneider François (2010), *La décroissance. Dix questions pour comprendre et en débattre*. Paris: La Découverte.

Beck Ulrich, Giddens Andrew, and Lash Steven (1996), *Reflexive Modernisierung. Eine Kontroverse*. Frankfurt/Main: Suhrkamp.

Boulanger Paul-Marie (2008), Une gouvernance du changement sociétal: le transition management, *La Revue Nouvelle* 11: 61–73.

Boulding Kenneth E. (1981), *Evolutionary Economics*. London: SAGE.

Boyce James K. (2002), *The Political Economy of the Environment*. Northampton: Edward Elgar.

Cochet Yves (2005), *Pétrole Apocalypse*. Paris: Fayard.

Cohen David (2009), *La prospérité du vice. Une introduction (inquiète) à l'économie*. Paris: Albin Michel.

Cour des comptes (CdC) (2005), *La coordination de la politique fédérale de développement durable. Rapport de la cour des comptes transmis à la Chambre des représentants*. Brussels.

Daly Herman (1991), *Steady-State Economics*. Washington: Island Press.

Eising Reiner and Kohler-Koch Beate (1999), *Governance in the European Union: A Comparative Assessment*. London: Routledge.

Hajer Marteen (1995), *The Politics of Environmental Discourse: Ecological Modernization and the Policy Process*. Oxford: Oxford University Press.

Halpern Charlotte (2007), *On the Europeanisation of environmental policy instruments: the limited effects of instrumental innovation in the case of France*. NEWGOV research report 09/D04.

Hopwood Bill, Mellor Mary, and O'Brian Geoff (2005), Sustainable development: mapping different approaches, *Sustainable Development* 13(1): 38–52.

Intergovernmental Panel on Climate Change (IPCC) (2013), *Fifth Assessment Report (AR5). Summary for Policymakers*. Available at: www.ipcc.ch/ [Accessed 5 October 2013].

Jackson Tim (2009), *Prosperity without Growth, Economics for a Finite Planet*. London: Earthscan.

Latouche Serge (2006), *Le pari de la décroissance*. Paris: Fayard.

Loorbach Derk (2007), *Transition Management, New Modes of Governance for Sustainable Development*. Utrecht: International Books.

Lovins Amory B., Lovins L. Hunter, and Hawken Paul (1999), A road map for natural capitalism, *Harvard Business Review* 77(3): 145–158.

Martinez-Alier Joan, Pascual Unai, Vivien Franck-Dominique, and Zaccai Edwin (2010), Sustainable de-growth: mapping the context, criticisms and future prospects of an emergent paradigm, *Ecological Economics* 69(9): 1741–1747.

McGlade Jacqueline (2007), Experience with the use of economic instruments, European Agency for the Environment. Speech delivered on 19 March 2007.

McNeill John Robert (2001), *Something New Under the Sun: An Environmental History of the Twentieth-Century World*. Allen Lane: Penguin Press.

Meadows Dennis H., Meadows Donnella L., Randers Jorgen, and Behrens III Williams H. (1972), *The Limits to Growth (Report to the Club of Rome)*. New York: Universe Books.

Neumayer Eric (2010), *Weak Versus Strong Sustainability: Exploring the Limits of Two Opposing Paradigms*. Cheltenham: Edward Elgar.

Newig Jens, Voss Jan-Peter, and Monstadt Jochen (2008), *Governance for Sustainable Development: Coping with Ambivalence, Uncertainty and Distributed Power*. London: Routledge.

Organisation de coopération et de développement économiques (OCDE) (2008), *Perspectives de l'environnement de l'OCDE à l'horizon 2030*. Paris: OCDE.

Purdey Stephen (2010), *Economic Growth, the Environment and International Relations: The Growth Paradigm*. London: Routledge.

Rist Gilbert (2003), *The History of Development: From Western Origins to Global Faith*. London: Zed Books.

Rist Gilbert (2010), *L'économie ordinaire. Entre songes et mensonges*. Paris: Presses de Sciences-Po.

Schumacher Eric F. (1973), *Small Is Beautiful: A Study of Economics as if People Mattered*. London: Blond and Briggs.

Shove Elizabeth and Walker Gordon (2007), CAUTION! Transitions ahead: politics, practice, and sustainable transition management, *Environment and Planning A* 39(4): 763–770.

Spaargaren Gert, Mol Arthur P.J., and Buttel Frederick H. (2006), *Governing Environmental Flows: Global Challenges to Social Theory*. Cambridge: MIT Press.

Stern Nicholas (ed.) (2006), *The Stern Review Report: The Economics of Climate Change*. London: HM Treasury.

Wilkinson David (2007), Environmental Policy Integration at EU level – State-of-the-art Report. *EPIGOV Paper 4*. Berlin: Ecologic – Institute for International and European Environmental Policy.

World Bank (2012), *Turn down the Heat: Why a 4°C Warmer World Must be Avoided*, Report. Washington: World Bank.

World Commission on Environment and Development (WCED) (1987), *Our Common Future*. Oxford: Oxford University Press.

Zaccai Edwin (2010), Pour protéger l'environnement, faut-il abattre la croissance? In: Alexandra De Heering and Stéphane Leyens (eds), *Stratégies de développement durable. Développement, environnement ou justice sociale?* Namur: Presses Universitaires de Namur, 51–82.

Zaccai Edwin (2012), Over two decades in pursuit of sustainable development: Influence, Transformation, Limits, *Environmental Development* 1(1): 79–90.

Zaccai Edwin and Haynes Isabelle (eds) (2008), *La société de consommation face aux défis écologiques*. Paris: La Documentation française.

8 Prosperity and the crisis of politics

Laurent de Briey[1]

"Prosperity": the term is difficult to define, even in its formal sense. At the very least, it suggests favourable circumstances, genuine flourishing, some degree of abundance, and having one's needs met. It is the opposite of poverty and also stagnation. When we use it without further qualification, it tends to have economic and, more generally, material connotations. Yet this is, perhaps, only one way to interpret the term: one can also speak of cultural, religious, and even political prosperity.

For the purposes of this article, in any case, I will use "prosperity" to refer very broadly to development's ultimate end. Not that prosperity is development's endpoint – development is a continual process, so it makes no sense to speak of it as coming to an end. But prosperity represents what development is seeking to achieve. Yet this is only a formal definition. It needs to be refined by characterising the kind of development we have in mind. Any attempt to define prosperity thus requires an examination of the mode of development we are collectively pursuing. Defining prosperity is thus not simply a technical issue involving development indicators. In defining prosperity, we are trying to understand what should count as social progress. In this sense, defining prosperity strikes me as a fundamentally political task.

Consequently, this essay will re-situate the question of prosperity's definition within the context of a crisis of politics, which is best illustrated by the increasing difficulty that the central institutional actor in politics, the state, confronts in carrying out its key missions. I will show that this crisis of politics is rooted, on the one hand, in the peripheralisation of the state due to globalisation and, on the other, in the generalisation of neoliberal individualism which, in the name of emancipation and autonomy, has devalued the affirmation of collective values (section 1). Politics, in this context, is reduced to governance. This model limits the state's legitimacy to its efficiency in managing and producing economic resources at the expense of the collective elaboration of a social project (section 2).

This reduction of politics excludes the definition of collective values from its sphere of competence while favouring moral deregulation. The latter is premised on the same form of individualism that underlies economic deregulation. It may even promote the economic colonisation of culture more than it fosters individual autonomy (a question I will consider in section 3). True autonomy must ensure that people are responsible for the effects of their actions on others and requires a social ethos founded on a sense of participating in the same project – namely, making society more prosperous (section 4).

There is also a need to reaffirm politics as the ability to imagine prosperity as a collective endeavour that is not restricted to the question of the distribution of resources, but which also takes into account the affirmation of collective values (section 5). Awareness of the need for a political definition of prosperity, we shall conclude, contributes to political prosperity – and is the very opposite of political poverty. Prosperity in this sense refers to a degree of political development at which all functions are efficiently and sufficiently exercised and in which citizens are confident and recognise themselves in their institutions and representatives (section 6).

Space does not allow us to prove these various claims systematically – this has, in any case, often been done elsewhere. This article's ambition, rather, is to show the inner logic connecting these claims. To this end, I will rely in particular on the work of Jacques Généreux, *La dissociété*, and of Bernard Stiegler, *La télécratie contre la démocratie*, as well as on the findings of my own previous work, particularly *Le sens du politique*, whose argument I will summarise.

1 The crisis of politics

The classic, ideal-typical political model is the nation-state. In this context, the state is seen as a central, sovereign authority, one that, in other words, has the power to determine the norms and rules governing social relations in a given community. This community constitutes a nation that is characterised by a high degree of cultural and moral homogeneity which, far from being natural, is the result of conscious political construction, relying notably on mandatory education to assimilate minorities.

This model's persistence in the collective imagination surfaces in the metaphor of the island – or the space ship – to which political philosophers occasionally refer.[2] This metaphor enables them to think about the principles of justice that would govern an isolated society and to defer to a later stage of their thought process – when they discover that the island is part of an archipelago – the question of interstate relations.[3] Yet such a representation of the state must be seen now as the reason for the confusion that blinds us to the "peripheralisation" of the state resulting from globalisation and the cosmopolitanisation of reality that it induces.

Cosmopolitanisation consists in integrating people into a global human community above and beyond their national, ethnic, social, and cultural differences.[4] Mobility of any kind (goods, people, capital, information, and so on), on the one hand, and the development of risks affecting the entire planet (climate heating, nuclear energy risks, international terrorism, genetic change, etc.), on the other, have rendered obsolete the state and nation as our primary conceptual reference points. Sovereignty is gone; the winner is the ever increasing interdependence of states and people. States are no longer isolated central authorities, endowed with a monopoly of legitimate violence, but actors participating in global interactions with parties as various other states, international institutions, multinational corporations, NGOs, and so on (Sassen, 2006). This "peripheralisation" of states affects their ability to perform their three traditional functions: (1) preserving internal and external security; (2) controlling macroeconomic balances; (3) strengthening social cohesion (Vercauteren, 2001: 293–315).

At present, maintaining internal as well as external security can only be ensured through international cooperation, which unsettles the state's primary symbol, i.e. its sovereignty. Even the United States must seek international support when it undertakes a major military operation. Though such support may not be technically necessary, it is nonetheless essential to ensure the operation's legitimacy and provide it with the internal support required to bear the resulting human and economic costs. States can maintain a capacity for action only if they acknowledge the reality of their independence and if they are conscious of the fact that they can serve the national interest only by pursuing common goals.

Since the gradual integration of national economies into a single global economy over the past forty years has not been accompanied by a comparable process of political integration, states have also seen their ability to regulate their economics decline. While it cannot be denied that market deregulation – which made economic and financial globalisation possible – was not always forced upon states, but that some consciously chose it (particularly Thatcher's United Kingdom and Reagan's United States, even though the United States essentially favoured deregulation in other countries) (Généreux, 2008: 63–68), once the process had begun, states found themselves engaged in a competitive game leaving them with little elbow room. States are encouraged to cut social expenditures, taxes, and salaries in order to benefit capital. States thus find themselves in a "lose–lose" situation, in that they must model their behaviour on that of their neighbours, not to increase their competitiveness, but simply to preserve it.

The decline in the state's ability to control a nation's economy does not, however, mean that the state no longer has an economic role. To the contrary, as the relationship of subordination between them has become reversed, economics has become politics' almost exclusive concern. Since politics is no longer capable of subordinating economic relationships to a normative framework that shapes them, politics now finds itself subordinated to economic constraints and is assigned the goal of preserving economic competitiveness. But as a result, the state's third function – strengthening social cohesion – is undergoing a crisis.

Strengthening social cohesion is not simply directed at socio-economic inequalities. More broadly, it has to do with the capacity of creating a collective sense of belonging to the same society, of defining collective identity, and of making the experience of living together meaningful. Social cohesion exists when the members of a society feel they play a role in achieving a shared project. Strengthening social cohesion thus depends on fighting the inequalities that are responsible for social exclusion. It also requires the collective elaboration of a project in which citizens can recognise themselves.

Economic competition's distinctive constraints, however, place a downward pressure on the mechanisms of interpersonal solidarity. The result is increased socio-economic inequality and social exclusion. But social cohesion is also weakened by globalisation's cultural implications. As a result of both secularisation and migratory movements, the state has lost its rootedness in a political community that is, culturally speaking, relatively homogenous. Moral pluralism and multiculturalism make it problematic to define values that are shared by most citizens. Consequently, relationships between individuals tend to oscillate between indifferent tolerance, which is made possible by the lack of a sense of living together, and a defiant lack of understanding – or even full-blown xenophobia – which, too, can result in social exclusion.

Moral pluralism and multiculturalism would, however, be nothing more than factors making it a little harder for the state to maintain social cohesion had this function not been profoundly delegitimated, normatively speaking, by liberal individualism. Indeed, the primacy of economics over politics is only the most visible manifestation of the cultural pre-eminence of liberalism's uniquely individualistic anthropology.

This anthropology is founded on the methodological and perhaps even ontological claim that the individual is prior to social relations and has as its corollary the political value attached to liberty as independence, which, according to Benjamin Constant (1988), is the form of liberty characteristic of the "moderns". Whereas Antiquity equated liberty with political participation, which ensured that powers that could not be controlled would never emerge, liberal individualism sees the free individual as one whose will is submitted to no constraint. To be free is to be capable of acting on one's preferences, regardless of the value or reasonableness of such actions, and to be protected in a private sphere in which no one, not even the state, has the right to interfere (Renaut, 1997).

While liberalism's philosophical origins go back three centuries, it only became the dominant cultural framework in the second half of the twentieth century, as a result of secularisation and in reaction to totalitarianism. Constant's thought was itself already motivated by the desire to preserve the French Revolution's emancipatory aspirations from their perversion by the Terror. Thus Marcel Gauchet declares: "Today, thinking about politics must in the first place be thinking about the totalitarian state" (2005: 433). More generally, liberal individualism asserts that each individual exists independently of all transcendent values, be they social, political, or religious. Individuals are expected to acknowledge their freedom from any form of determinism. Their identity and worth depends solely on their own choices and their aspirations are limited to the satisfaction of their personal preferences, notably through political representation, which frees them from the obligation to participate in public affairs.[5]

The source of liberal individualism thus lies in an emancipatory ideal that rejects all forms of determinism, yet at the price of downplaying politics as a space of collectively elaborated projects. The individual's desire for emancipation deconstructs any sense of collective belonging and any ambition to collectively imagine a future that would be the realisation of an ideal or a sense of progress. This collective incapacity is the reason for what Bernard Stiegler (2006: 14) calls the "political misery" of our time. Our sense of "living together" is confined to the simple fact that individuals coexist on the same finite territory and have a need to share natural resources (such as air and water) as well as artificial ones (money, roads, etc.).

2 The reduction of politics to governance

With its room for manoeuvre restricted in practice and its goal of creating collective identity challenged on normative grounds, what function can politics still have? Essentially, one of governance. This fashionable term is the expression *par excellence* of the disqualification of politics as a space for elaborating a shared project in favour of the pragmatic management of resources and conflicts. Rather than embodying a political vision of society, politics is presumed to be capable, for issue after issue, of achieving pragmatic compromises between interested parties, preserving order, and guaranteeing economic competitiveness.

According to the logic of liberal individualism, an individual's liberty must be limited externally only by the liberty of other individuals, consistent with the saying that "your liberty begins where mine ends". The state is an instrument needed to ensure mutual limitations on liberty where these do not occur spontaneously.[6] These restrictions are a necessary evil required to ensure that peaceful coexistence prevails in society.

This individualistic logic is shared by neoliberalism and the left-liberalism that inspires most of the traditional parties of the left. What fundamentally distinguishes left-liberals from neoliberals is that they have far less faith in the market's spontaneous order, leading them to support a more extensive role for the state in regulating private interactions and in offsetting the shortcomings of an imperfectly competitive market. But the regulatory and redistributive roles of the state are limited by the need for economic competitiveness, which compels left-liberals to seek a compromise between efficiency and social justice. This compromise finds philosophical justification in John Rawls' difference principle (1971: 234), which holds that inequalities are justified when they improve the conditions of society's least advantaged members.[7] Thus the accumulation of wealth at the high end of the social ladder can be justified if it promotes economic activity that creates jobs and finances social security programmes.

Since the reduction of politics to governance is as pervasive on the left as on the right, the legitimacy of politics no longer depends on citizens' participation in collective will formation through political institutions, but on representatives' efficiency in managing public resources, particularly by reducing the state's operating costs, to which all citizens contribute, as much as possible (Vercauteren, 2007). The most important of political virtues has become "good governance", a term that connects managerial competence and ethics, understood as the refusal to conflate one's personal interests with those of one's constituents.

The importance that ethics has assumed in politics is typical of the logic of governance. First, the governance model, in allowing politics to become professionalised, has turned the management of public affairs into a profession. The personal careers of politicians and public affairs have converged, in a way that could turn the often denounced collusion of interests into a permanent reality. Second, to the extent that this model downplays ideological conflict between different social projects, competition between representatives is primarily based on their respective management skills. Personal ethics have become all the more important as the efficiency of management skills is hard to objectify. Jacques Généreux notes (2008: 43) that "it is easier to become a world champion in political morality than in full employment".

If the efficiency of management skills is hard to objectify, it is not, however, for lack of indicators. Key indicators include employment rates, inflation, government budget deficits, and, most importantly, GDP growth. Yet establishing a connection between such macroeconomic indicators and specific policies is a particularly speculative exercise. A government can, for example, benefit from positive economic news resulting from a previous government's policies or, more prosaically, from global economic trends over which it has little control. Despite these limitations, the governance model views economic indicators as the measures of a society's prosperity. As such, they are the ultimate goal from which political management is evaluated.[8]

In this way, a concept of prosperity that is restricted exclusively to the abundance of economic resources (Généreux, 2008: 329–343) has become pervasive. This is a direct consequence of liberal individualism and the reduction of politics to governance. Once the state is seen as a necessary evil for managing the coexistence of individuals sharing limited resources, it is only natural to try to eliminate the reason for this need: resource scarcity. Thus liberal individualism promotes a development model that is aimed at producing economic abundance, which is supposed to satisfy needs and realise desires in such a way that the reasons for rivalry between individuals declines, while others become the people with whom one can cooperate in producing the desired abundance and achieving prosperity.

3 Moral deregulation and economic colonisation

One of the normative implications of the reduction of prosperity to an abundance of economic resources is the requirement that the state be value-neutral. This requirement stands opposed, at least at the political level, to any collective assertion of values aimed at providing individuals guidance about the ways they use their freedom. Liberal individualism maintains that the state must guarantee the coexistence of private spheres, while making no pronouncements as to what should pass for "good" in these spheres, lest it overstep its role and threaten individual autonomy. The state must concern itself with the "right" rather than the "good".[9] The distinction between the right – i.e. treating each individual impartially while respecting fundamental human rights – and the good – that is, judgements about the proper way to live in a way that provides a differential evaluation of various kinds of individual behaviour – is supposed to prevent the liberal state from sliding towards the despotism that arises from endorsing a particular conception of the good life and discriminating against alternative forms of life. Rather, the state should only intervene in the realm of values to support minority cultures and lifestyles, protecting them from any discrimination by the majority culture. Like individuals, different cultures must be able to coexist peacefully in society. Ultimately, the goal is to establish a cultural market of sorts, offering individuals a wide range of cultures and conceptions of the good to which they are free to subscribe.[10]

Consequently, there is no place, at the level of the political community, where the collective quest for a form of prosperity that would incorporate cultural and moral development and an examination of the values that are constitutive of a good life could occur. This quest is confined to the private sphere's outer reaches, and possibly to social, cultural, and religious communities, despite the fact that they have been significantly weakened by pluralism and secularisation, which are consequences of the modernising process.

State neutrality is an emancipatory ideal that is difficult to reject. In a society dominated by tradition and social conformity, this ideal, moreover, represents genuine social progress. The deconstruction of traditional values which, since May '68, has triumphed symbolically is undeniably a positive thing. Yet it is strange that, particularly on the left, one finds so little concern about the curious parallels between this process and economic deregulation. Both are premised on the consecration of a purely individual conception of liberty and the fiction of an autonomous individual. Do we not have reason to fear that such similar ways of thinking will produce similar effects? If the benefits of economic deregulation are not evenly distributed, can moral deregulation really serve personal autonomy?

The justification of economic growth supposedly lies in the production of ever greater resources, allowing individuals to satisfy their preferences without economic interference. Yet the development of the capitalist economy has also transformed social values. Just as the Protestant ethic benefited early capitalism by approving the accumulation of wealth (Weber, 1992), contemporary capitalism is supported by materialistic hedonism, which emphasises the immediate enjoyment of consumer goods (Bell, 1979).

At present, consumption would appear to constitute both a duty and a value: a duty that contributes to the indispensable growth that our economy feeds off and a value to the extent that, since liberalism has reduced social life to cooperation for resource production, the possession and consumption of resources constitutes a privileged criteria for social recognition. The goal is thus a form of imagination that elicits a desire for endless consumption (Stiegler, 2005: 110–111).[11] The alienating character of a consumer economy is thus apparent in the need to keep individuals in a state of dissatisfaction by waving before their eyes the possibility of being satisfied by possessing or consuming of a particular product (Arnsperger, 2005; de Briey,[12] 2007: 460–468). Such a process is contingent on the economic colonisation of a culture.

As Habermas has continuously demonstrated in his work,[13] colonisation consists in imposing one system's developmental principles on another[14] (de Briey,

2009a: 159–164). Economic colonisation thus refers to a cultural system, including the entirety of a group's beliefs, norms, values, and lifestyles, the development of which is driven by the economic system's demand for profitability. Yet as a result of the weakening of the traditional foundations of social norms, such as the family and the school, the only institution with the power to define and spread social norms is the mass media, particularly television. It is no longer exaggerated to claim that the television set – and, more generally, the mass media as a whole – has taken the place once occupied by the priest.

This far from harmless substitution is all the more perverse in that, contrary to priests, whom one could at least presume to be sincere, the mass media is very explicitly commercial in its outlook. Even public television stations, for obvious budgetary reasons, provide a public service – i.e. that of educating rather than entertaining viewers – only incidentally and must adopt a commercial outlook lest they lose their "mass" character. Movie directors – who, as we know, are paid to incorporate the brand names of cars and drinks into their movies – marketing directors, and advertisement creators – not to mention video game designers – forge the collective consciousness and shape our conception of what counts as a successful life.

This subordination to economic demands is constitutive of the economy's "colonisation" of culture. As a result of this colonisation, we have gone from being a market economy to being a market society – that is, a society in which all subsystems are regulated by the market's distinctive principles. Liberal individualism, in seeking to preserve individual autonomy from state interference, prevents us from engaging in the essential political task of building genuinely collective frameworks and, in so doing, it surrenders individuals to a kind of economic despotism. Moral deregulation thus ultimately benefits individual autonomy less than it does the market.

4 From independence to responsibility

Liberal individualism can thus be situated at the intersection of the following triptych:

- The reduction of prosperity to material well-being;
- The reduction of the state to an instrument for managing the coexistence of free individuals;
- The legitimation of the desire to satisfy one's individual preferences.

These three components refer to the same ideal[15]: that of an individual protected from any interference by other individuals; an individual who is able to live in accordance with her own conception of the good, without being required to justify it, at least to the extent that it is compatible with the liberty-as-independence of others. Yet the adoption of a development model that is exclusively confined to material prosperity facilitates the economic colonisation of culture, while the reduction of the state to the governance model widens the breach between citizens and their representatives, with whom they have ceased to identify. Finally, allowing individuals to preoccupy themselves exclusively with their personal interests is one of the causes of the recent economic and financial crisis.[16]

To emphasise the lack of market (and particularly financial market) regulation, after thirty years of neoliberal deregulation, and to present it as one of the reasons for the crisis is to overlook the fact that neoliberal deregulation is a moral phenomenon far more than it is an economic and financial one. The crisis is not simply evidence of the self-destructive character of a development model based on infinite growth in a finite world and of a mode of production and consumption that disregards environmental and social costs; rather, it strikes me as a perfect illustration of the philosophical fraud implicit in the liberal legitimation of the pursuit of pure self-interest.

Yet the hope that the economic and financial system might be heavily regulated by the state and that a new redistribution of riches be seriously considered runs up against two limitations. First, the peripheralisation of the state discussed earlier limits its room for manoeuvre, in that effective regulation seems possible only through international cooperation. Second, in a context in which politics has been devalued and the pursuit of self-interest is more legitimate than ever, the compliance of citizens has been undermined. An individualistic logic does not encourage citizens to respect laws voluntarily when it is possible to break them without consequences. To the contrary, it favours a parasitic attitude, that is, an official recognition of existing norms combined with an individual desire to free oneself of them. Only a state capable of extremely repressive measures can, from an individualistic perspective, render conformity with the law rational. At present, this is neither possible nor desirable.

Since, fortunately, the fist of the state is simply not strong enough, it is no better suited to bring the individualistic pursuit of self-interest into line with the general interest than the invisible hand of the market. What we need is to revisit the origins of the financial and economic crisis, as well as the social and political crisis, and renounce the logic of individualism. We must recognise that the current crisis is a crisis of values, to the extent that we are all, to some degree, contaminated by the ideology of individualism. All of us, to some degree, have learned never to look beyond our own individual interest. Political decision-makers, as well as economic actors and ordinary citizens, must become conscious of the fact that living in a society means more than living side-by-side by one another as we go about satisfying our own personal preferences. The value placed on individual independence must be replaced by a sense that we, as individuals, are interdependent (Généreux, 2008: 438–440) and that we must take into account the long-term consequences of our actions and be conscious of our responsibility to one another.

This makes it necessary to break with the conception of liberty as "independence" and to embrace a definition of liberty as "autonomy" (de Briey, 2009a: 38–42). Consistent with the principles of Kantian morality upon which it is based (Kant, 1998, 2004), liberty-as-autonomy consists in following one's own principles of action in the possible hope that they may be universalised. For the most part, this means that liberty, in addition to external limits, must also have internal limits: a willingness to act consistently with one's conception of the good, not only for oneself and one's personal interests, but also in the name of universal values. Whether such values do or do not exist, whether the resulting obligations are or not known, is not relevant to this discussion. What matters is the willingness of every actor to conform to such values and to adopt the requisite behaviour, independently of the validity of their individual opinion and the prevailing social consensus on its validity. We will break with individualism only when we recognise that freedom is inseparable from the sense of moral responsibility experienced by individuals who are aware that their behaviour interacts with that of others.

The fact of the matter is that, up to this point, proponents of liberal individualism would find such a stipulation fully compatible with their own conception of politics. They might concede that, morally speaking, it is desirable that the individual prefers a conception of liberty as autonomy rather than as independence, while maintaining that, from a political perspective, the state should concern itself solely with ensuring that independent individuals coexist with one another in a spirit of justice. Yet this implies a failure to recognise that an appeal to become aware of our collective responsibility can only be meaningful from the standpoint of a social ethos that does not reduce collective life exclusively to cooperation for the purpose of producing material resources, but which takes questions of moral responsibility seriously.

If many people these days believe that it is entirely legitimate to be exclusively concerned with their own self-interest, it is because the prevailing culture is dominated by individualistic assumptions. If many at present see material prosperity as a privileged path to social recognition, it is because the quest for economic prosperity is our society's primary – if not exclusive – collective project. Similarly, it is only to the extent that society makes the desire to live a "good" life – and not simply a comfortable or even just life – central to its development project (and thus to its definition of prosperity) that we will be able to break with moral individualism. Only to the extent that society begins to value action that considers its long-term effects and its consequences for others will we be able to question the legitimacy of our individual preferences. It is, moreover, the feeling of belonging to a shared community that can create, among its members, the empathy that will dispose them to subordinate their desire to maximise their self-interest to their sense of moral responsibility.

Furthermore, the inseparability of individual thinking from collective explorations of moral responsibility rests on an epistemological foundation. Individuals do not reflect solipsistically on the values that constitute a good life. They can transcend the limits of their own particular perspective only by comparing their own points of view to those expressed in a process of intersubjective deliberation. Even if, at the end of the day, specific individuals must take responsibility for the positions (which may well be critical) they take in relation to collective discussions, these individual responses can only emerge over time through a collective process of reflection (de Briey, 2006).

In this way, the meaning of relationships between individuals is transformed. Others will no longer be seen simply as limitations of my individual liberty, with whom I can, at best, cooperate when their interests overlap with my own. Others can, rather, be seen as enabling my own liberty, as it is in relation to them that I must position myself. They are a community in which each person plays a unique role. The logic of individualism is turned on its head. Self-affirmation cannot be separated from a sense of collective belonging which can only be cultivated through a shared development project. If the latter can still be understood as the quest for prosperity, the definition of prosperity that is sought through social development is profoundly transformed. Prosperity is not simply material or economic; it is also moral.

5 A political definition of prosperity

The term "prosperity" is not easy to define, as I explained in my introduction, before proposing to define it in formal terms as "development's end". This definition makes prosperity the social progress's end result, but tells us nothing about the kind of development and progress we are seeking. To the contrary, I rejected a more substantive definition of prosperity that confined it to material or economic abundance. The ambition shared by this volume's essay of "redefining prosperity" cannot be limited to a technical assessment of the strengths and weaknesses of development indicators. It must involve a broader examination of the very kind of development and social progress – and hence prosperity – that we would like to promote.

The answer to such questions does not, however, depend on scientific expertise. On the contrary, a political community's ability to adopt such a process of questioning as its own can ground a sense of belonging and collective identity. Under the nation state, this sense of belonging expressed itself as patriotism, which united the community around shared values. These shared values were supposedly based on race, religion, and a tradition or history that the nation has in common. Liberal individualism has, however, undermined all social determinisms of this kind. Lest we adopt a reactionary position, liberal individualism can only be abandoned if our appeal to moral responsibility is based on a sense of belonging to a community founded on participation in the collective definition and construction of a project, rather than on a particular, exclusive identity.

To the extent that we see others not simply as people who share our world and whose liberty limits our own, this collective quest for prosperity must involve something more than self-interested mutual cooperation. At stake is not only an agreement on the mode of producing the resources required to live *next to* others, but some understanding as to the way in which we want to live *with* others. The common project that can serve as a basis for a sense of shared belonging must not be the search for prosperity defined solely as sustainable resource creation and distribution, but must also include an agreement on the ends we are pursuing in using these resources.

We are not advocating a conservative project that would impose a particular set of values on society. We have at our disposal neither a substantive conception of prosperity that specifically describes the level of development to which we aspire, nor a substantive conception of morality. There is no tradition, religion, or any other heteronomous foundation with the legitimacy required to impose a homogeneous set of values on society. Rather, we must consecrate the kind of social pluralism that makes it possible to engage in a collective discussion about the values that society should promote. The legitimacy of these values resides solely in the fact that they emerged from public discussion and their validity lasts only until the moment when they are called into question – a moment that is essential, since public debate always implies power relations between conflicting interests. The social deconstruction of dominant ideologies and the collective reconstruction of shared values thus constitute two inseparable moments of a single process. The important thing is not to reaffirm specific values, but to reintroduce values into public debate. Re-examining the legitimacy of action of our action is far more important than the specific (and always debatable) answers we find.

6 Towards political prosperity?

Whereas liberal individualism turns politics into an instrument for managing the coexistence of individual wills, a truly democratic understanding of politics consists, in my view, in the ways in which a collectivity acts upon itself to build the kind of society in which it wants to live. Political institutions must be spaces in which social debates are formalised and where the kind of prosperity that is collectively desired can be defined explicitly and redefined constantly.

Such an understanding of politics, which draws on republicanism, attempts to acknowledge the peripheralisation of the state. It is based on a rough outline of the three stages by which the modern state has developed:

1 The nation-state, which is characterised by state sovereignty and national homogeneity. This form is characteristic of societies that are relatively enclosed upon themselves.
2 The managerial state, consistent with the governance model, which ensures the coexistence of free agents and promotes economic production. This form became dominant in the wake of economic globalisation and increasing interdependence between states.
3 The participatory state, characterised by its capacity to express in formal terms a collective will and by the fact that citizens see their institution as reflecting their choices.

The first form is shaped by the legacy of seventeenth- and eighteenth-century royal absolutism. It sees the state as a force capable, because of the coercive powers conferred upon it by its monopoly on legitimate violence, of governing social relations in a decisive way within the framework of a society that is relatively protected from external interference. In light of the totalitarian experience of the twentieth century, this form of the state poses the philosophical problem of how state power can be limited. From this point on, the democratic ideal proves decisive. Yet its role is primarily confined to ensuring that citizens control the state apparatus, notably through elections. This control makes it possible to believe that the collectivity is capable, through the state, of freely acting upon itself.

The second form is a residual version of the first that prevails once the state has been peripheralised in the wake of globalisation. The state continues to be seen essentially as an instrument of constraint, yet as societies become increasingly interdependent, it loses its sovereignty. By passively submitting to its peripheralisation rather than acknowledging its implications, the state sees each of its primary functions thrown into crisis.

By contrast, the third form embraces the view that, as a result of its peripheralisation, any attempt to define the state in terms of its coercive powers has become obsolete. The mobility inherent in globalisation has at least partially subordinated the state's capacity for constraint to its citizens' compliance. Once a significant number of citizens have emancipated themselves from a particular state's control, the state is no longer able to manage social relations unless citizens voluntarily submit themselves to its laws. Once the state has been reduced to a service provider, interstate competition gradually destroys all capacity for political action. Such a capacity for action can be rediscovered only by developing a sense of belonging to a political community. States are thus no longer characterised by their coercive powers power, but by the extent to which they are able to formalise and articulate a collective will.

Consequently, the shift from the second to the third form depends on grammar – and specifically pronouns. It is necessary to learn once again to say "we". The individualistic framework premised on the separation of state and society expresses itself in the collective consciousness by the use of "they" and "them" to refer to politicians, as opposed to the "we" of civil society. Representation, moreover, is understood as the delegation of the management of public affairs, thus allowing citizens to devote themselves to managing their own private affairs. By contrast, the success of the participatory form of politics must manifest itself by the use of a collective "we", integrating the state and political representatives into civil society, while emphasising each individual's shared responsibility for society present and future prosperity. More than anything, participation means contributing to the ways in which a community acts upon itself.

The function of politics as a space collective will-formation and expression can be distinguished from coercive powers of any kind. Force only belongs to the essence of politics to the extent that politics is seen as an instrument for counteracting the weakness of individual wills. When the purpose of politics is to enable the expression of a collective will – and to formalise this expression through institutions – there is no need for this will to be systematically reinforced through a coercive apparatus that each individual is required to obey. Since the expression of a collective judgement is an end in itself, the desire to make it constraining is a separate question. The affirmation of a collective norm must be seen as a reference point that enables individuals to adopt their own positions, rather than as a constraint placed on individual liberty. In a globalised society, respect for norms is, in any case, ensured by approval rather than the threat of sanctions. Thus the characteristic form of the twenty-first-century state, expressed metaphorically, can no longer be that of a bureaucrat imposing restrictive regulations, but that of a legislator engaging in debate. Society must feel that, through its representatives, it is participating in a debate.[17]

Conclusion

By reinvesting politics as a space where the definition of the kind of prosperity we are seeking through our model of societal development can be collectively debated, we can break with the logic of liberal individualism and affirm politics' socialising function – that is, the creation of a society in which individuals not only live *next to* one another, but also *with* one another, and by engaging in relationships of communication and recognition based on a shared past and a shared project.

Whereas the lack of a shared project – which Bernard Stiegler (2006: 14) believes is constitutive of the "political misery" of our age – makes it possible to mobilise society to invent our future, the conception of politics as a community's ability to act on itself – though in fact, it is as much an ability to think as to act collectively – makes it possible to promote a new form of political development, one that is consistent with globalisation and the peripheralisation of the state it entails. Placing the definition of prosperity at the heart of political debates reaffirms the importance of the function, which at present has lost its legitimacy, of strengthening social cohesion through politics. It even represents its primary function, insofar as it creates favourable conditions – if not a strictly necessary condition – for realising other political functions. A sense of social belonging built around a shared project can only favour peaceful social relations and respect for the law. Collective deliberation over an expansive conception of prosperity can only undermine the pre-eminence of economics and reaffirm the primacy of politics.

Contrary to the way in which politics is devalued at present, the success of the political development promoted here expresses itself in the ability of citizens to recognise themselves in their institutions and representatives, as well as their senses of the appropriateness of the ways in which politics fulfils its functions, most importantly by reinforcing social cohesion through a definition of the kind of prosperity to which society aspires. To paraphrase Stiegler, this level of political development would be constitutive of political prosperity. This is why the search for a political definition of prosperity is central to political prosperity itself.

Notes

1 Université de Namur. For further information see author's biography at the front of this volume.
2 See, for example, Bruce Ackerman (1980).
3 This dissociation is evident in Rawls, who really only addresses international relations

in *The Law of Peoples*, which was first published in 1993, over twenty-two years after *A Theory of Justice*.

4 For what follows, see Ulrich Beck (2006).

5 For a more detailed analysis, see de Briey (2009a: 35–51).

6 This is why the governance model tends to favour private self-regulation: ethical codes, good conduct codes, the social responsibility of corporations, labelling, and so on are supposed to render state interference unnecessary.

7 That the difference principle can lend itself to such an interpretation can be explained, in my eyes, by the fact that Rawls initially conceived of his theory of justice as applied to an autarkic society symbolised by an island. This theory cannot thus by purely transposed onto societies participating in globalised economies without taking into account the resulting peripheralisation of the state.

8 I obviously do not dispute the fact that elected representatives must be capable of good governance, as much from the standpoint of ethics as effective management. Similarly, I do not dispute that economic development is central to making society prosperous. I am criticising, rather, the exclusive reduction of politics to governance and of prosperity to economic growth. Good governance and economic development are not ends in themselves.

9 See, for example, John Rawls (1988).

10 For a more detailed analysis of this point, see de Briey (2009a), beginning on p. 143.

11 This is why Stiegler sees the development of Hollywood as the main investment of American politics.

12 See my critique of Arnsperger's book.

13 See, notably, Jürgen Habermas (1984, 1985).

14 I am summarising an argument explored in de Briey (2009b).

15 Individualism's most serious advocates do not hold that individuals exist prior to any social relations. Their claim is normative: even if individuals are interdependent social beings, they should be considered independent beings in order to acknowledge that they have their own spheres of liberty and to protect them from social determinism and/or political despotism. Consequently, summarising the current state of scientific research, as Jacques Généreux has done, in order to show that individualism is purely counterfactual and emphasise that human beings are essentially interdependent, cannot be an adequate refutation. See Jacques Généreux (2008: 383–402).

16 I explore this claim in de Briey (2009b: 10–13). Here and in the follow section I draw on several points made in this article.

17 I explore this conception of politics in de Briey (2009a), particularly beginning at pages 118 and 164.

References

Ackerman Bruce (1980), *Social Justice in the Liberal State*. New Haven/London: Yale University Press.

Arnsperger Christian (2005), *Critique de l'existence capitaliste: Pour une éthique existentielle de l'économie*. Paris: Cerf.

Beck Ulrich (2006), *The Cosmopolitan Vision*. Cambridge: Polity Press.

Bell Daniel (1976), *The Cultural Contradictions of Capitalism*. New York: Basic Books.

Constant Benjamin (1988), The liberty of the ancients compared with that of moderns. In: *Politics Writings*. Cambridge: Cambridge University Press, 308–328.

de Briey Laurent (2006), *Le conflit des paradigmes*. Bruxelles: Université de Bruxelles.

de Briey Laurent (2007), Une économie authentique? Entre libération et sublimation du désir, *Revue philosophique de Louvain* 105(3): 460–468.

de Briey Laurent (2009a), *Le sens du politique*. Wavre: Mardaga.

de Briey Laurent (2009b), Aux sources philosophiques de la crise, *Places to Be*, June, 10–13.

Gauchet Marcel ([1976] 2005), L'expérience totalitaire et la pensée politique. In: *La condition politique*. Paris: Gallimard.

Généreux Jacques (2008), *La dissociété*. Paris: Points.

Habermas Jürgen (1984), *The Theory of Communicative Action, Volume 1: Reason and the Rationalization of Society*. Boston: Beacon Press.

Habermas Jürgen (1985), *The Theory of Communicative Action, Voume 2: Lifeworld and System: A Critique of Functionalist Reason*. Boston: Beacon Press.

Kant Immanuel (1998), *Groundwork of the Metaphysics of Morals*. Cambridge: Cambridge University Press.

Kant Immanuel (2004), *Critique of Practical Reason*. Mineola: Dover Publications.

Rawls John (1971), *A Theory of Justice*. Cambridge: The Belknap Press.

Rawls John (1988), The priority of the right and ideas of the good, *Philosophy and Public Affairs* 17(4): 251–276.

Rawls John (1993), *The Law of Peoples*. Cambridge: Harvard University Press.

Renaut Alain (1997), *The Era of the Individual: A Contribution to the History of Subjectivity*. Princeton: Princeton University Press.

Sassen Saskia (2006), *Territory, Authority, Rights: From Medieval to Global Assemblages*. Princeton: Princeton University Press.

Stiegler Bernard (2005), *Constituer l'Europe. 1. Dans un monde sans vergogne*. Paris: Galilée.

Stiegler Bernard (2006), *La télécratie contre la démocratie*. Paris: Flammarion.

Vercauteren Pierre (2001), La crise de l'État dans l'Union européenne. *Annuaire Français de Relations Internationales II*: 293–315.

Vercauteren Pierre (2007), Gouvernance et démocratie: quel ordre? *Fédéralisme Régionalisme* 7(2) [Société civile, globalisation, gouvernance: aux origines d'un nouvel ordre politique?]. Available at: http://popups.ulg.ac.be/federalisme/document.php?id=591

Weber Max (1992), *The Protestant Ethic and the Spirit of Capitalism*. London: Routledge.

9 Collective action and the redefinition of prosperity

On the democratic governance of the transition

Christian Arnsperger[1]

Redefining prosperity: what collective action?

The notion of prosperity that currently rules industrial-democratic[2] societies – that is, the identification of prosperity with the increase of national wealth, itself identified with the growth in GDP – is the result of a long-term historical process. Its roots are economic as well as political and cultural. The economic culture that nowadays dominates our planet has evolved over centuries. It was no one's personal decree, even though thinkers and pundits have, at one time or other, offered synthetic generalisations of some of its core elements – think of Adam Smith in the eighteenth century or Karl Marx in the nineteenth. Nevertheless, this notion of prosperity was only able to endure and to find its way deep into our cultural imagery because it enjoyed political support and was bolstered by concrete decisions. So while the idea of prosperity as growth in market wealth within the framework of an industrial-capitalist economy was never planned and forced upon us by fiat, it was certainly promoted through the *public management of growth.*

This management operates essentially through economic incentives and social formatting. It embeds citizens – in a more or less conscious way – within the cogs and wheels of a logic they did not choose, but which provides the framework that lends meaning to their lives. There is little need nowadays to dwell on the close linkages that exist between growth, employment, and debt. They impel political and economic decision makers to move ahead in ways that constantly reinforce the logic at hand, while mere citizens, in turn, attempt spontaneously (and because ruling norms coerce them) to find their "place" inside the ongoing process. Personal prosperity de facto is measured by one's success within the logic of national – or, for the richest among us, global – prosperity, and in order to last this national prosperity needs to be managed collectively.

These days, more and more of us realise that this logic is no longer ecologically or humanly sustainable. Ecological hard-nosedness and social criticism are called upon to join forces in the face of the threefold scarcity that is, at present (and has been for a long time already), staring us in the face. First, we are fast running out of fossil energy carriers, and especially of oil (Heinberg, 2003, 2004, 2007). But even before fossil fuels start running out after having peaked, it might very well be that we will "run out of planet" because global warming, caused by emissions of carbon dioxide and other greenhouse gases, might prove destructive well in advance of the disappearance of oil and coal (Holmgren, 2009; Dessler and Parson, 2010). Finally, since this climatically problematic exploitation of scarce fossil energies is taking place within an increasingly globalised and all-encompassing industrial and financial capitalism backed by unmistakable political and military force (Klein, 2007), it seems that we have been, for some time already, running out of humanity: well before climate change started to deploy its deleterious effects, we became deeply alienated "capitalist beings" (Arnsperger, 2009).

Therefore, we are facing a threefold task: first, to massively and rapidly reduce our carbon emissions, all the way to a 90 per cent drop (at least) by 2030; second, to massively and rapidly replace non-renewable energies with renewable ones; and third, to create modes of production and consumption stripped of the alienating features we are experiencing today. We need to urgently combine ecological and anthropological sustainability: the environment as well as human beings need to be protected against the preoccupying impacts of climate change, of fossil fuel depletion and of reckless profit seeking. Within the framework of the industrial-capitalist system, the logic of GDP growth is not able to respond to all these challenges simultaneously. That is why it is so important, right now, for us to redefine prosperity.

Here we seem to be facing a paradox: it is precisely the most positive aspects of our current political life that make such a redefinition impossible. In parallel with industrial capitalism, we have witnessed the development of a form of democracy that is both entrusted with promoting and reinforcing capitalism and capable (at least to some extent) of reining it in and disciplining it. The social-democratic state carries a fundamental ambiguity in that it neither passively serves the interests of the large actors that dominate the system nor acts as a "knight in shining armour" defending citizens against the system's corrosive effects. In an imperfect democracy, it is always possible to pursue a plurality of alternative conceptions of prosperity even though it is, of course, impossible to envisage the sudden, wholesale replacement of GDP with another indicator. No democratic parliament will ever consent to a monolithic and unilateral redefinition of national or regional prosperity.

Some people argue for the pluralisation of macroeconomic indicators. This would certainly be a good thing because it would make it possible for citizens who wish to measure their own and their community's prosperity differently to refer in a more legitimate fashion to alternative measurements. However, the question is upon what new cultural and economic assumptions such alternative indicators would rest. To ask this question is to ask *which ecologically and anthropologically sustainable ways of life* could serve as new frameworks within which to elaborate new conceptions of prosperity. It is only in *real-life, full-scale experiments* within communities structured towards specific goals that new conceptions of prosperity can gradually be "put into circulation" in industrial-capitalist societies. The pluralisation of modes of socioeconomic organisation, hence of alternative forms of economy, within the dominant society, is the crucial pre-condition for the pluralisation of macroeconomic indicators.

1 Radicalising the idea of a "plural economy"

Isn't this idea of a plurality of ways of life within the current system the epitome of utopianism? It is, without a doubt – but only because the collusion between our democracy with the mechanics of industrial capitalism has become all too tight. While we cannot expect our states to save citizens from capitalism, we can nevertheless object to their inability to sufficiently disconnect socioeconomic rights from participation in capitalism. It is true that social democracy nowadays maintains a vast public employment sector as well as a large social economy sector where people can work in not-for-profit activities that are usually not highly paid but that carry alternative values. Sure enough, there is considerable democratic value nowadays in the logic of the "plural economy" which contemporary democracy empowers through subsidies financed from taxing private profits. It demonstrates that the idea of public support for alternative socioeconomic conceptions is not absurd.

However, as we know from observing what happens "when the music stops" (Blinder, 2013), the logic of public subsidies and employment is deeply dependent on GDP growth. If they want to maintain thriving public services and a stable social economy sector, states need to not just avoid killing the hen that lays the golden eggs – in our case, industrial capitalism – but to possibly help it grow more plump so that it might keep on giving away some of its eggs to be redistributed. Can this social-democratic logic survive the threefold challenge I outlined above, and especially the two first ones – global warming and the depletion of fossil fuels? This question might seem a bit far-fetched, but this is only because we do not yet fully perceive the extent to which ecological scarcity will, in a not-so-distant future, start eating away at the profit margins of the industrial-capitalist private sector, and therefore at the tax revenues of states. The hen will probably lay fewer and fewer golden eggs because the way it gets its food will come up against ecosystem barriers. The alternative *but intra-systemic* alternative conceptions of wealth embodied in public service and in the social economy will become less and less viable as classical, *intra-systemically conceived* prosperity measured by GDP growth starts to dwindle.

The logic of a "plural economy" needs to be pushed further – not in order to establish for all eternity some "reservations" in which associations or public actors can deploy an "alternative" logic, but in order to deepen the democratic ethos itself. Democracy should not mean only giving all citizens equal opportunities to fully participate in the cogs and wheels of industrial capitalism. Such generalised participation, to which a majority of citizens claims to aspire (especially when they are poor, disenfranchised or unemployed), boils down to seeking to generalise a way of life which, despite all its internal diversity, is globally unsustainable. Democracy should allow those citizens who feel so inclined to take up full-scale experimentation with sustainable, frugal ways of life that carry a small carbon footprint, are low on alienation, and have a lot of relational content. A full-blown democracy – which is not what goes today under the guise of social democracy – ought to facilitate and accompany its citizens' socioeconomic experiments.

Today, redefining prosperity means allowing the emergence of citizens' initiatives that are sufficiently structured and long-lasting so that new conceptions of prosperity, of human flourishing and wealth, of work, and so on, can be borne out by socioeconomic experimentation. Within the framework of democracy, it is this pluralisation – and not some hypothetical replacement of one definition of prosperity by another – that will make it possible to move beyond the all too monolithic universe of contemporary economic policy. To redefine prosperity means to democratically orchestrate the grassroots pluralisation of conceptions of prosperity – it means to steer in an open way a transition towards a genuine *plural economy* in which non-capitalist, frugal, convivial ways of life can emerge and stabilise without fearing marginalisation. This is my central thesis in this chapter.

2 The age of conscious evolution

We are going to have to reconstruct biological, agricultural, but also – more broadly – economic and social systems that incorporate the three imperatives put forward earlier: the shift towards renewable energy sources, the mutation towards frugal ways of life, and the development of non-capitalist modes of production and consumption. In particular, the notion of *resilience* – so central today within the "transition towns" movement (Hopkins, 2007) – is linked to this idea of designing social and economic mechanisms that are deliberately self-limiting. Furthermore, we will need to be especially watchful in order to remain aware of the "true nature" of the interacting entities, so that we can devise global interaction mechanisms that make self-limitation feasible and workable. This is not at all the case in our growth-oriented civilisation where fiscal, financial and market incentives are directed at agents who are assumed to be seeking maximum wealth, profit, resources, and goods:

> Because of the growth and development culture of the last 300 years, we tend to think that people have always exploited every opportunity for growth in numbers and material wealth and that it was only environmental and external constraints that contained humanity. However, there is ample evidence of traditional and indigenous people[s] living in the midst of abundance that they did not seek to exploit.
>
> (Holmgren, 2002: 187)

What characterises such peoples – and this is something which we could very well emulate nowadays – are individual mentalities and a shared way of life, as well as a cosmology, such that the non-depletion of nature's abundance, the letting-be of wildlife and non-human species, and so on, are a spontaneous part of daily existence (see, e.g. Anderson, 2010; Berkes, 2012). The peoples of which Holmgren is speaking were de facto endowed with global, cultural, and religious schemes that made it unnecessary to regulate the actions of individuals from the top down. These societies could therefore afford not to go into regulatory details – these details would spontaneously flow from the global scheme of a culture and a spirituality (see, e.g. Wolff, 2001).

Nowadays in the age of social engineering, this sort of innocence is no longer accessible to us as such. What traditional peoples did spontaneously we need to do intentionally – even if it means programming ourselves individually and collectively for a new spontaneity.... This strange "re-programming" is a delicate task if ever there was one, but it will have to be part and parcel of any ecological and economic transition towards sustainability. We modern humans no longer blindly obey taboos or traditions. We therefore have no choice but to shape our own development – to create ourselves, so to speak, right down to the values to which we deliberately choose to submit.

If ecological and economic transition is going to have any significance for us, we need to recognise that we have entered a new epoch in evolution: the epoch of *conscious evolution* (Marx, 1998; Cullinan, 2011). We are in charge of our own human nature and our own way of being human. Right down to our brains, we possess a "plasticity" (Malabou, 2004) that allows us to make our lives into a terrain of permanent experimentation – social experimentation on the one hand, through the design of communal ways of life, of rules and of political orientation; human experimentation on the other hand, through the design of ways of inner life and of spiritual orientations. Our philosophies of life, all the way to our very cosmologies, are today objects of evolution, and we understand that we make them consciously evolve ourselves, thanks to our autonomy and freedom.[3]

3 Dissensus and "muddling through"

Let me insist that in our democratic day and age, this conscious evolution cannot be decreed as *forced* evolution. One of the unassailable and irreversible conquests of modernity is that evolution requires very wide-ranging freedom to experiment. In order to collectively orchestrate the transition we will therefore have to value plurality and diversity when it comes to ways of life and to choices of community structure. The ecological principle of biodiversity needs to also be applied to what I call *socio-diversity* (Arnsperger, 2010a). In this context, John Michael Greer calls for a culture of "dissensus": given that there is radical uncertainty about future scenarios (global warming, decline in non-renewable energy sources) and about the practical solutions (socioeconomic practices, styles of community, tools, etc.) that will need to emerge as we go along,

> encouraging people to pursue conflicting and even diametrically opposed options increases the chance that someone will happen on an answer that works. Dissensus is not simply the vacuum left by a lack of consensus. It has its own methods, values and style, and its results differ in kind from

> those of consensus or other methods of decision-making such as majority rule.
>
> (Greer, 2009: 96)

A genuine democracy accepts dissensus among its citizens all the way down to their ways of life and to the kinds of identity quests they pursue (for a philosophical discussion of dissensus in politics, see especially Ziarek, 2001).

This connects up with another key concept, that of "muddling through". Greer's idea is that "the strategy of muddling has much to recommend it" because

> no one knows what an ecotechnic civilisation would look like. (…) What we do know is that certain things are not working now and need to be changed; and that certain other things that still work may not work for long, so that having replacements handy is probably wise. In a situation of this sort, betting everything on one grandiose plan for the future is a poor bet. A wiser approach would encourage many different responses to the situation.
>
> (Greer, 2009: 93–94)

According to Johnson (2010), in spite of their having been largely co-opted by the economic system, our democracies possess one important virtue: they allow sufficient "muddling" – made of multiple deliberations, committees, votes, double-checks, appeals, and so on – so that the diversity of options within the dissensus can play itself out fully without risking uniformity or conformity from a totalitarian regime or from a conspiracy of powerful economic actors.

Of course, there is a very close kinship between the idea of muddling and that of experimentation. In fact, they might as well be synonyms. Many ecologists are mistaken, it seems to me, when they interpret these ideas too narrowly in terms of "adaptation". The picture that tends to emerge is that of human beings trying to tinker around resourcefully in order to stay alive and to transmit their survival techniques to the next generation. However, as underscored for instance by the voluntary simplicity movement (Grigsby, 2004), what is involved in personal transformation and in the evolution of individual consciousness is not distinct from what is involved in creating new communities and new rules.

In sum, personal and spiritual experimentation is not separable from collective and communal experimentation (Arnsperger, 2009). To put it differently, we are patching ourselves together in the space of spiritualities, all the while patching our communities together in the space of socioeconomic modes of organisation. The citizens of our social democracies should claim the right to this twofold muddling process – in which "patchiness" is actually a virtue – throughout their whole lives. Is this, rather than the constant formatting of lives by the imperatives of industrial-capitalist growth, not the true meaning of lifelong training?

Therefore, our societies should facilitate both free collective-communal experimentation and free personal-spiritual experimentation. We need to re-think our modern societies in the form of *egalitarian laboratories of personal as well as collective experimentation* within utopian groups that respect the norms of freedom and autonomy imposed by our democracies. Equality of opportunity does not only mean the equal possibility for all of participating in "social cooperation" within the current socioeconomic system, given a determined conception of "human nature". It means first and foremost an equal access for all to the *meaning resources* (philosophical ideas, psychological and symbolic tools, networks of political practices, spiritual conceptions and practices) that encourage a re-thinking and a re-shaping of the social and, intermeshed with it, the human. To militate for "another world" within our pluralist democracies means having – as a citizen – the right and the effective possibility of shaping oneself and the collective within a democratic entity that tolerates and encourages experimentation: to work for the whole, to work on oneself.

4 A common ground for shared claims

Accordingly, all citizens' movements interested in the transition should have two things in common: (1) the awareness that each one of them is experimenting on the backdrop of radical uncertainty; (2) the call for radical democracy – rooted in an ethic of dissensus instead of an ethic of consensus or majority – as a means of letting these different experiments co-exist and perhaps converge over time. Therefore, there should be a shared claim as to means and rights that will make this radical democracy possible and that will allow motivated citizens to disconnect from the dominant logic without losing their rights and their basic security. This will be the only way of initially protecting the gradually emerging alternative (non-capitalist, local, domestic, etc.) economies and of seeing the development of economic activities that carry new meanings and generate merely sufficient – rather than maximal – material wealth.

Just because people might share these general values does not mean that they can find easy answers to the many concrete questions that are bound to come up when they attempt to articulate the various options, to choose among them, and so on. A transition town will still have to decide whether it promotes permaculture as strongly as it promotes the Natural Step or biodynamic agriculture. An eco-neighbourhood might not be able to accommodate all movements on an equal footing and so there are likely to be tradeoffs, frustrations, and rivalries. Still the objective has to be clear: the transition towards a sustainable plural economy and a culture of sustainability will only be viable if our democracies make room for an *ecology of experimentations* – a genuine socio-diversity composed of as many experiments as can realistically be given the right to exist and develop. This is the diversity that has to be demanded above all.

5 A new conception of equality of opportunity

An ecological and economic transition will only be possible if, within today's industrial-capitalist society, the "pro-growth consensus" has started to fall apart.

This is the sort of de-legitimisation towards which Ivan Illich was already pointing back in the 1970s:

> [The] political choice of a frugal society remains a pious dream unless it can be shown that it is not only necessary but also possible: (1) to define concrete procedures by which more people are enlightened about the nature of our present crisis and will come to understand that limits are necessary and a convivial life style desirable; (2) to bring the largest number of people into now suppressed organizations which claim their right to a frugal life style and keep them satisfied and therefore committed to convivial life; and (3) to discover and revalue the political and legal tools that are accepted within a society and learn how to use them to establish and protect convivial life where it emerges.
>
> (Illich, 1973: 101)

Spiritual work on oneself and personal experimentation are crucial to this threefold process of awareness-building and mobilisation – especially for Illich's point (1). Once the pro-growth consensus as to what defines prosperity has begun to crack, and once the idea that model change will occur through the emergence of local and voluntary convivial initiatives has gained ground and taken root, what needs to be fundamentally changed is the role we attribute to the state in regulating and orchestrating prosperity. As to point (2) above, the *de jure* attribution to citizens of a scheme of income support – for instance in the form of a basic income or of a negative income tax (Arnsperger, 2010a; Arnsperger and Johnson, 2011) – would be important, but such support would only be meaningful if the unconditional income were seen at the same time as a kind of "economic transition income" (ETI) that allows every individual to free inside themselves the potentials of self-creation and collective creation that had been left dormant in the dynamic of industrial productivity and of competitive enhancement of the value of private capital. Thus, as underscored by Illich's point (3), the primary task of citizens is to root their call for an ETI within the very structure of liberal pluralism:

> We, the citizens in search of conviviality, demand within this industrial-capitalist society and in the name of the democratic ideal it proclaims in its official institutions, the right to experiment with non-industrial and non-capitalist ways of life. Refusal by the industrial-capitalist institutions to grant us the effective possibility of viably carrying out this experimentation will have to be interpreted as a deep discrimination and as a manifest breach of the notion of equality of opportunity upon which so much rests in our liberal democracies.

The state's primary task should be to secure for us, as citizens, an equal opportunity of access to a non-growth-centred way of life that can actually be lived in real time and on a real scale. This is the main purpose of democracy today, and not the subservient steering of the mechanisms of heteronomous, growth-centred capitalism, which blind human beings as to the potentials they carry inside them. Growth has merely become a bad utopia, that is, an ideology that misrepresents and distorts what is really at stake in our trajectories of social and personal experimentation.

What lies at the root of today's notion of transition is the pluralistic imperative of a *real – as opposed to merely formal – egalitarianism of convivial experimentations*. This is what equality of opportunities means, or ought to mean. This is what citizens in search of a transition should demand, regardless of their specific personal options in the realms of spirituality and ecology. In this sense, the diversity of paths will not be a weakness but a strength – on the condition that each path shares with all other paths the aim of ushering in a viable transition, rather than "winning" on the "market" for agricultural methods or in the "competition" between philosophies of nature.

6 Principles for the collective orchestration of transition

Given how radically uncertain future scenarios are, it is very difficult to say what these alternative economies, these frugal communities, and so on, will look like in detail. However, a couple of basic principles that are likely to rule most – if not all – these initiatives can be outlined.

What individual behaviours?

In the area of individual behaviour, the basic principle is the *bull's eye*. (I draw my inspiration directly from the idea of a "bull's-eye diet" developed by Sharon Astyk (2008: 186–193).) The idea is simply to lead a life centred, as much as possible, around the centre of our being – on the one hand, the "inner centre" that spiritual practices point toward, on the other hand the "bioregional centre" which is either the home (in case one chooses a domestic economy), the neighbourhood or town (in case one chooses a community economy such as an eco-neighbourhood or an ecovillage) or the region (if one chooses, more classically, a regional or sub-regional economy). Contrary to the logic of the globalised industrial-capitalist economy in which – to paraphrase the fifteenth-century theologian Nicholas of Cusa – "the center is everywhere and the circumference nowhere", the logic of sustainability requires that the centre of our existence and the circumferences of the successive concentric circles be clearly identified, and that we use them in order to establish limits in our lives, boundaries that ought not to be crossed except in case of dire necessity. In practice, this leads to a rather complex choice rule:

(a) First psychological-spiritual question: Do I really need *X*?
(b) First technical-economic question: If the answer to (a) is Yes, can *X* be produced closer rather than further away?

(c) Ethical-political question: If the answer to (b) is Yes, can this more local production be carried out with less labour alienation and exploitation rather than more?

> If the answer to (c) is Yes, obtain your supply of *X* at this local level
> If the answer to (c) is No, then

(d) Second technical-economic question: Is there some less local level where the production of *X* can be carried out with less labour alienation and exploitation rather than more?

> If the answer to (d) is Yes, obtain your supply of *X* at this less local but more ethical level
> If the answer to (d) is No, then

(e) Second psychological-spiritual question: Upon reflection, do I really, *really* need *X*?

> If the answer to (e) is Yes, have *X* produced at the most local level possible despite the poor working conditions
> If the answer to (e) is No, feel satisfaction at your moral progress and pursue your local existence without *X* – while, of course, militating for an improvement in working conditions…

Obviously, contrary to the de-centring or even the *loss of centre* involved in the globalised industrial-capitalist model, the transition will inevitably be accompanied by a movement of re-centring and re-rooting. Such a movement is inscribed within the choice rule itself and implies two things: on the one hand, a resurgence – without machismo and without the type-casting of women – of the domestic economy, of the family hearth as a place where food and various other commodities and services are produced instead of being, as they are currently, imported from outside the family; on the other hand, a resurgence of small-scale, bio-organic agriculture as well as of numerous professions linked to "soft" mobility and to the maintenance of local economic and social ties.

Re-localisation and protection

Through this process, the "world economy" will again become for us what it has never stopped being for the many so-called "poor" countries or regions of the planet – a federation of local economies, each of which practices a healthy and just dose of protectionism. According to the US farmer and philosopher Wendell Berry,

> the idea of a local economy rests upon two principles: neighborhood and subsistence. In a viable neighborhood, neighbors ask themselves what they can do or provide for one another, and they find answers that they and their place can afford. This, and nothing else, is the *practice* of neighborhood.

> This practice must be, in part, charitable, but it must also be economic, and the economic part must be equitable; there is a significant charity in just prices. Of course, everything needed locally cannot be produced locally. But a viable neighborhood is a community; and a viable community is made up of neighbors who cherish and protect what they have in common. This is the principle of subsistence. A viable community, like a viable farm, protects its productive capacities. It does not import products that it can produce for itself. And it does not export local products until local needs have been met. The economic products of a viable community are understood either as belonging to the community's subsistence or as surplus, and only the surplus is considered to be marketable abroad. (...) In charity, moreover, it must refuse to import goods that are produced at the cost of human or ecological degradation elsewhere.
>
> (Berry, 2002: 260)

The crucial phases, which are directly connected with questions (a) and (e) in the above individual-choice rule, are of course the following: "until local needs have been met" and "only the surplus is considered to be marketable abroad". Indeed, the dynamics of transition toward the local is unthinkable in the absence of two elements: on the one hand, the preoccupation with reducing our needs so that the rest of the planet can have enough and is not exploited in the name of our alleged "needs", which often are merely inessential cravings; on the other hand, the preoccupation with maximising the surplus that we put at the disposal of the citizens of other parts of the planet, so that they can have enough of what their own local economy is unable to produce. Concerning this second element, as Berry writes,

> the idea that local needs should be met first and only surpluses exported does not imply any prejudice against charity toward people in other places or trade with them. The principle of neighborhood at home always implies the principle of charity abroad. And the principle of subsistence is in fact the best guarantee of giveable or marketable surpluses. This kind of protection is not "isolationism".
>
> (Berry, 2002: 260–261)

As to the first element, the precise extent of the reduction each individual citizen or group ought to carry out is difficult or even impossible to compute. However, there are methods linked to the evaluation of one's desired ecological footprint and to the reductions in consumption that could roughly allow one to attain it. (See for instance Merkel (2003) who offers a very detailed and easy-to-use numerical method. For an up-to-date discussion in the business area, see, e.g. Epstein (2008).) At any rate, short of making very precise personal footprint reductions compulsory via an authoritarian government backed by some hypothetical infallible science committee, no citizen or group will ever know with absolute certainty whether its efforts will contribute sufficiently to global reduction, especially given the potential negligence of numerous other citizens and groups. Whatever the case may be, what matters above all is that our democracies stimulate critical education (Bonnett, 2004) and – via the free circulation of philosophical and spiritual tools – the ability of citizens to evaluate, criticise, and reduce their needs without taking genuine enjoyment out of their lives. Citizens are bound to notice that, on the contrary, the reflected reduction of one's needs is a major source (time-honoured in all philosophical and spiritual traditions) of joy and contentment, independently even of whether others are also, and in equal measure, reducing theirs.

Land reform

As I said, it is difficult to know exactly what future would be in store for a network of quasi-self-sufficient ecovillages or for a federation of transition towns linked together by local, justice-oriented trade agreements, in which families would grow food in private or communal vegetable gardens and farms. In any case, our democracies are going to have to carry out a fundamental reform of citizens' access to land. This is a very touchy topic because it brings up images of agrarian reforms implemented by the socialist revolutions back in the 1920s and 1930s, or by Mugabe's dictatorship in Zimbabwe at the end of the century. Nevertheless, it is unavoidable that many more citizens than is currently the case – that is, apart from large farms, agro-industrial businesses and real-estate firms – will have to be given a right to cultivate the soil, to raise cattle and to keep the corresponding produce for local self-consumption. What use is it to give everyone an unconditional basic income if the only option for spending that income is to remain in the dominant economy and to be a customer of the large chains of agro-business distribution?

An important step will be to establish a register of plots of land to be made available for alternative initiatives, and to legally force all towns and cities to host a quota of ecovillages and/or eco-neighbourhoods on their territory. Another complementary measure of considerable urgency will be to stop allocating plots of land to energy-consuming industrial and commercial activities that have no evolutionary potential – with the certainty that one will have to confront the anger of the holders of entrenched economic interests (mega-retail companies, road and air transport companies, etc.).

Re-thinking the race to productivity

An indispensable complement to all of the above is that our democracies renounce the race to constantly boost labour productivity (Jackson, 2009; Schor, 2010). We therefore need to urgently deepen our analysis of and reflection on the links between employment and environment in order to see how local and low-productivity sectors could be assisted and protected in our regions. One temptation to be shunned is that of creating sectors that feed into a globalised "green capitalism" – essentially because in such sectors the perverse effects of today's industrial-capitalist logic will remain intact (Rogers, 2010; Dauvergne and Lister, 2013). On the contrary, there should be a focus on sectors that are spontaneously "green" simply because they operate on principles of proximity and subsistence and are, by that token, characterised by small-scale production without growth ambitions or compulsions, by local anchoring that emphasises short-distance human ties (including in employment and finance) over long-distance mechanical ties (Shuman, 1998, 2006, 2012; Cortese, 2011; Souchier, 2013).

Interestingly, the currently much-hailed "green industries" such as insulation, bioclimatic construction, solar panels, or windmills will not in the least occupy centre stage here. As shown persuasively by Astyk (2008), the vast majority of collectives and citizens will not – especially in a context where GDP growth falters and where the dominant system in which they are still participating enters a crisis – have the means to invest heavily in such high-tech options. In addition, it is clear that these green industries will for a long time yet remain large consumers of fossil fuels, so that their net energy and resource savings will be extremely low, or even nil or negative. Better, therefore, to bank on the long-term reparatory virtues of re-localisation, self-provision, and self-consumption instead of costly green-tech "ecological restoration". Consistently applying the bull's-eye principle by masses of citizens will likely do more for sustainability than the pricey development of green industries.

Sure enough, such industries would be – and, in fact, already are – better received by the economic and financial establishment than measures of income support for voluntary simplifiers, permaculturists, de-consumers, inhabitants of radical ecovillages, and the defenders of domestic and village economies. These citizens have little or nothing to contribute to incumbent industrial-capitalist dynamic; they are, so to speak, beyond repair for the dominant logic and, therefore, much more of a threat – if not yet in terms of numbers, at least in terms of ideas. The key choice will be whether to focus on the rebirth of local professions and "traditional", low-productivity activities that have high human content or on the emergence of green industries that can, just like today's gray and brown ones, swiftly be made more efficient and global.

What role for the state?

There is little doubt that the payment of the ETI in the form of a basic income or of a negative income tax, as well as the various measures we have been discussing, will need to be orchestrated by the state. The particular way in which this is done, and the particular levels of power involved, will depend on each particular democracy.

Is it not time to demand that – as a complement to the ministries of economics and finance and endowed with similar budgetary powers – a genuine *ministry of economic transition* be put into place, entrusted with the task of financing (via the ETI and various subsidies, and why not via a public bank oriented towards transition issues), coordinating and accompanying these economically and socially innovative citizens' initiatives? Ideally, of course, all levels of power from the municipalities upward to the European Commission, through the subregions, the regions and the members states, should create such transition ministries and network them in such a way that – in accordance with the subsidiarity principle – the projects of level n can "move upward" democratically to level $n+1$ and be coordinated with the help of democratically instituted rules and procedures. The function of such a ministry would be to stimulate, frame, and coordinate the creation of new logics of production, consumption, and distribution, of new relational logics conducive to heightened non-market and, above all, non-capitalist social links, of new employment logics and modes of labour organisation, and so on.

As a first step, we could certainly enhance the viability of the existing – and constantly, albeit slowly, expanding – network of transition towns and communities which gather citizens who want to develop and scale up various social and economic innovations: resilient local communities structured to withstand the shocks and benefit from the opportunities of a post-carbon world (Wilson, 2012); integrative approaches to population, food, energy, monetary-financial, as well as transport and health, with a view to globally reducing circuits and intensifying "alternative" social logics such as mutual credit and gift-giving (Greco, 2009; Eisenstein, 2011); re-localisation of economic activities and financing circuits, implying the creation of local complementary currencies (Lietaer and Dunne, 2013); creation of participatory models within these shorter circuits, inspired by workers' and consumers' councils and by democratic self-management (Magnuson, 2008, 2013).

Of course, "transition citizens" have not yet reached a critical mass. They could, however, do so soon enough. According to recent studies the "cultural creatives", who admittedly contain other categories than just the transition citizens, have reached 24 per cent of the population in the United States and 17 per cent in France. One can thus estimate that the Transition Towns movement is supported by a relatively small fraction of the European population, but that this fraction is probably growing rapidly. The expansion of Transition projects is significant and is drawing interest even from outside of the "transition" crowd proper – which suggests that the business as usual of political decision making "among good friends" (elected officials, lobbyists, and party apparatuses) is stalling. Green capitalism would therefore be profitable only in the very short run, even when looked at from an electoral angle.

In the short run, green capitalism should be encouraged to the extent that it is a lesser evil compared to grey and brown capitalism. However, this encouragement should never be at the cost of stifling the transition to a post-capitalist plural economy. This is a politically complex problem because it concerns the links between politicians, industrial and academic lobbyists, and trade unions. If the political decision makers lend too sympathetic an ear to pro-capitalist lobbies and think tanks, they will fall short of the lucidity required by the third priority I outlined at the beginning – namely, the creation of modes of production and consumption stripped of the alienating features we are experiencing today. If so, they will probably compromise the possibility of a genuine transition. This means that more room should probably be made, within the political decision process itself, for citizens' groups and associations that explicitly carry forward transition projects and ideas. The question is not simply whether we want to create and maintain an "associative sector" in general, or even whether we will foster a "social economy" sector, but whether political decisions will be increasingly informed and influenced by collaborations or even co-optations involving *transition* associations. These grassroots citizens' groups could certainly represent a significant counterweight to *status quo oriented* lobbies and think tanks, and they could help the government not to take irreversible measures that would forever sway the economy away from a transition trajectory.

In their current configuration, trade unions – and, more generally, actors involved in "social dialogue" – can hardly offer sufficient counterweights because classical social forces in the capital-labour faceoff are too exclusively focused on short-term issues such as stimulating capitalist economic growth and employment. There would be urgent need for a renewal of reflection within trade union structures, and this should be encouraged by citizens' movements.

More generally, as I said earlier, there should be intense financial support – if possible via an ETI scheme – for concrete initiatives that actually build, and seek to scale up, transition micro-projects. Unless budgets can be increased (which is always desirable), there would necessarily have to be a transfer of public resources within the budgetary masses currently allocated to the social economy, in order to put more emphasis on radical experimentation initiatives and less on "soft" support associations. Here the dilemma is a cruel one: should more resources be given to initiatives that have, in the past, done excellent work in supporting and revalidating those who are injured by the dominant system, or should more public financing be forthcoming for those initiatives that are working towards truly alternative and innovative projects? This sort of dilemma is always unsolvable except in times of increased overall public spending – but this is precisely what capitalism renders difficult if not impossible with its competitiveness imperatives and its calls for lower fiscal burdens in exchange for a (very largely illusory) growth in jobs. The only realistic short-term option is to go full-throttle for a conversion of grey and brown to green capitalism, all the while maximising public receipts from the profits of these new and profitable actors in order to finance radical transition experiment initiatives (especially through the ETI). In this way at least, the passage to green capitalism would not serve only to reaffirm the dominant logic, but rather it would ultimately assist in its supersession (Arnsperger, 2010b).

This idea seems outlandish, and both neoliberal and green think tanks will tell us that "overtaxing" the actors of green capitalism – mainly businesses – would bring the whole growth engine to a halt. This illustrates the profoundly contradictory character of green capitalism: it promises us an ecological transition which it then forces us to revise downwards, giving priority to a narrow version of the two first tasks outlined at the beginning – claiming to fulfil the urgent need for reduced carbon emissions and for a shift from nonrenewable to renewable energy sources with the creation of a few highly capitalistically profitable pockets of green-tech development and growth – but once again neglecting the third: alienation. However, a "green new deal" (see Nollet, 2008; Barbier, 2010) can only be meaningful if it is actually a "deal": public authorities support the creation of profitable green-industry-and-service sectors but these sectors – assuming they are truly motivated by "greenness" and not by money – in return accept to fit into a longer-term project in which they will, *for the sake of the ecological transition they claim to be heralding*, gradually vanish after having made it possible (through their taxes) to finance a genuinely alternative transition rooted in citizens' initiatives. Therefore, what we need is a *two-tier transition process*:

1 Engineer the transition from grey-brown to green capitalism.
2 Use the means thus made available to engineer the transition from green capitalism towards a plurality of initiatives that will be spontaneously "green" because they are, in and of themselves, frugal and post-capitalist.

It is because this two-tier transition process is so complex that it would be so essential to create a ministry of transition and various – in particular, municipal and regional – institutions to orchestrate these two stages. In fact, only a public agency backed by democratic legislative and executive powers can – provided the political will is there – drive home to the actors of today's grey-brown capitalism, and especially to those of today's and tomorrow's green capitalism, that their social mission is not simply to make profits, to grow by being competitive and to act as "job creators", but also and mainly to contribute (in particular via the ETI scheme) to a transition toward a plural economy in which production, distribution and consumption will no longer be organised by green capitalism but by a galaxy of post-capitalisms – associative, democratic, self-managed, frugal, and therefore spontaneously "green".

Conclusion: the opportunity of a salutary turning point

In the 1970s and 1980s, thanks to the two oil shocks of 1973 and 1979, the industrial world seemed ripe for a radical U-turn. The flooding of the world market with cheap (mostly Saudi) oil stopped the transition in its tracks and re-started the industrial-capitalist growth machine as if nothing had happened. This led us into a deep economic and financial crisis (Rubin, 2009; Rifkin, 2011).

Will our children say that the 2010s and 2020s marked another missed opportunity during which ecologists and green parties themselves re-started the growth engine yet again as if nothing had happened, transforming "green" into a bunch of global industrial sectors with zero or even negative net energy, and at a huge public and private cost? Will it turn out that in these years we once again missed the chance for decisive re-centring and re-localisation and that, once more, we bequeathed to the next generation the task of paying off our ecological and financial debts? If the general principles sketched in this chapter find no hearing among the citizens and the decision makers of our democracies, there is a great risk that, indeed, we might have to await an even more disturbing collapse of our system and of the mechanisms that uphold it. It might then take yet more decades, or even centuries, before a world in equilibrium can be rebuilt.

However, many clues – among which the growing number of individuals who call themselves "cultural creatives", the increasing mobilisation of citizens for voluntary simplicity, the growing attention of the media for ecological issues and the increasing involvement of young people in reflection and alternative socioeconomic initiatives – show that the current ecological and human crisis will be an opportunity. When Juliet Schor writes of "plenitude" or when Tim Jackson coins an expression such as "prosperity without growth", these authors are not looking to minimise the urgency and depth of the issues. On the contrary, the challenge right now is to realise just how much of a resource frugal post-capitalist initiatives can be for a collective reflection on prosperity – or, rather, on *prosperities* (in the plural).

Notes

1 Université catholique de Louvain and Belgian National Fund for Scientific Research. For further information see author's biography at the front of this volume.

2 All general labels are ultimately defective, but I nevertheless offer this one to characterise the logic within which we lead our lives nowadays: a system anchored in industrial production (that is, equipped with machines and heavy tools, hence tending towards economies of scale and the substitution of capital for labour) and ruled by the principle of maximum net valuation of both physical and financial capital (that is, a logic that is "genetically" geared towards globalisation and what some of us might want to call imperialism).

3 This does not at all exclude, of course, that autonomy and freedom be rooted in collective dimensions, and in education in particular. Neither does it exclude that we might also conceive of ourselves as receiving our autonomy and freedom from a "transcendence". See e.g. Bruteau (1997), Berry (1999), or Dowd (2007).

References

Anderson Eugene N. (2010), *The Pursuit of Ecotopia: Lessons from Indigenous and Traditional Societies for the Human Ecology of Our Modern World*. Santa Barbara: Praeger.

Arnsperger Christian (2009), *Éthique de l'existence post-capitaliste: Pour un militantisme existentiel*. Paris: Cerf.

Arnsperger Christian (2010a), Revenu d'existence et promotion de la sociodiversité, *Mouvements* 64(4): 100–106.

Arnsperger Christian (2010b), Être réellement écologiste, c'est être anticapitaliste, *Politique* 63: 64–65.

Arnsperger Christian and Johnson Warren A. (2011), The guaranteed income as an equal-opportunity tool in the transition toward sustainability. In: Axel Gosseries and Yannick Vanderborght (eds), *Arguing About Justice: Essays for Philippe Van Parijs*. Louvain-la-Neuve: Presses Universitaires de Louvain, 61–69.

Astyk Sharon (2008), *Depletion and Abundance: Life on the New Home Front*. Gabriola Island: New Society Publishers.

Barbier Edward (2010), *Scarcity and Frontiers: How Economies Have Developed Through Natural Resource Exploitation*. Cambridge: Cambridge University Press.

Berkes Fikret (2012), *Sacred Ecology*. London: Routledge.

Berry Thomas (1999), *The Great Work: Our Way Into the Future*. New York: Random House.

Berry Wendell (2002), The idea of a local economy. In: *The Art of the Commonplace*. New York: Continuum, 249–261.

Blinder Alan S. (2013), *After the Music Stopped: The Financial Crisis, the Response, and the Work Ahead*. New York: Penguin.

Bonnett Michael (2004), *Retrieving Nature: Education in a Post-Humanist Age*. Oxford: Blackwell.

Bruteau Beatrice (1997), *God's Ecstasy: The Creation of a Self-Creating Universe*. New York: Crossroads.

Cortese Amy (2011), *Locavesting: The Revolution in Local Investing and How to Profit from it*. Hoboken: Wiley.

Cullinan Cormac (2011), *Wild Law: A Manifesto for Earth Justice*. Totnes: Green Books.

Dauvergne Peter and Lister Jane (2013), *Eco-Business: A Big-Brand Takeover of Sustainability*. Cambridge: MIT Press.

Dessler Andrew and Parson Edward A. (2010), *The Science and Politics of Climate Change: A Guide to the Debate*. Cambridge: Cambridge University Press.

Dowd Michael (2007), *Thank God for Evolution: How the Marriage of Science and Religion Will Transform Your Life and Your World*. New York: Viking.

Eisenstein Charles (2011), *Sacred Economics: Money, Gift and Society in the Age of Transition*. Berkeley: Evolver Editions.

Epstein Marc J. (2008), *Making Sustainability Work: Best Practices in Managing and Measuring Corporate Social, Environmental, and Economic Impacts*. San Francisco: Berrett-Koehler.

Greco Thomas H. (2009), *The End of Money and the Future of Civilization*. White River Junction: Chelsea Green.

Greer John Michael (2009), *The Ecotechnic Future: Envisioning a Post-Peak World*. Gabriola Island: New Society Publishers.

Grigsby Mary (2004), *Buying Time and Getting By: The Voluntary Simplicity Movement*. Albany: State University of New York Press.

Heinberg Richard (2003), *The Party's Over: Oil, War, and the Fate of Industrial Societies*. Gabriola Island: New Society Publishers.

Heinberg Richard (2004), *Powerdown: Options and Actions for a Post-Carbon Society*. Gabriola Island: New Society Publishers.

Heinberg Richard (2007), *Peak Everything: Waking Up to the Century of Decline in Earth's Resources*. Gabriola Island: New Society Publishers.

Holmgren David (2002), *Permaculture: Principles and Paths beyond Sustainability*. Hepburn: Holmgren Design Services.

Holmgren David (2009), *Future Scenarios: How Communities Can Adapt to Peak Oil and Climate Change*. Totnes: Green Books.

Hopkins Rob (2007), *The Transition Handbook: From Oil Dependency to Local Resilience*. Totnes: Green Books.

Illich Ivan (1973), *Tools for Conviviality*. New York: Marion Boyars.

Jackson Tim (2009), *Prosperity without Growth: Economics for a Finite Planet*. London: Routledge/Earthscan.

Johnson Warren A. (2010), *Muddling Toward Frugality: A New Social Logic for a Sustainable World*. Weston: Easton Studio Press.

Klein Naomi (2007), *The Shock Doctrine: The Rise of Disaster Capitalism*. New York: Penguin.
Lietaer Bernard and Dunne Jacqui (2013), *Rethinking Money: How New Currencies Turn Scarcity into Prosperity*. San Francisco: Berrett-Koehler.
Magnuson Joel (2008), *Mindful Economics: How the U.S. Economy Works, Why it Matters, and How it Could Be Different*. New York: Seven Story Press.
Magnuson Joel (2013), *The Approaching Great Transformation: Toward a Livable Post Carbon Economy*. New York: Seven Story Press.
Malabou Catherine (2004), *Que faire de notre cerveau?* Paris: Bayard.
Marx Hubbard B. (1998), *Conscious Evolution: Awakening the Power of Our Social Potential*. Novato: New World Library.
Merkel Jim (2003), *Radical Simplicity: Small Footprints on a Finite Earth*. Gabriola Island: New Society Publishers.
Nollet Jean-Marc (2008), *Le Green Deal: Proposition pour une sortie de crises*. Bruxelles: Le Cri.
Rifkin Jeremy (2011), *The Third Industrial Revolution: How Lateral Power is Transforming Energy, the Economy, and the World*. New York: Palgrave Macmillan.
Rogers Heather (2010), *Green Gone Wrong: Dispatches from the Front Lines of Eco-Capitalism*. London: Verso.
Rubin Jeff (2009), *Why Your World is About to Get a Whole Lot Smaller: Oil and the End of Globalization*. New York: Random House.
Schor Juliet (2010), *Plenitude: The New Economics of True Wealth*. New York: Penguin.
Shuman Michael H. (1998), *Going Local: Creating Self-Reliant Communities in a Global Age*. New York: Routledge.
Shuman Michael H. (2006), *The Small-Mart Revolution: How Local Businesses are Beating the Global Competition*. San Francisco: Berrett-Koehler.
Shuman Michael H. (2012), *Local Dollars, Local Sense: How to Shift Your Money from Wall Street to Main Street and Achieve Real Prosperity*. White River Junction: Chelsea Green.
Souchier Raphaël (2013), *Made in Local: Emploi, croissance, durabilité – et si la solution était locale?* Paris: Eyrolles.
Wilson Geoff (2012), *Community Resilience and Environmental Transitions*. London: Routledge/Earthscan.
Wolff Robert (2001), *Original Wisdom: Stories of an Ancient Way of Knowing*. Rochester: Inner Traditions.
Ziarek Ewa P. (2001), *An Ethics of Dissensus: Postmodernity, Feminism, and the Politics of Radical Democracy*. Stanford: Stanford University Press.

10 Conclusion

Who will redefine prosperity?

Robert Boyer,[1] *Isabelle Cassiers,*[2] *and Isabelle Ferreras*[3]

The journey that the reader has just undertaken is somewhat dizzying. The definition of prosperity prevalent in Western society today has proven deeply problematic. This book has sought to nourish a debate which has the potential to spark significant social change, and we leave the reader to think over the conclusions below, offered in broad strokes, which we hope will galvanise and orient public debate over our choices for thought and action.

For centuries, our economic model has promoted the concept of prosperity prevalent today, as synonymous or concurrent with the growth of material wealth. As Dominique Méda explains, the flattening of this potentially broad concept to its material dimension was made possible by a shift in morality beginning in the seventeenth and eighteenth centuries, in which the individual desire to pursue material wealth began to be seen as legitimate. The pursuit of wealth was freed from its status as a means to satisfying one's needs, and became an end in itself. The "condition of being prosperous, successful or thriving" that defined prosperity could no longer be conceived of outside the continuous pursuit of material goods. Every chapter in this book highlights both the inadequacy of the framework this historical turning point handed down to us and the wealth of perspectives that open up when the definition of prosperity is reworked.

These commonalities raise important questions that invite the reader to take a position. First, they reinforce our conviction that we have arrived at a new historical turning point, one that signals a shift as profound as the one that marked our societies three or four centuries ago. Second, on the substantial level, these contributions converge to force us to abandon an overly narrow and outmoded concept of prosperity and to fundamentally rethink this vehicle of our collective goals, adapting it to current constraints and aspirations. Third, from a procedural and political perspective, these chapters lead us to consider the redefinition of prosperity in practical terms: what actions must be undertaken, what decisions made, and what barriers overcome to give substance to a new understanding of an old term?

1 An historical crossroads: finding the turning point, daring to follow it

Expanding on Dominique Méda's contribution, Isabelle Cassiers and Géraldine Thiry explain how the goal of economic growth and the use of GDP as a key indicator are historically circumscribed, tied to social compromises and geo-political relationships that are no longer current. The current context is so different from the period of exceptional growth that occurred between 1945 and 1975 that nostalgia is fruitless: the recession of the 1970s and subsequent reconfigurations of the socio-economic system shifted the terrain too drastically, sweeping away the negotiated redistribution of wealth, strengthening the role of financial institutions, weakening or silencing the voices of many members of the population and paralysing Nation-States in the face of the naked power of globalised capital.

Solidarity as we know it – which brought society collective bargaining agreements and universal social welfare – has broken down. This is a poignant reminder that there is no market mechanism capable of fairly distributing the dividends of growth. As Thomas Périlleux and Julien Charles show, when the institutionalised compromise between social solidarity and production capacities was called into question, a deep malaise emerged, revealing the immense gap between managerial promises of "self-realisation" and the all-too-frequent experience of alienation through an often-toxic organisation of labour. Again it must be recalled that the evolution of capitalism over the course of the past thirty years has done nothing but exacerbate its inherent tendencies, laying to rest any nostalgia for a lost and utopian "golden age", and to this end, Jean De Munck's critique of consumerism questions the desirability of the lifestyle produced by the development of such a principle.

Today, the need for profound change is starkest when seen in light of the financialisation process, which has been pushed to the point of absurdity. Within the American model, financial innovation was supposed to overcome poverty by providing the least well off with easy – but ultimately predatory – home loans. The results speak for themselves: the West plunged into a major economic and social crisis that brought long-term unemployment for the most vulnerable, a new wave of poverty, tensions, and conflicts at the national and international level, and worrisome political instability.

This instability brings us to the political crisis discussed by Laurent de Briey, who locates its source in the twin trends of the State's growing subservience to the imperatives of financial globalisation and the spread of a brand of liberal individualism that makes it difficult to assert collective values. And yet there is no lack of collective challenges to these trends: the finiteness of natural resources, for example, is a *collective* constraint, and one that raises life-or-death questions for humanity. These questions are particularly evident in the field of agriculture, where, as Gaëtan Vanloqueren and Philippe Baret show, the limits of modernisation are closing in. More generally, Tom Bauler and Edwin Zaccai, as well as Christian Arnsperger, recall just how dubious the possibility of overcoming environmental problems through technological progress alone really is.

An implicit question is raised in the pages of this book, which remains open to debate: is the capitalist system capable of rising to these challenges or should we begin cultivating "post-capitalism" without delay? Whatever the response to this question, lack of anticipation will only lead to further upheaval, as has been amply demonstrated in the way governments and other dominant actors have responded to the current crisis. In short, the authors of this book have no doubts about the reality and scope of the historic shift currently underway. At stake here is not whether a shift will happen, but whether it will be navigated, and if so, then how and by whom. This brings us to the substantive and political questions of how to redefine prosperity, which are addressed below.

2 The substantive question: towards a definition closer to being than having

This work is an appeal. Our era faces the urgent task of loosening the constraints currently holding back our collective understanding of prosperity. Stéphane Leyens suggests we must restore depth to the concept by recognising its inherently axiological side. To define prosperity is necessarily to designate a desired state for society, a goal for which to reach. This exercise requires that we as scholars acknowledge and inhabit our specific critical standpoints; that is, that we recognise that no discussion of and about society can be "objective". With this in mind, the authors propose to push past a definition that has too long been limited to the quantifiable aspects of life, centred on having. The task here is to define prosperity so that it may be used to qualify existence holistically; that is, to define it on the level of being. This work does away with the analytically unfounded view that supposes individuals to (inter) act freely and autonomously within markets and instead considers them as social actors; that is, as *people,* both shaped and constituted by social interactions. It is important to clarify that an understanding of prosperity centred on emancipated being (rather than accumulative having) in no way denies that *having* is an integral part of *being*. There is no question that misery and poverty are antonyms to prosperity. The question raised here pushes beyond the sustainable creation and allocation of resources; we must ask to what end we are using them.

Amartya Sen's capability approach overcomes certain weaknesses in the utilitarian and liberal traditions; it has brought about a kind of Copernican revolution in social development research. Where health and education were previously viewed as the potential *results* of growth strategy, the capability approach makes access to these goods an essential *condition* of development. From this perspective, a society can be considered prosperous if it strengthens the capability of each of its members to achieve his or her aspirations. This definition does not entirely free us from the individualist paradigm, however; questions persist about the common good and about how to rebuild from collective action – in short, Sen deals insufficiently with the question of *agency*. We will return to this question further on. Offering substance to this essential issue, Jean De Munck identifies, on the level of emancipated being, three dimensions necessary for an individually and collectively prosperous life: the biological, environmental and material dimension (a *healthy life*); the cultural dimension (a *good life*); and the political dimension (a *just life*). A state of prosperity would be one in which individuals have the capability to lead a fulfilling life on each of these levels, which are seen as inherently complementary. This same idea of multiple and complementary dimensions appears again in this volume in the chapter analysing of new wealth indicators. While GDP remains prisoner of a one-dimensional, productivist and consumerist logic, the quest to move "beyond GDP" may be understood as an attempt to evaluate a variety of *results* in a comprehensive, quantified way – the state of the environment, the allocation of resources, objective quality of life, subjective perception of well-being – each specifically viewed as a component of a broader vision of development. The range of indicators being proposed shows how fragmented contemporary values and compromises truly are, and exposes the difficulty of producing new unifying principles and of measuring "value" non-monetarily. We nevertheless hope that this fragmentation is due to the incipient nature of the effort, rather than indicating the fundamental impossibility of advancing together in more coordinated fashion.

The consequences of an understanding of prosperity based on emancipated being rather than accumulative having are immediate. This book is far from exhaustive, and explores a few specific fields – work, innovation, the environment – by raising radical questions. What good is any hypothetical prosperity in a society where life is wasted on earning a living? This is the muffled cry echoing from new work-related pathologies (stress, burn-out, harassment, work-related suicide). Thomas Périlleux and Julien Charles explore the conditions for "living work" and what it would mean for a person to experience full engagement of the self, of a kind that allows her to achieve existential coherence across multiple relations to the self, to others and to the material world. Gaëtan Vanloqueren and Philippe Baret investigate the ways in which agricultural innovation is shackled by an ever-more exclusive focus on the criterion of financial profitability. Their contribution, which is potentially applicable to other fields, raises questions about the creation, dissemination, and implementation of knowledge, and calls for science and innovation to break free from the constraints by which they are currently bound. In each of their fields of analysis, the authors highlight the importance and urgency of strengthening new agricultural models, such as agroecology, and of modifying our eating habits, both for individual health and for that of the planet. Yet another chapter uses two lines of inquiry to examine the growing challenge of limited natural resources, examining the diverse range of approaches to the relationship between growth and the environment as well as the status of and possibilities for environmental "governance". This last question leads us, in turn, to the fundamentally political questions raised by this volume.

3 The political question: increasing collective autonomy and democratic participation

The substantive question discussed above inevitably raises the question of power: Who has the power to influence the societal goals that orient our public policies? Who decides on the standards by which we determine whether life is *healthy*, *good*, and *just*? How is legitimacy to make this choice determined? This question is central to the redefinition of prosperity today.

Western society likes to believe it is democratic. However, it would seem that one decisive factor, sometimes left to lurk in the shadows of this volume, is reining in all effective redefinitions of prosperity and limiting the de facto exercise of democratic power: we are referring to money, whose power over the past decades has been increased by financial globalisation.

Contemporary States are locked into a subservient relationship with globalised capitalism, making it difficult – if not impossible – to break free of its constraints. The weakening political power of governments may be seen in the way financial institutions and markets have imposed their standards on State management of the current economic crisis. This situation raises concerns about national and regional governments' effective capacity to adopt policies that might promote alternative ideas of prosperity. Examples of these limitations are myriad: the difficulty of imposing healthier food quality regulations in the face of agricultural, food, and chemical industry interests; the difficulty of limiting exposure to violence in cultural productions for fear it would affect the profits of major media outlets; the difficulty of promoting economic equality, for example by guaranteeing employees control over their quality of life at work even in cases where that would go against the interests of financial investors. If public powers cannot make decisions in these areas even when their constituents are pushing them to do so, what power do they really have? If this is the case, the locus of their power has shifted, and can no longer be defined as public.

Any discussion of the idea of prosperity is empty if it does not confront the ultimate question of society's capacity to decide for itself. The democratic ideal cannot be separated from the ideal of collective autonomy; that is, members of a community participating in determining the conditions of their shared life. Any attempt to redefine prosperity that seeks to be democratic must consider the means available to contemporary societies to conceive and undertake such a project. While hoping to open the path to further reflection in this direction, this book questions whether contemporary Western societies are capable of the autonomy necessary to put their choices into practice.

There is no point in trying to conceal the range and scope of the stumbling blocks to a viable alternative model of development that is founded on a broader concept of prosperity. For one thing, the multi-dimensional nature of any such model, which aims to encourage the autonomy of individuals within a dense web of social relations while protecting the long-term viability of the ecosystem, makes it difficult to define a comprehensive indicator capable of replacing GDP – emblematic of the paradigm to be transcended – let alone to induce governments to adopt it. Beyond that, is it a good idea to encourage governments to do so, or should we be wary of the possibility of "governance by indicator"? Isabelle Cassiers and Géraldine Thiry recall how, over the past two decades, governments and public services have undergone a massive shift towards management models developed in the private sector to meet shareholders' demand for performance and earnings. In their study of environmental issues, Tom Bauler and Edwin Zaccai illustrate how the notion of "governance" is being used to cover up deep ambiguities. Is this notion, as some would assert and the principle of soft law professes, a way to ensure flexible coordination among independent actors in a way that respects their diversity? Or, to the contrary, does it conceal the true origin of the rules being imposed on the actors, carving an anti-democratic chasm between citizens and their political representatives? Laurent de Briey argues that the evolution of governance is evidence that the political has been disqualified as a space in which collective projects may be elaborated, and has been replaced by an imperative to pragmatically manage resources and conflicts.

The difficulty of mobilising and bringing together actors to effect change is another impediment to the project of redefining prosperity. The collective actors behind the former productivist model, although destabilised by the economic crisis and the consequences of financialisation, will not spontaneously usher in a new model; they are, naturally, inclined to defend their jobs and the social benefits laboriously acquired through more than a century of social struggle. For the moment, those who might be expected to advance a new paradigm, whose existence and creativity has been helpfully highlighted here by several authors, are still at the stage of resistance or of experimentation at the local level. Their efforts have yet to be united, just as institutional reform capable of generating a comprehensive alternative project has yet to be promoted. There is no doubt, however, that our horizons are expanded by their presence and practices, which are in some ways *already* bringing about a redefinition of prosperity. Christian Arnsperger calls for the promotion of "socio-diversity" in our societies, seen as "egalitarian laboratories of experimentation". His contribution advances the idea of strengthened individual and collective autonomy, and stresses the importance of developing a "transition" plan today; an itinerary for moving from a present defined by this narrow concept of prosperity to a future organised according to a democratically redefined, multi-dimensional concept of prosperity.

From this perspective, the role of the State seems indispensable once again. Several of this book's authors suggest it has the specific role of overseeing the implementation of collective autonomy. Laurent de Briey invites us to consider the conditions under which the State might promote "political prosperity" by fostering the diversification of concepts of prosperity among citizens. Stéphane Leyens and Dominique Méda both show how public *participation* is the true force behind any democratic re-conception of prosperity – at least of a prosperity that reflects the deep aspirations of individuals and populations. While we recognise it is impossible to establish a single definition of prosperity, we argue that everyone should be able to exercise his or her *capability to participate* in the definition of prosperity at work in society.

We conclude this journey by highlighting three pitfalls to be avoided. First, we recall that no redefinition of prosperity can be purely procedural, undertaken without regard to the value system underlying it. Any distinction between the substantive and the procedural is a blurry one at best. By proposing a shift towards a definition based on emancipated being and refined through public debate, the authors of this work have *already* assumed a normative posture. Second, we warn against accepting any definition of prosperity that leads humanity into an impasse. Well-informed public debate is pivotal, and a growing body of literature, widely cited in this work, is available to inform and enlighten this debate. Finally, we must never overestimate the strength of popular initiative against the system we would like to move beyond: such initiatives run the risk of suffocation in a system that has retained much of its vigour. In other words, it is more important than ever to provide the resources these initiatives need to thrive, through both collective action and government support.

Awareness is growing of the gravity of the economic, environmental, and democratic crises confronting us at this point in our history. In each of its chapters and as a whole, this book attempts to suggest that our understanding of prosperity lies at the heart of these three crises. In this context, the mobilisation of civic and non-profit organisations around these issues will prove vital. Grassroots groups, unions, cultural, political, and spiritual movements – the organisations that make up civil society – are called upon to engage in the crucial project of re-defining prosperity; together, it is they who will nourish our societies' capability for collective autonomy.

It is up to each of us, and thus to you, our readers, to help forge the capability for collective autonomy with regard to the most fundamental aspects of life in society. We have marked out the path towards a redefinition of prosperity. But what do you think? How do you plan to promote what we all aspire to – a *healthy*, *good*, and *just* life?

Notes

1 Institut des Amériques (Paris) and French National Centre for Scientific Research
2 Université catholique de Louvain and Belgian National Fund for Scientific Research
3 Université catholique de Louvain and Belgian National Fund for Scientific Research. For further information see authors' biographies at the front of this volume.

Selected bibliography

Ackerman Bruce (1980), *Social Justice in the Liberal State*. New Haven/London: Yale University Press.

Agarwal Bina, Humphries Jane, and Robeyns Ingrid (eds) (2005), *Amartya Sen's Work and Ideas: A Gender Perspective*. London: Routledge.

Altieri Miguel A. (2002), Agroecology: the science of natural resource management for poor farmers in marginal environments, *Agriculture, Ecosystems & Environment* 93: 1–24.

Arnsperger Christian (2013), Small is beautiful: but is it responsible? A critical reappraisal of E.F. Schumacher's contributions to ecological economics and political ecology. In: Hendrik Opdebeeck (ed.), *Responsible Economics: E.F. Schumacher and His Legacy for the 21st Century*. Bern/Brussels/Vienna: Peter Lang, 127–149.

Arnsperger Christian and Johnson Warren A. (2011), The guaranteed income as an equal-opportunity tool in the transition toward sustainability. In: Axel Gosseries and Yannick Vanderborght (eds), *Arguing About Justice: Essays for Philippe Van Parijs*. Louvain-la-Neuve: Presses Universitaires de Louvain, 61–69.

Arnsperger Christian, Brunnhuber Stefan, Goerner Sally, and Lietaer Bernard (2012), *Money and Sustainability: The Missing Link*. Axminster: Triarchy Press.

Astyk Sharon (2008), *Depletion and Abundance: Life on the New Home Front*. Gabriola Island: New Society Publishers.

Ayres Robert U. (2000), Commentary on the utility of the ecological footprint concept, *Ecological Economics* 32(3): 347–349.

Barry John (2012), *The Politics of Actually Existing Sustainability: Human Flourishing in a Climate-Changed, Carbon-Constrained World*. Oxford: Oxford University Press.

Beck Ulrich (2006), *The Cosmopolitan Vision*. Cambridge: Polity Press.

Bell Daniel (1976), *The Cultural Contradictions of Capitalism*. New York: Basic Books.

Boltanski Luc and Chiapello Eve (2005), *The New Spirit of Capitalism*. London: Verso.

Boltanski Luc and Thévenot Laurent (2006), *On Justification: Economies of Worth*. Princeton: Princeton University Press.

Boyce James K. (2002), *The Political Economy of the Environment*. Northampton: Edward Elgar.

Comim Flavio, Qizilbash Mozaffar, and Alkire Sabina (eds) (2008), *The Capability Approach: Concepts, Measures and Applications*. Cambridge: Cambridge University Press.

Coote Anna and Franklin Jane (2013), *Time on our Side: Why we all need a Shorter Working Time*. London: New Economic Foundation.

Costanza Robert, Alperovitz Gar, Daly Herman, Farley Joshua, Franco Carol, Jackson

Tim, Kubiszewski Ida, Schor Juliet, and Victor Peter (2012), *Building a sustainable and desirable Economy – in society – in nature*. Report to the United Nations as part of the Sustainable Development in the 21st Century (SD21) project implemented by the Division for Sustainable Development of the United Nations Department of Economic and Social Affairs.

Cowan Robin and Gunby Philip (1996), Sprayed to death: path dependence, lock-in and pest control strategies, *The Economic Journal* 106(436): 521–542.

Daly Herman (1991), *Steady-State Economics*. Washington: Island Press.

De Munck Jean and Ferreras Isabelle (2012), The democratic exchange, as the combination of deliberation, bargaining, and experimentation. In: Jean De Munck, Claude Didry, Isabelle Ferreras, and Annette Jobert (eds), *Renewing Democratic Deliberation in Europe: The Challenge of Social and Civil Dialogue*. Oxford/Brussels: Peter Lang, 149–170.

De Munck Jean, Didry Claude, Ferreras Isabelle, and Jobert Annette (eds) (2012), *Renewing Democratic Deliberation in Europe: The Challenge of Social and Civil Dialogue*. Oxford/Brussels: Peter Lang.

De Schutter Olivier and Vanloqueren Gaëtan (2011), The New Green Revolution: how twenty-first-century science can feed the world, *Solutions* 2(4): 33–34.

Dejours Christophe (2006), Subjectivity, work, and action, *Critical Horizons* 7(1): 45–62.

Dejours Christophe (2007), For a critical conception of work. Sydney. Available at: www.crsi.edu.au/Recognition/conf2007/audio.html

Dejours Christophe (2010), Suicide at work and the crisis of culture. *Congrès Marx International VI: « Crises, révoltes, utopies »*, Université Paris X-Nanterre. Available at: www.actuelmarx.u-paris10.fr/cm6/index6.htm

Dejours Christophe and Deranty Jean-Philippe (2010), The centrality of work, *Critical Horizons* 11(2): 167–180.

Deranty Jean-Philippe (2008), Work and the precarisation of existence, *European Journal of Social* 11(4): 443–463.

Desrosières Alain (2003), Managing the economy: the state, the market, and statistics. In: Theodore Porter and Dorothy Ross (eds), *The Cambridge History of Science, Modern Social and Behavioral Sciences,* vol. 7. Cambridge: Cambridge University Press, 553–564.

Douthwaite Richard ([1992] 1999), *The Growth Illusion: How Economic Growth Enriched the Few, Impoverished the Many and Endangered the Planet.* Totnes: Green Books.

Easterlin Richard A. (1974), Does economic growth improve the human lot? Some empirical evidence. In: Paul A. David and Melvin Warren Reder (eds), *Nations and Households in Economic Growth: Essays in Honor of Moses Abramovitz*. New York: Academic Press, 89–124.

Ferreras Isabelle (2012), The Collective Aspects of Individual Freedom. A Case Study in the Service Sector. In: Serafino Negrelli, Ota De Leonardi, and Robert Salais (eds), *Democracy and Capabilities for Voice: Welfare, Work and Public Deliberation in Europe*. Oxford/Brussels: Peter Lang, 101–116.

Foley Jonathan A., Ramankutty Navin, Brauman Kate A., Cassidy Emily S., Gerber James S., Johnston Matt, Mueller Nathaniel D., O'Connel Christine, Ray Deepak K., West Paul C., Balzer Christian, Bennett Elena M., Carpenter Stephen R., Hill Jason, Monfreda Chad, Polasky Stephe, Rockström Johan, Sheehan John, Siebert Stefan, Tilman David, and Zaks David P.M. (2011), Solutions for a cultivated planet, *Nature* 478: 337–342.

Francis Charles, Lieblein Geir, Gliessman Stephen, Breland Tor A., Creamer Nancy, Harwood Richard, Salomonsson Lennart, Helenius Juha, Rickerl Diane, Salvador Ricardo, Wiedenhoeft Mary, Simmons Steve, Allen Patricia, Altieri Miguel, Flora Cornelia, and Poincelot Raymond (2003), Agroecology: the ecology of food systems, *Journal of Sustainable Agriculture* 22(3): 99–118.

Frey Bruno S. and Stutzer Alois (2002), *Happiness and Economics: How the Economy and Institutions Affect Human Well-Being*. Pinceton: Pinceton University Press.

Gadrey Jean and Jany-Catrice Florence (2006), *The New Indicators of Well-Being and Development*. London: Macmillan.

Galaz Victor, Biermann Frank, Crona Beatrice, Loorbach Derk, Carl Folke, Olsson Per, Nilsson Måns, Allouche Jeremy, Persson Åsa, and Reischl Gunilla (2012), Planetary boundaries: exploring the challenges for earth system governance, *Current Opinion in Environmental Sustainability* 4(1): 80–87.

Georgescu-Roegen Nicholas (1971), *The Entropy Law and the Economic Process*. Cambridge: Harvard University Press.

Greer John Micael (2009), *The Ecotechnic Future: Envisioning a Post-Peak World*. Gabriola Island: New Society Publishers.

Habermas Jürgen (1984), *The Theory of Communicative Action, Vol. 1: Reason and the Rationalization of Society*. Boston: Beacon Press.

Habermas Jürgen (1985), *The Theory of Communicative Action, Vol. 2: Lifeworld and System: A Critique of Functionalist Reason*. Boston: Beacon Press.

Habermas Jürgen (1991), *The Structural Transformation of the Public Sphere*. Cambridge: The MIT Press.

Heinberg Richard (2011), *The End of Growth*. Gabriola Island: New Society Publishers.

Helliwell John F., Layard Richard, and Sachs Jeffrey (eds) (2013), *World Happiness Report 2013*. New York: Sustainable Development Solutions Network.

Hezri Adnan A. and Dovers Stephen R. (2006), Sustainability indicators, policy, governance: issues for ecological economics, *Ecological Economics* 60(1): 86–99.

Holmgren David (2002), *Permaculture: Principles and Paths Beyond Sustainability*. Hepburn: Holmgren Design Services.

Holmgren David (2009), *Future Scenarios: How Communities Can Adapt to Peak Oil and Climate Change*. Totnes: Green Books.

Hopkins Rob (2007), *The Transition Handbook: From Oil Dependency to Local Resilience*. Totnes: Green Books.

Hopwood Bill, Mellor Mary, and O'Brian Geoff (2005), Sustainable development: mapping different approaches, *Sustainable Development* 13(1): 38–52.

Illich Ivan (1973), *Tools for Conviviality*. New York: Marion Boyars.

Jackson Tim (2009), *Prosperity without Growth: Economics for a Finite Planete*. London: Earthscan Ltd.

Johnson Warren A. (2010), *Muddling Toward Frugality: A New Social Logic for a Sustainable World*. Weston: Easton Studio Press.

Kahneman Daniel and Deaton Angus (2010), High income improves evaluation of life but not emotional well-being, *Proceedings of the National Academy of Sciences* 107: 16489–16493.

Kahneman Daniel, Krueger Alan A., Schkade David, Schwarz Norbert, and Stone Arthur A. (2006), Would you be happier if you were richer? A focusing illusion, *Science* 312: 1908–1910.

Kant Emmanuel (1998), *Groundwork of the Metaphysics of Morals*. Cambridge: Cambridge University Press.

Kant Emmanuel (2004), *Critique of Pratical Reason.* Mineola: Dover Publications.

Lamine Claire (2011), Transition pathways towards a robust ecologization of agriculture and the need for system redesign: cases from organic farming and IPM, *Journal of Rural Studies* 27(2): 209–219.

Layard Richard ([2005] 2011), *Happiness, Lessons from a New Science.* New York: Penguin.

Litfin Karren (2014), *Ecovillages: Lessons for Sustainable Community.* Cambridge: Polity Press.

Loorbach Derk (2007), *Transition Management, New Modes of Governance for Sustainable Development.* Utrecht: International Books.

Madron Roy and Jopling John (2003), *Gaian Democracies: Redefining Globalisation and People-Power.* Totnes: Green Books.

Martinez-Alier Joan (1987), *Ecological Economics: Energy, Environment, and Society.* Oxford: Blackwell.

Martinez-Alier Joan (2002), *The Environmentalism of the Poor: A Study of Ecological Conflicts and Valuation.* Cheltenham: Edward Elgar.

Martinez-Alier Joan, Pascual Unai, Vivien Franck-Dominique, and Zaccai Edwin (2010), Sustainable de-growth: mapping the context, criticisms and future prospects of an emergent paradigm, *Ecological Economics* 69(9): 1741–1747.

Marx Karl (1961), *Economic and Philosophic Manuscripts of 1844.* Moscow: Foreign Languages Pub.

Meadows Dennis H., Meadows Donnella L., Randers Jorgen, and Behrens III Williams H. (1972), *The Limits to Growth (Report to the Club of Rome).* New York: Universe Books.

Meadows Dennis H., Randers Jorgen, and Meadows Donnella L. (2004), *Limits to Growth: The 30 Year Update.* White River Junction: Chelsea Green Publishing Company.

Neumayer Eric (2004), *Weak versus Strong Sustainability: Exploring the Limits of Two Opposite Paradigms.* Cheltenham: Edward Elgar.

Newig Jens, Voss Jan-Peter, and Monstadt Jochen (2008), *Governance for Sustainable Development: Coping with Ambivalence, Uncertainty and Distributed Power.* London: Routledge.

Nussbaum Martha (2000), *Women and Human Development: The Capabilities Approach.* Cambridge: Cambridge University Press.

Nussbaum Martha and Sen Amartya (eds) (1993), *The Quality of Life.* Oxford: Oxford University Press.

O'Neill John ([1993] 2004), *Ecology, Policy and Politics: Human Well-Being and the Natural World.* London: Routledge.

Pikkety Thomas (2014), *Capital in the Twenty-First Century.* Cambridge: Harvard University Press.

Rawls John (1971), *A Theory of Justice.* Cambridge: The Belknap Press.

Rawls John (1988), The priority of the right and ideas of the good, *Philosophy and Public Affair* 17(4): 251–276.

Rawls John (1993), *Political Liberalism.* New York: Columbia University Press.

Rawls John (1999), *The Law of Peoples.* Cambridge: Harvard University Press.

Rawls John (2001), *Justice as Fairness: A Restatement.* Cambridge: Belknap Press of Harvard University Press.

Raworth Kate (2012), *A Safe and just Space for Humanity: Can we Live within the Doughnut?* Oxford: Oxfam International.

Renault Emmanuel (2009), Political philosophy of social suffering. In: Boudewijn de

Bruin and Christopher Zurn (eds), *New Waves in Political Philosophy*. Basingstoke: Palgrave, 158–176.

Rockström Johan, Steffen Will, Noone Kevin, Persson Åsa, Chapin F. Stuart, Lambin Eric F., Lenton Timothy M., Scheffer Marten, Folke Carl, Schellnhuber Hans Joachim, Nykvist Björn, de Wit Cynthia A., Hughes Terry, van der Leeuw Sander, Rodhe Henning, Sörlin Sverker, Snyder Peter K., Costanza Robert, Svedin Uno, Falkenmark Malin, Karlberg Louise, Corell Robert W., Fabry Victoria J., Hansen James, Walker Brian, Liverman Diana, Richardson Katherine, Crutzen Paul, and Foley Jonathan A. (2009), A safe operating space for humanity, *Nature* 461: 472–475.

Röling Niels (2009), Pathways for impact: scientists' different perspectives on agricultural innovation. *International Journal of Agricultural Sustainability* 7(2): 83–94.

Sale Kirkpatrick (2000), *Dwellers in the Land: The Bioregional Vision*. Athens: University of Georgia Press.

Sassen Saskia (2006), *Territory, Authority, Rights: From Medieval to Global Assemblages*. Princeton: Princeton University Press.

Schor Juliet (2010), *Plenitude: The New Economics of True Wealth*. New York: Penguin.

Schor Juliet (2011), *True Wealth: How and Why Millions of Americans Are Creating a Time-Rich, Ecologically Light, Small-Scale, High-Satisfaction Economy*. New York: Penguin.

Schultz Maria, Rockström Johan, Öhman Marcus C., Cornell Sarah, Persson Åsa, and Norström Albert (2013), *Human Prosperity Requires Global Sustainability – A Contribution to the Post-2015 Agenda and the Development of Sustainable Development Goals*. A Stockholm Resilience Centre Report to the Swedish Government Office.

Sen Amartya (1981), *Poverty and Famines: An Essay on Entitlement and Deprivation*. Oxford: Oxford University Press.

Sen Amartya (1982), *Choice, Welfare and Measurement*. Oxford: Blackwell.

Sen Amartya (1987), *On Ethics and Economics*. Oxford: Blackwell.

Sen Amartya (1992), *Inequality Reexamined*. Cambridge: Harvard University Press.

Sen Amartya (1999), *Development as Freedom*. New York: Knopf Press.

Sen Amartya (2009), *The Idea of Justice*. London: Allen Lane.

Shuman Michael H. (1998), *Going Local: Creating Self-Reliant Communities in a Global Age*. New York: Free Press.

Skidelsky Robert and Skidelsky Edward (2012), *How Much is Enough? The Love of Money and the Case for the Good Life*. London: Allen Lane.

Smith Nicholas H. and Deranty Jean-Philippe (2012), Work and the politics of misrecognition, *Res Publica* 18(1): 53–64.

Speth James Gustave and Haas Peter M. (2006), *Global Environmental Governance*. Washington: Island Press.

Stern Nicholas (2007), *The Economics of Climate Change: The Stern Review*. Cambridge: Cambridge University Press.

Stiglitz Joseph, Sen Amartya, and Fitoussi Jean-Paul (2010), *Mismeasuring our Lives. Why GDP doesn't add up. The Report by the Commission on the Measurement of Economic Performance and Social Progress*. New York/London: New Press.

Sumberg James, Thompson John, and Woodhouse Philip (2012), Why agronomy in the developing world has become contentious, *Agriculture and Human Values* 30(1): 71–83.

Thévenot Laurent (1984), Rules and implements: investment in forms, *Social Science Information* 23(1): 1–45.

Thévenot Laurent (2007), The plurality of cognitive formats and engagements: moving between the familiar and the public, *European Journal of Social Theory* 10(3): 413–427.

Thiry Géraldine and Cassiers Isabelle (2010), Alternative indicators to GDP: values behind numbers. adjusted net savings in question, *IRES Discussion Paper* 18: 1–21.

Thiry Géraldine, Bauler Tom, Sébastien Léa, Lacroix Valérie, and Paris Sébastien (2013), *Indicators Beyond GDP. Characterizing Demand: Institutional Analyses and Actors' Consultation by "Road Show"*. Brainpool Project (FP7), Deliverable 1.2, February.

van den Bergh Jeroen (2012), Growth, a-growth or degrowth to stay within planetary boundaries? *Journal of Economic Issues* 46(2): 909–920.

Vanloqueren Gaëtan and Baret Philippe V. (2009), How agricultural research systems shape a technological regime that develops genetic engineering but locks out agroecological innovations, *Research Policy* 38: 971–983.

Wackernagel Mathis and Rees William (1995), *Our Ecological Footprint: Reducing Human Impact on the Earth*. Gabriola Island: New Society Publishers

Weber Max (1992), *The Protestant Ethic and the Spirit of Capitalism*. London: Routledge.

Wijkman Anders and Rockström Johan (2012), *Bankrupting Nature: Denying our Planetary Boundaries*. London: Routledge.

Wilkinson Richard G. and Pickett Kate (2009), *The Spirit Level: Why Greater Equality Make Societies Stronger*. New York: Bloomsbury Press.

Williams Bernard (1985), *Ethics and the Limits of Philosophy*. Cambridge: Harvard University Press.

World Commission on Environment and Development (1987), *Our Commune Future*. Oxford: Oxford University Press.

Ziarek Ewa Płonowska (2001), *An Ethics of Dissensus: Postmodernity, Feminism, and the Politics of Radical Democracy*. Stanford: Stanford University Press.

www.ingramcontent.com/pod-product-compliance
Lightning Source LLC
LaVergne TN
LVHW011133300926
849160LV00008B/625
* 9 7 8 1 1 3 8 7 4 4 0 2 8 *